Esther D. Rothblum
Jacqueline S. Weinstock
Jessica F. Morris
Editors

Women in the Antarctic

Pre-publication
REVIEWS,
COMMENTARIES,
EVALUATIONS . . .

"**I**f personal stories fascinate you, as they do me, you will be unable to put down *Women in the Antarctic* until you've read every word. You will learn that women who go to the Antarctic are Navy personnel, students, scientists, contractors, and adventurers. Their experiences are not always positive in this remote, male-dominated land of deep silence but, nevertheless, I finished the book feeling exhilarated and inspired.

By moving 'outside the bounds of what is usually considered to be a woman's place—metaphorically, but also literally,' these women learned self-reliance and interconnection. They talk of having found themselves. They toughened their skins. Most exciting to me, they learned, one and all, the power of leaving one's comfort zone, of self-challenge, of questing after the unknown. There are strong messages here, from women on the ice to women everywhere."

Ellen Cole, PhD
Professor of Psychology,
Alaska Pacific University,
Anchorage, AK;
Author, *Wilderness Therapy for Women: The Power of Adventure*

More pre-publication
REVIEWS, COMMENTARIES, EVALUATIONS . . .

"The interviews in this book provide a rich and multifaceted picture of North American women's experience in the Antarctic. Through these women's stories we learn about the early days of United States women scientists working in the Antarctic as well as the present-day odysseys of women coming to the austral continent for research, work, their military careers, and expedition challenges. The stories these women tell about their experiences are enthralling. Whether it is the pioneering scientists who had to convince the Antarctic old guard that women had a valuable role to play on the continent, or the discipline and heart of the first women's expedition team to trek to the South Pole, these women have exciting and inspiring stories to tell. The variety of reasons why women chose to work in the Antarctic and the diversity in the quality of their experiences makes for fascinating reading. This book provides a lucid description of the culture of women in the Antarctic."

Sybil Carrère, PhD
Research Scientist,
University of Washington,
Seattle, WA

"I can think of no one better able to tell the story of life in the Antarctic than the women who lived there themselves. *Women in the Antarctic* offers a realistic and at times unpretty picture of a less-than-welcoming, male-dominated land as beautiful as it is dangerous.

Women in the Antarctic fills an important gap in the annals of women adventurers by offering the personal stories and true experiences of the women who have been there. Reading the book was both inspiring and informative, uplifting and motivating. Something for everyone can be found in these moving accounts of 'life away from home.'

I was amazed and inspired by the spirit and courage of these women who traveled to the Antarctic in pursuit of career opportunities, studies, and adventure. It is a valuable book about the spirit of women that I will keep on my shelf and pass on to my daughter as soon as she can read!"

Kathryn Malin
Second-year graduate student,
Department of Counseling
Psychology, Alaska Pacific
University, Anchorage, AK

Harrington Park Press
An Imprint of The Haworth Press, Inc.

Appendix

Interview Questions: Women in Antarctica

Introduction

1. To get started, would you tell me a little bit about the kind of work you were doing in the Antarctic? We'll go into some of this in more depth later on, but I'd like to get a sense of your work to start out with.
2. How many people were in your field team? (How many people were you working with day to day?)
3. How well did you know these people before going to the Antarctic?

Part I: Leading Up to the Antarctic

1. How did you end up going to the Antarctic? What led up to it?

   Probes:
   - I imagine going to the Antarctic is not something one does lightly. What was this decision process like for you? What kinds of things did you think about when you were deciding about going?
   - Did any part feel risky? (Were there any parts, any things you worried about or were concerned about?)
   - How did people close to you—such as co-workers, family, and friends—react to your decision to travel to the Antarctic?
   - How supportive were these people?
   - Did anyone surprise you in the way they reacted? Or did everyone react pretty much as you expected?
2. Did you think about this whole experience, going to the Antarctic, as an adventure?

Probes:
- [If not, ask: What would you call it? How would you describe it?]
- What would you consider an adventure? [If necessary, ask: Why that and not going to the Antarctic?]
- [If yes, ask: Have you been on other *adventures*? (Before going to the Antarctic, what was the most adventurous thing you've done?)

Part II: In the Antarctic

1. From the information you shared with us already (via telephone or questionnaire), you were in the Antarctic from _____ to _____ and you did/did not winter over, did I get this correct?
   - What season was it when you were there? What was the average temperature?
2. Now for a nice open-ended question. What was it like being in the Antarctic? What would you say to help me understand your experience?
3. Now let me ask you to get more specific so I can understand your experience on a more daily level. Could you describe a typical day in the Antarctic? Starting with when you woke up, lead me through the day so that I can see what you saw.
   - [If there in both summer and winter, ask about each; also ask for a comparison.]

Probes:
- How did you spend your free time?
- What was the twenty-four-hour daylight/nighttime like?
- What did you do for recreation?
- What kinds of recreation or free-time activities were available?
- [If At McMurdo, ask:]
  - What about the bars? Did you go to any of the bars? Was that a frequent pastime for folks? What about for you—did you find yourself spending a lot of your free time in the bars? Would you say you drank more, less, or about the same as you did at home?
- [If Not At McMurdo, ask:]
  - Were there any places to gather where people could hang out and maybe get a drink?
  - What was the drinking situation like? Was that a frequent pastime for folks? What about you—did you drink more, less or the same as you did at home?
  - What about exercise? What kinds of exercise were available? Did you do any exercise? What kinds?

- While you were in the Antarctic, were there any important holidays or occasions that occurred?
- Did you get to travel around the Antarctic at all? What was that like?
- Did you consider anything you did while in the Antarctic a risk?

4. I've asked you a lot about what you did while you were in the Antarctic. Now I'd like to ask you about the kinds of social support you got while you were there.

Probes:

- First, let me ask about support from home. Who did you have contact with from home and what kind of contact did you have with them? How much contact did you have? How did that feel? [Explore contact with family, friends, co-workers.]
- Did you feel pretty well supported by the folks back home while you were in the Antarctic? Was it harder or easier than they thought it was going to be having you so far away for so long? Was it harder or easier than you thought it would be?
- What about the support you received from others in the Antarctic?
  - WORK: Were the people you were working with supportive of you and your work? What about personal support as well as work support? Did co-workers support each other on a more personal level or did people pretty much keep those kinds of issues to themselves?
  - PERSONAL ISSUES: Would you say you made any friends while you were in the Antarctic? Did you have people you could talk to if you felt the need? How did you feel about that?
- Did you keep any sort of diary or journal while in the Antarctic? Was that helpful to you?
- During your stay in the Antarctic, I would imagine there were both ups and downs. Were there times that you felt down? What kinds of things made you feel down? How did you deal with these days/ these feelings?

5. How well do you think you worked with the others on your project?

Probes:

- Did people pretty much work independently or did you work more as a team?
- Did you get along with your co-workers?
- What was the male to female ratio? I know in my readings it seems that only recently more and more women are going to the Antarctic, but there's still usually many more men. How did you feel about the male to female ratio?

- I would imagine that in such a small environment there can be a lot of tension and rumors can spread quickly. How did you find it?

6. I asked you earlier if you had people you could go to talk to who would listen to you if you needed someone. Did other people you were with in the Antarctic come to you as someone they could talk to? How did you feel about that?

Part III: After the Antarctic

1. What was it like returning from the Antarctic?

   Probes:
   - What was your life like when you returned?
     - Was it hard readjusting to being back home?
     - Did others have a hard time adjusting to your return?
     - How were things different (if they were), or were things pretty much the same as before?
   - Did you keep in contact with people from the Antarctic?

2. So often in life it seems that major decisions involve weighing options and making trade-offs. Were there trade-offs in going to the Antarctic?
   - What did you give up to go to the Antarctic?
   - What do you think you gained from going to the Antarctic?
   - Did you change as a person?

3. Is there anything else that you feel is important that I haven't asked about?

Index

Women in the Antarctic

HAWORTH Innovations in Feminist Studies
Esther Rothblum, PhD and Ellen Cole, PhD
Senior Co-Editors

New, Recent, and Forthcoming Titles:

Prisoners of Ritual: An Odyssey into Female Genital Circumcision in Africa
by Hanny Lightfoot-Klein

Foundations for a Feminist Restructuring of the Academic Disciplines
edited by Michele Paludi and Gertrude A. Steuernagel

Hippocrates' Handmaidens: Women Married to Physicians by Esther Nitzberg

Waiting: A Diary of Loss and Hope in Pregnancy by Ellen Judith Reich

God's Country: A Case Against Theocracy by Sandy Rapp

Women and Aging: Celebrating Ourselves by Ruth Raymond Thone

Women's Conflicts About Eating and Sexuality: The Relationship Between Food and Sex
by Rosalyn M. Meadow and Lillie Weiss

A Woman's Odyssey into Africa: Tracks Across a Life by Hanny Lightfoot-Klein

Anorexia Nervosa and Recovery: A Hunger for Meaning by Karen Way

Women Murdered by the Men They Loved by Constance A. Bean

Reproductive Hazards in the Workplace: Mending Jobs, Managing Pregnancies
by Regina Kenen

Our Choices: Women's Personal Decisions About Abortion by Sumi Hoshiko

Tending Inner Gardens: The Healing Art of Feminist Psychotherapy
by Lesley Irene Shore

The Way of the Woman Writer by Janet Lynn Roseman

Racism in the Lives of Women: Testimony, Theory, and Guides to Anti-Racist Practice
by Jeanne Adleman and Gloria Enguidanos

Advocating for Self: Women's Decisions Concerning Contraception by Peggy Matteson

Feminist Visions of Gender Similarities and Differences by Meredith M. Kimball

Experiencing Abortion: A Weaving of Women's Words by Eve Kushner

Menopause, Me and You: The Sound of Women Pausing by Ann M. Voda

Fat—A Fate Worse Than Death?: Women, Weight, and Appearance by Ruth Raymond Thone

Feminist Theories and Feminist Psychotherapies: Origins, Themes, and Variations
by Carolyn Zerbe Enns

Celebrating the Lives of Jewish Women: Patterns in a Feminist Sampler edited by Rachel
Josefowitz Siegel and Ellen Cole

Women and AIDS: Negotiating Safer Practices, Care, and Representation edited by Nancy
L. Roth and Linda K. Fuller

A Menopausal Memoir: Letters from Another Climate by Anne Herrmann

Women in the Antarctic edited by Esther D. Rothblum, Jacqueline S. Weinstock,
and Jessica F. Morris

Breasts: The Women's Perspective on an American Obsession by Carolyn Latteier

Lesbian Step Families: An Ethnography of Love by Janet M. Wright

Women, Families, and Feminist Politics: A Global Exploration by Kate Conway-Turner
and Suzanne Cherrin

Women's Work: A Survey of Scholarship By and About Women by Donna Musialowski Ashcraft

Women in the Antarctic

Esther D. Rothblum
Jacqueline S. Weinstock
Jessica F. Morris
Editors

Harrington Park Press
An Imprint of The Haworth Press, Inc.
New York • London

Published by

Harrington Park Press, an imprint of The Haworth Press, Inc., 10 Alice Street, Binghamton, NY 13904-1580

Cover design by Monica L. Seifert.

COVER PHOTO:

top left: The United States Antarctic Program is in charge of all U.S. activities on the Antarctic Continent (photo by Berneice Albright).

top right: The first all-female VXE6 crew, 1991. Front, from left to right: Lt. Rhonda Buckner, Aircraft Commander; Lt. Patty Turney, Copilot; AE2 Tammy Tudor, Flight Engineer; PH2 Tammy Trefts, Crewman/Photographer. Back, from left to right: AT2 Jane Alstott, Loadmaster; AD3 Nancy Kelson, Loadmaster; Lt. Wells, Navigator (photo by David Armer).

bottom left: The four members of the American Women's Trans-Antarctic Expedition upon their arrival at the geographic South Pole, January 14, 1993. From left to right: Sunniva Sorby, Anne Dal Vera, Sue Giller, Ann Bancroft.

bottom right: Berneice Albright and an emperor penguin.

The Library of Congress has cataloged the hardcover edition of this book as:

Rothblum, Esther D.
  Women in the Antarctic / Esther Rothblum, Jacqueline Weinstock, Jessica Morris.
    p.   cm.
  Includes bibliographical references and index.
  ISBN 0-7890-0247-7 (alk. paper).
  1. Antarctica—Discovery and exploration. 2. Women explorers. 3. Women scientists.
  I. Weinstock, Jacqueline S., 1961-   . II. Morris, Jessica. III. Title.
G860.R78   1998
919.8'904—dc21   97-39233
                                                                               CIP

ISBN 1-56023-914-X (pbk.)

CONTENTS

Jacqueline S. Weinstock
Department of Integrated
Professional Studies,
University of Vermont

ABOUT THE EDITORS

Esther D. Rothblum, PhD, is Professor of Psychology at the University of Vermont in Burlington, Vermont. She received a Kellogg Fellowship that involved travel to the Antarctic and a National Science Foundation grant that involved research on women in the Antarctic. Dr. Rothblum has edited over twenty books related to women's mental health and is currently Editor of the journal *Women and Therapy* (The Haworth Press).

Jacqueline S. Weinstock, PhD, is Assistant Professor in the Human Development and Family Studies Program at the University of Vermont in Burlington, Vermont. Her research and writing revolve around friendships and other forms of relationships, especially the roles they play in shaping individual and community responses to various oppressions. With Mary Field Belenky and Lynne Bond, she co-authored the 1997 book, *A Tradition That Has No Name: Nurturing the Development of People, Families, and Communities.* She is currently investigating the friendship experiences of lesbian, gay, bisexual, and transgender individuals.

Jessica F. Morris, is a graduate of Vassar College and a doctoral candidate in Clinical Psychology at the University of Vermont in Burlington, Vermont. Her research and writing have focused on the various aspects of the psychology of women. Jessica has worked with substance abusers at Yale University and college students through the counseling center at the University of Massachusetts, Amherst. Although she has never been there, Jessica has learned much about life in the Antarctic.

Preface

For centuries it was frowned upon for women to travel without escort, chaperone, or husband. To journey was to put oneself at risk, not only physically but morally as well. . . . I find it revealing that the metal bindings in women's corsets were called "stays." Someone who wore "stays" wouldn't be going far.

Mary Morris (1993, pp. xv-xvi)

Despite their socialization to stay home, a few women have always traveled in search of adventure. Sometimes they did so secretly, sometimes they were disguised as men, and often they did not publish their experiences, so that we have little record of their journeys. They faced considerable odds. When Annie Peck climbed the Matterhorn in 1895, she was not the first woman to do so, but she was the first woman to do so wearing pants (Olds, 1985). At the turn of the century, Ethel Brilliana Tweedie (in Morris, 1993) critiqued the habit of women riding horses sidesaddle and urged society to permit women to ride astride as men did: "Riding man-fashion is less tiring than on a side-saddle, and I soon found it far more agreeable, especially when traversing rough ground. My success soon inspired Miss T. to summon up courage and follow my lead. She had been nearly shaken to pieces in her chair pannier, besides having only obtained a one-sided view of the country through which she rode . . ." (pp. 91-92). Despite these odds, women persevered, writing about their experiences in such books as *On Sledge and Horseback to Outcast Siberian Lepers* (Marsden, in Morris, 1993).

This book is about women in the Antarctic. For centuries, people believed that there must be an unknown land (terra incognita) at the bottom of the globe to offset the land mass in the northern hemisphere. Maps from the sixteenth century depict this land filled with fire and monsters. Antarctica wasn't explored until the nineteenth

century and so remained the last unknown continent. Governments and private companies began funding explorers to be the first to spend a winter in the Antarctic, the first to reach the South Pole, or the first to fly to the South Pole.

For the first century of explorations to the Antarctic, there were no women on the continent. A widely read text on the Antarctic (*Reader's Digest,* 1985) has only one article about women, titled "The Women They Left Behind: Unsung Heroines of Exploration," about women married to Antarctic explorers. These women were portrayed as waiting patiently for their husbands to return and received media attention when they became widows. Ernest Shackleton wrote to his wife Emily in 1907 that he had found the willpower to retreat before reaching the South Pole because "I thought you would rather have a live donkey than a dead lion" (in *Reader's Digest,* 1985, p. 237).

Just as women traveled incognito to other parts of the world, there were definitely women who traveled to the oceans around Antarctica about whom all records are lost. In 1986, Elizabeth Chipman wrote *Women on the Ice,* a chronological account of the individual women who went to the Antarctic. She states:

> Certainly women were on board some of these far-searching vessels, for their names are known. Certain it is, also, that many more women ventured south than those whose names have been recorded. The captains and ships' officers of whaling vessels sometimes were accompanied by their wives during voyages south; however, this was not always mentioned in the ships' logs. Men sent to the islands for months at a time—and sometimes for a few years—to work at the killing of seals and allied trades, often took women with them." (p. 12)

Ironically, one use of whalebone was to make "stays" for women's corsets in Europe.

How did we come to be interested in women in the Antarctic? After graduating from college, I (Esther) took a trip with friends from Austria (where I lived) to Scandinavia. We drove north through Finland, finally arriving at the fjords above the Arctic Circle, and took the boat across the Arctic Ocean to the North Cape. Although it was mid-June, the snow-covered island was cold and windy. Nearly

a decade later, I was teaching in southern Australia. I took a trip to southern Tasmania, where a signpost indicated the Antarctic thousands of miles away. The weather and the sky reminded me of the Arctic, and I yearned to see the Antarctic Continent.

For years, I read everything I could find on the Antarctic, which was mostly explorations by men in the past century. I wrote to people described in the media as having been there, indicating that I would be willing to go along on future expeditions. When I received a Kellogg Fellowship that included international travel, I knew I had found my opportunity to go to the Antarctic.

I eventually went to the Antarctic aboard an Argentine merchant marine vessel—the *Bahia Paraiso*. It had been the ambulance ship during the Malvinas/Falklands War. The ship left Ushuaia, the southernmost city in the world, every two weeks, crossing the Drake Passage (one of the roughest parts of the ocean) and stopping at various Argentine Antarctic stations to airdrop supplies by helicopter and to resupply personnel by zodiac (small, inflatable boats). The ship had limited ice-breaking capability so it could cross semifrozen seawater only during the Antarctic summer. It also took along two dozen or so tourists on each trip, who were dropped off to sightsee along the subantarctic islands and then on the Antarctic Peninsula. We were one of the first tour groups to visit the U.S. Palmer Station, which had previously not permitted tourists.

Although the conditions were spartan (vastly different from the expensive cruise ships that tour the Antarctic Continent), the scenery was spectacular. The Antarctic oceans contain the majority of the world's marine life. We saw whales, seals, penguins, albatrosses, and other seabirds as well as icebergs, sea cliffs, and old whaling stations. Two weeks after I left the ship, it ran aground outside Palmer Station and sank. Although all passengers and crew were rescued by zodiacs from Palmer Station, all possessions were lost, and the fuel and oil leaking out of the ship's hull created a disaster for the ocean wildlife (including penguins that U.S. scientists had been studying for years to examine the effects of the ozone hole on animals). As most of the women whose accounts follow, I had viewed the Antarctic trip as very safe; the sinking of the ship (although I was not a passenger at the time) was to prove me wrong.

Similar to many people who have been to the Antarctic, I spent a lot of effort trying to go back. I wrote about the Antarctic for the popular media and for a psychology journal. For years, I had conducted research on the fear of failure among women, and what struck me about the women in the Antarctic (including women aboard the ship bound for Argentine stations) was their sense of adventure and their willingness to take risks. I applied for a National Science Foundation grant that focused on risk-taking among women. I was interested in how women, who are socialized to place importance on interpersonal and social relationships, manage to go so far away from their family and friends, and what the consequences are when they leave these social relationships. Jackie Weinstock and Jessica Morris, both graduate students in psychology at the time, were funded by the grant to develop, conduct, and analyze the interviews.

*   *   *

I (Jackie) grew increasingly fascinated by the Antarctic with each additional interview I conducted. Admittedly, I was not at first drawn to the project because of the Antarctic itself but rather because of the opportunity to listen to the stories of women who had ventured to a place both unknown and unusual—a place so far away and distinct from their "off the ice" lives. Interested in various interpersonal relationships in particular, I was fascinated by the reflections the women might have engaged in when deciding whether to go to the Antarctic and the ways in which they experienced social relationships before, during, and following their trips.

By my fourth or fifth interview, I was drawn into the Antarctic experience itself. The stories the women were sharing and the passion they expressed for the place intrigued me. This passion seemed twofold. First, the beauty and magnificence of the place, the specialness of being somewhere that few others have been was deeply felt and expressed by many of the women with whom I spoke. And second, I was drawn to the sense of community, of time and space to relate to each other and to enjoy both intimate conversation and playful activities, that many expressed. These passions were so evident that by the time the fifth woman I interviewed asked me, after the interview was over, if I wanted to go to the Antarctic, I found myself saying yes. I admitted to her that I really hadn't

thought about it before, but that I was getting more and more interested with each interview. Indeed, both during and since those interviews, I began to explore the Antarctic more deeply through readings. And I started then—and continue now—to imagine what it would be like to spend some time there, what I would need to do to be able to go, how I would handle being so far away from friends and family, what new things I might learn about myself in this kind of setting, and what I might be like in the course of—and after— spending a few months in the summer or, perhaps, over a winter season.

I haven't made any plans at this point to actually pursue a trip to the Antarctic. But I believe my experiences with this project—and the opportunity I had to meet with and hear about women who have ventured to Antarctica—were the underlying motivators for a recent trip I took to St. Petersburg, Russia. I caught a little bit of that spirit of adventure from the Antarctic women we interviewed.

* * *

I (Jessica) was once one of those people who knew little about the Antarctic (that's the South Pole, right?). When Esther first invited me to serve as research assistant on the project, it was the chance to participate in research built upon the voices of women that was of interest to me. I had only just found out that I had been admitted to the PhD program in Clinical Psychology at the University of Vermont. In order to take the job, I moved to Vermont three months early and immediately took a class in qualitative research methods.

As soon as I found out I would be working on the project, I started learning all I could about Antarctica. All over my house were piles of books about Antarctica: picture books, historical books, magazine articles, and booklets from the National Science Foundation. The more I read, the more fascinated I became. There was something enthralling about the continent. At first it was the physical uniqueness that occupied me. Then the thrilling stories of brave explorers captured me, as I tried—unsuccessfully—to imagine what it must have been like. I read the information that the National Science Foundation provided. I was able to find out about the mundane aspects of life in the Antarctic. I pored over the maps

of the various U.S. bases to become familiar with what they looked like. Nothing, however, prepared me for what it would be like to hear the stories of women who have lived in the Antarctic.

Because I was unable to travel, all of the interviews I conducted were over the telephone. I was a little concerned about this—whether I would be able to make some sort of connection with the women I interviewed. I am actually a telephone person; that is to say, I like talking on the phone and do so a lot. But talking to friends and family is different. I was pleasantly surprised, however, to find out how easy it was to develop rapport over the phone. As I followed each woman's story, asking questions about her experiences, it often got quite personal. Again and again, I found myself being privilege to some of the most intimate and private aspects of these women's lives. It is quite difficult to explain how honored I felt to be able to listen to their stories.

Not only was the process of talking to women fascinating, but so too was the content of their stories about Antarctica. For a number of months I was quite consumed with life in Antarctica. I kept a photo of the four women of the American Women's Trans-Antarctic Expedition standing at the South Pole over my desk. I often joked that I knew more about life in Antarctica than anyone who'd never been there. I'm sure that my friends and family were tired of hearing me say, "Did you know that in Antarctica. . . ."

This book is about the women who have been to the Antarctic. Other than a brief description of the Antarctic, which follows, and accounts by women who study those who travel to distant places, most of the accounts are by the Antarctic women themselves. This book is about the voices of women in the Antarctic.

REFERENCES

Chipman, E. (1986). *Women on the ice.* Melbourne, Australia: Melbourne University Press.

Morris, M. (1993). *Maiden voyages: Writings of women travelers.* New York: Vintage Books.

Olds, E.F. (1985). *Women of the four winds: The adventures of four of America's first women explorers.* Boston: Houghton Mifflin Company.

Reader's Digest. (1985). *Antarctica: Great stories from the frozen continent.* New South Wales, Australia: Reader's Digest Services Pty. Limited.

Acknowledgments

Our thanks go to the women who started it all—the pioneers and adventurers—and who opened up the Antarctic for women to live and work there today.

Esther Rothblum would like to thank Dr. Irene Peden, whose enthusiasm and experience in the Antarctic allowed Esther to organize a trip to the Antarctic Peninsula in 1989. This trip was conducted while Esther had a Kellogg National Fellowship and also a small group grant from the Kellogg Foundation to travel to the Antarctic. Dr. Tito Guerrero, also a Kellogg Fellow, was a helpful co-planner of the trip, and Dr. Polly Penhale, Program Manager at the Office of Polar Programs at the National Science Foundation, invited us to attend the fall 1988 Antarctic Orientation Session in Washington, DC. Esther would also like to thank the members of the Kitchi Gammi Club breakfasts in Duluth, Minnesota—Drs. Barbara Elliott, Skip Hofstrand, Art Aufderheide, and Sister Mary Odile Cahoon, whose Nordic and Antarctic experiences were incentives for the Antarctic trip.

The scientists, Navy personnel, and civilian support staff whose accounts follow were interviewed by Jacqueline Weinstock and Jessica Morris, who were funded by a National Science Foundation Women's Career Advancement Award granted to Esther Rothblum during the period 1992 to 1993. We would like to thank Dr. Polly Penhale at the National Science Foundation for her tremendous help with this project, as well as Dr. Neil Swanberg who provided advice and information in the planning and execution stages of this grant. We would also like to thank the members of Naval Support Force Antarctica in Port Hueneme, California, particularly Lieutenant Pamela Patrick, our primary contact person, and employees of the Antarctic Support Associates in Denver, Colorado, particularly Mr. Chris Shepard and Ms. Sandra Kenady.

We want to thank all the people who expressed their willingness to be interviewed for this National Science Foundation study, and

especially the thirty-six women (scientists, Navy personnel, and civilian support staff) whose interviews formed the basis of our research project. We thank Dr. Sondra Solomon who performed the inter-rater reliability ratings for our interviews. All three of us (at different times) took Dr. Corinne Glesne's course on qualitative research methods at the University of Vermont. We thank her for her assistance with research methods. We would also like to thank Elaine van der Stok who transcribed the interviews and Leah Nickerson who entered the data for ethnographic analysis.

Most of all, our thanks go to the women who agreed to have their interviews constitute the chapters that follow. Eleven women from the National Science Foundation grant are included in this book, as are Dr. Irene Peden and Sister Mary Odile Cahoon, who were early women "pioneers" in the Antarctic. We would like to thank Dr. Naomi McCormick at the State University of New York, Plattsburgh, for connecting us with Sue Giller and members of the American Women's Trans-Antarctic Expedition, whose accounts are also included in this book.

Introduction

Esther D. Rothblum
Jacqueline S. Weinstock
Jessica F. Morris

Antarctica is the coldest, highest, and driest continent on earth. Unlike the Arctic, which consists of frozen water surrounded by land, the Antarctic is land surrounded by water. Land is colder than water, so Antarctica has temperatures ranging from 40 degrees Fahrenheit in the warmest part of the continent in summer to minus 100 degrees Fahrenheit (not including the wind-chill factor) in the winter. Ninety-eight percent of the continent is covered with ice, and in fact, Antarctica contains 90 percent of the world's ice. The ice is several miles thick in parts of Antarctica's interior, so that the altitude is similar to high mountainous regions. Even though the Antarctic Continent contains 68 percent of the world's fresh water locked up as ice, the almost total lack of precipitation classifies it as a desert. Frequent blizzards and high winds form "white-outs" that make it difficult to see, and the view is often a monotonous sheet of white snow and ice.

Antarctica has no native wildlife or vegetation, except on the coast. Whereas the Arctic regions have native human cultures—and even cities north of the Arctic Circle—Antarctica has never had a native culture. Its distance from other land masses—thousands of miles from all continents except South America, which is 800 miles away across the Drake Passage—meant that it was unexplored by humans for 140 million years. One of the roughest oceans in the world surrounds Antarctica, making travel to the region difficult even with modern technology such as icebreakers and radar.

Why would anyone choose to go to this barren continent? In 1913, explorer Ernest Shackleton placed an ad in a newspaper that stated:

Men wanted for hazardous journey. Small wage, bitter cold, long months of complete darkness. . . . Safe return doubtful . . . and recognition in case of success.

He received about 5,000 applications.

The "heroic age" of the first half of this century was marked by explorations of the Antarctic, which was not fully mapped until the 1950s. Explorers searched for a tropical paradise, for places to find seals and whales, or to claim new territory for their empires. The first half of the twentieth century was marked by competitive explorations by men, each vying to be the first to reach some as yet uncharted part of the continent, to be the first ashore, the first to reach the magnetic South Pole, the first to fly there, or the first to sail there solo. The media has focused the most on the Amundsen and Scott expeditions to reach the geographic South Pole.

In 1947, two U.S. women went to the Antarctic with the Ronne Antarctic Expedition. Edith (Jackie) Ronne was the wife of the expedition leader, Captain Finne Ronne, and she had planned to organize the expedition's affairs in the United States while the men were away. When she was saying goodbye to her husband, he asked her to come along as far as Panama, and then Chile, and finally to the Antarctic itself. So Jackie wouldn't be the only woman, Jenny Darlington came along; she had recently married one of the expedition's pilots. The Ronne Antarctic Expedition wintered over on the Antarctic Peninsula and almost had to spend another winter in the Antarctic when the ice around the peninsula stayed frozen during the summer (Chipman, 1986). Jenny became pregnant near the end of the stay, a fact that was initially only known by her husband and the expedition's doctor, who was alarmed at the prospect of the team spending another winter on the ice. Fortunately they were picked up by a U.S. icebreaker that was in the vicinity of the peninsula. Jackie Ronne wrote numerous articles about the expedition for newspapers and is currently at work on a book about her trip. Jenny Darlington published the book *My Antarctic Honeymoon: A Year at the Bottom of the World* in 1956 with Jane McIlvane. In this book, she describes the conflict between Finne Ronne and Harry Darlington and the resultant strained relations between the two women.

Explorations continue today, although they have decreased considerably, and the U.S. Antarctic Program in particular discourages "tourism" of this nature. Explorers are rarely funded by governments but instead by private fundraising or the media.

Several years ago, U.S. television covered the international expedition headed by Will Steger, in which six men traversed the Antarctic Continent by dogsled. A few recent explorers have been women.

In 1908, Britain made the first formal claim to Antarctic territory, and by 1943, over 80 percent of the continent had been nationally divided. In some cases these claims conflicted, particularly at the Antarctic Peninsula, which is currently claimed by Argentina, Chile, and the United Kingdom. The first claim to the Antarctic by Britain not only contributed to the Falklands War in 1982, by ignoring Argentinian claims, but earlier, resulted in the 1961 Antarctic Treaty. This treaty, first proposed by the United States, makes the Antarctic the subject of an international trust for the establishment of scientific bases, environmental protection, and international cooperation. While the treaty is active, all claims to the Antarctic have been suspended.

Most people who have come "to the ice" in recent decades engage in scientific research or support those who do. About a dozen nations have built research "stations" that are permanent, insulated, and heated. A small station might consist of three or four buildings, divided between facilities for research, housing, and storage. Small stations are often highly specialized in the kind of research that is possible to conduct there—marine biology at the coastal Chinese Great Wall Station or metereology at the Russian Vostok Station. The U.S. Antarctic Program maintains a small station, Palmer, on the Antarctic Peninsula, for marine biology research. People going to work at Palmer Station usually fly to Punta Arenas, the southernmost city in Chile, and then board a U.S. ship, the Polar Duke. The Antarctic Peninsula is much further north and consequently much warmer than the continent. The summer season lasts longer and the station's surroundings are scenically beautiful (with icebergs, islands, penguins, and seals).

For those people going to the Antarctic Continent via the U.S. Antarctic Program during the early 1990s, a contingent of Navy personnel would arrive in the Antarctic at "winfly" or winter fly-in and

build an ice runway so that planes could land.* Scientists and civilian personnel usually flew to Christchurch, New Zealand aboard a commercial airliner, and then to the Antarctic aboard a Hercules propellor Navy cargo plane. They landed at McMurdo Station on frozen sea ice during the Antarctic summer (late October to late February), when the station had over 1,000 members and felt very crowded and busy. The constant daylight allowed people to work in two shifts around the clock, and people worked very hard, since the alloted use time of laboratory facilities, equipment, and transportation was very limited. People shared rooms in "Jamesways"—long, metal, prefabricated buildings. McMurdo Station looks like a small mining town—buildings include a church, gym, store, post office, library, and newspaper office. Holidays and special events become huge celebrations. People aren't allowed to travel far from base and need to file a foot plan (that is, leave an itinerary of where they are going) so they can be rescued if the weather deteriorates.

McMurdo Station serves as the "hub" for scientists going out to field camps, such as those studying geologic formations in the Dry Valleys. The U.S. Antarctic Program provides materials for the quick formation of small field camps and transports scientists and support personnel by helicopter. Some older, smaller stations (such as Byrd) now serve only as field camps. McMurdo Station is also the hub for personnel going to the Amundsen-Scott Station at the geographic South Pole. The South Pole station is much smaller, colder (temperature ranges from −21 degrees Celsius in the summer to −78 degrees Celsius in the winter), windier, and at a higher elevation (2,900 meters above sea level) than McMurdo. The summer season is shorter (only three months) and work space is very limited. The entire station is under a geodesic dome constructed of aluminum. There is tremendous prestige associated with the experience of actually having been at the "Pole," which is, in fact, marked by a red-and-white striped barber pole!

Thus, there are three groups of people who live and work in the Antarctic: Scientists, the U.S. Navy, and Antarctic Support Associates

---

*Although the Navy controlled the military flying operations in the Antarctic in the early 1990s during the time of our study, the Air Force has since assumed these duties.

(ASA). The U.S. Antarctic Program forbids any activities in the Antarctic that are not related to scientific research. Scientists apply for research grants through the Polar Programs Division of the National Science Foundation (NSF). Atmospheric chemists study the hole in the ozone layer, which is largest over the Antarctic Continent. Marine biologists study penguins, seals, whales, or krill (shrimp-like animals in the ocean around the Antarctic Peninsula). Metereologists use telescopes at the South Pole Station, where the skies are very clear due to the absence of cities. Geologists study rock formations in this oldest continent that has been undisturbed by civilization. And social scientists and health professionals study the people who go there and look for factors that predict good adaptation to the extreme conditions. Scientists who receive grants from NSF are called principal investigators (PIs) or co-principal investigators (Co-PIs), if they collaborate on a study. Sometimes they do their work alone, but more often they go to the Antarctic with field teams—laboratory technicians, graduate students, or other scientific support staff, some of whom are very highly specialized in their jobs. Prior Antarctic experience is often required in order to obtain an NSF grant, so some field-team members become PIs in their own right later on. The scientific personnel have the opportunity to explore the Antarctic Continent. Depending on the nature of their work, they may travel within the continent, climb mountains to collect rock samples, or dive for seals. Scientists along the coast use zodiacs—small, inflatable boats—to conduct oceanography or marine life research. In the past, there have been few women among the scientific research teams (and even fewer female PIs). Even today, the scientific disciplines are dominated by men. But the number of women increased substantially from forty-three in the 1979 to 1980 Antarctic season to 180 in the 1990 to 1991 season.

The U.S. Navy is in charge of operating the three U.S. Antarctic stations, as well as transporting civilians.* The Navy operates the Hercules cargo planes that transport people and supplies from New Zealand to McMurdo Station and also flies smaller propellor planes from McMurdo to the station at the South Pole. It operates the

---

*As noted, the Navy no longer controls military flying operations in the Antarctic, but it was in charge at the time of our study.

helicopters that transport people and supplies to field camps. Each year, about twenty-five women are among the VXE6 Antarctic Development Squadron as members of flight crews. The Navy personnel who operate the stations usually sign on for two-year tours of duty. Unlike the scientists and the naval personnel who are members of flight crews, these people rarely get to leave the station. They are part of the military hierarchy, with strict boundaries between officers and enlisted personnel. They rarely get to know the civilians well because the two groups lead very different lives while "on the ice."

Although women in the military are still in the minority, their numbers have increased dramatically. Until 1994, women in the Navy were prohibited from combat-related deployments. Going to the Antarctic was one of the few ways in which women could travel on Navy ships, and the Antarctic tour of duty represented a career advancement for Navy women. The 200 women from Naval Support Force Antarctica who are in the Antarctic each year represent about one-quarter of all naval personnel on the ice. Most of these women have never worked with so many other women. After the Antarctic tour, Navy personnel return to Port Hueneme, California.

Finally, the U.S. Antarctic Program has a contract with a company that is in charge of construction and maintenance. Formally ITT Antarctica, in recent years the contractor has been Antarctic Support Associates (ASA), based in Denver, Colorado. ASA hires the various people who go to the Antarctic as construction workers, computer operators, field engineers, clerical workers, or other maintenance crews, usually by placing advertisements in U.S. newspapers. In 1990/1991, ninety-five women were hired by ASA to work in the Antarctic, which represented about one-quarter of the ASA staff. Like Navy personnel, ASA workers rarely get to leave the stations. Unlike Navy personnel and scientists, for whom the Antarctic represents career advancement, most ASA workers go to the ice for a sense of adventure and to do something new. Some of them quit their old jobs in order to have this adventure.

At each of the three stations, a small contingent of people remains when Antarctic winter sets in. During the winter, the ice around the Antarctic Continent expands so that ships cannot access Palmer and McMurdo Stations, and the constant darkness and poor

weather conditions do not permit planes to land. Consequently, winter-over personnel cannot leave the Antarctic. A lot of research has gone into examining the characteristics that make people good candidates for the extended winter stay, since they cannot be evacuated. There is considerable prestige associated with wintering-over in the Antarctic. People find their own space in the emptier stations and often resent the crowds and bustle of the returning summer personnel. Each winter, a small percentage of winter-over personnel are women.

Our own study of women in the Antarctic began as an NSF grant. Though there have been well over 100 studies about men in the Antarctic, no research has focused specifically on women. Our NSF study focused on thirty-six women who were scientists and field-team members, Navy personnel, and ASA civilian support staff. We studied two issues: risk-taking and social consequences.*

WOMEN AND RISK-TAKING

First, we wanted to study risk-taking among women. The research on risk-taking has studied mainly dangerous risks taken by men, such as drunk driving, drug use, skydiving, and gambling. These are often thought of as *destructive* risks. Women are socialized to "play it safe," so that they avoid risks and, in fact, tend to avoid situations where there is any chance of failure. Yet risks do not have to be physically dangerous. It is risky to initiate a new relationship (because the other person could say no) or to submit an article to a magazine (because it could be rejected). These kinds of risks may be thought of as *constructive*. One study that asked women for their greatest regrets in life found that many women wished that they had taken more risks. In general, women take fewer destructive (dangerous) and fewer constructive risks.

We wanted to study women who do take risks, and the Antarctic seemed the ideal setting. The physical aspects of the Antarctic environment, such as the extreme cold, the blizzards and white-outs, travel in

---

*For a more detailed description of our study's results, see Rothblum, E.D., Morris, J.F., and Weinstock, J.S. (1995). Women in the Antarctic: Risk-taking and social consequences. *World Psychology, 1,* 83-112.

poorly marked terrain, crevasses (cracks in the ice that are hard to see), high-altitude rock climbing, icy ocean water, and flying in bad weather, constitute physical and somewhat dangerous risks.

The Antarctic also involves nonphysical risks. These include the isolation of the stations and the overcrowded conditions. Most people who work in the Antarctic cannot leave the immediate surroundings. The Antarctic is thousands of miles from their home environments and it is not possible to leave during the winter. Communication with home is difficult and sometimes impossible. Finally, most people would agree that leaving friends, family, and co-workers for months or years is stressful, and may jeopardize these relationships.

We wanted to know what factors about the Antarctic the women considered risks before they went, and what were the risks once they got there. We were also interested in what motivated women to seek Antarctic duty and whether they considered the experience an adventure. Because any risk has the potential of success or failure, we asked what they had gained and what they had lost as the result of going to the Antarctic. And we asked whether they would go back.

Women hear about and go to the Antarctic for various reasons—for career advancement, to escape poor jobs or poor relationships, to do something different and exciting. Once they get to the Antarctic, most women do in fact consider the experience an adventure. They realize the opportunity to work in an unusual setting, they know that few people ever go there, and they enjoy the beautiful scenery. Some of the women have done adventurous things all their lives; they have traveled widely, taken risks, skydived from airplanes, gone deep-sea diving. For others, this is their first adventure; they have never flown in an airplane or left their home state.

The women generally did not perceive the Antarctic to be a risk before they went. They were excited and were not fearful about anything, or else they knew people who had gone to the Antarctic and liked it. Many women had been in similar situations or in even more risky situations. If anything, the women were likely to contrast the Antarctic with even more dangerous situations. "It's not like climbing Mt. Everest," said one woman. Another said, "Not like the Arctic, where you could be eaten by a polar bear," or "Not like going to a war zone that has real dangers." Lest the reader think these reactions

by women are common, ask some friends whether they would spend a year in the Antarctic and see what they say!

Interestingly, the women's lack of concern about going to the Antarctic did not match the reality once they were there. All but one woman said that they did encounter risks in the Antarctic. Many of these risks were physical in nature and often related to leisure activities, such as exploring or going out on day trips. The risks included unauthorized exploring, being caught in storms, being lost, getting frostbite, or coming too close to crevasses, icebergs, or leopard seals. The women also became aware that travel to or within the Antarctic could be dangerous, and that accidents occasionally happened to planes, ships, or helicopters. One helicopter crashed and everyone aboard was killed while the women in this study were in the Antarctic. Women were aware of fuel leaks on ships, landed in a plane in bad weather, or were on a ship in a storm. Women also experienced risks in interpersonal relationships—starting and ending romantic relationships on the ice or with people back home while they were in the Antarctic. They saw others taking risks or they tried actively to avoid taking risks.

Yet most women felt they had benefited from going to the Antarctic, usually in terms of personal growth, self-reliance, and independence. They felt they had gained more than they had lost from the experience and did not regret going. In fact, the hardest part of the experience was often settling in back home, and so some women continued to travel or applied to go back to the Antarctic.

SOCIAL CONSEQUENCES OF GOING TO THE ANTARCTIC

Our second goal was to study the social and interpersonal consequences of going to the Antarctic. Women in the general public who avoid risks often say that what they fear most about taking risks are the interpersonal consequences. For example, they might fear ridicule if they can't do something well, or rejection if they initiate a relationship and then are turned down. We wanted to know how women who go to the Antarctic cope with the interpersonal consequences of this nontraditional behavior. How do family, friends, and co-workers react to this? Do these Antarctic women have a network of people in their lives

who are supportive during long absences? Or do the women get negative reactions from others but go anyway? If the latter is true, how are they able to do this, given that women are conditioned to pay great attention to maintaining social relationships?

We asked the women in our study how family, friends, and co-workers reacted to their decisions to go to the Antarctic, and whether the reactions were a surprise to the women. We were also interested in the kind of support women received from others while in the Antarctic, both from home and from others on the ice. And we asked how they felt about returning home.

About half the women in this book had spouses or partners, and about one-quarter had children. Women with children had from one to six children, who ranged in age (while the women were in the Antarctic) from six weeks old to over eighteen years old. Most women received considerable support and encouragement from their families to go to the Antarctic. If anyone worried about the risks, it was usually their mothers. Friends and co-workers were often supportive; on the other hand, sometimes they thought the women were crazy. Some women actually went to the Antarctic with co-workers or friends, a few with husbands. But in the new situation, relationships with these friends, co-workers, or even husbands sometimes became problematic. At other times, women felt that having a friend or spouse along made the trip tolerable or more enjoyable. Other women began short or long-term relationships in the Antarctic or met their future spouse on the ice.

Because of the isolated environment, communication with home was extremely important to the women. However, it wasn't easy. Letters and packages from home came by ship and plane and were sporadic. There was only one mail drop at midwinter at McMurdo Station, when a plane flew over the station without landing. Scientists often had access to electronic mail via computer and found this to be quick and useful. Telephone calls were very expensive and often used only for emergencies or important events. Some forms of communication, such as ham radio and satellite telegrams (Marsgrams), afforded little privacy. Generally, women told their friends and family to send lots of mail and as a result often communicated with certain people more while away than they would have back home.

In the absence of direct communication with home, support from people in the Antarctic became very important. Women often regarded their experiences on the ice as positive or negative depending on how well they got along with their immediate work group or field team. Work was time-consuming for women in the Antarctic, and women who went there for research opportunities or career advancement were enthusiastic about the work opportunities.

We also found that some women did not place a heavy emphasis on social relationships. They didn't have negative reactions from friends because they didn't have many friends. Sometimes this was because they hadn't lived very long in any one place. Psychologists once believed that social support was always positive, and the more social contacts and friends, the better. Interestingly, more recent research has found that for women, a large social network often means more work, as people in this network turn to them when they need help and support (Solomon and Rothblum, 1986; Wethington, McLeod, and Kessler, 1987). This has been termed "the cost of caring." It seems that for women, fewer friends may sometimes mean less stress.

THE ANTARCTIC EXPERIENCE IN GENERAL

The research on men in the Antarctic has focused on a number of general areas, such as personnel selection, isolation, conflict, activity, adaptation to the cold, the altitude, and the crowded living conditions, and reintegration to the home environment. Although our study focused primarily on risk-taking and the social consequences of this risk-taking for women, we also were curious about what it was like living and working in the Antarctic on a daily basis, and what it was like being female among so many men.

Women described daily life in the Antarctic, including their work, leisure time, holidays, friends, and relationships. Most women complained about the institutionalized food and the shortage of fresh produce. Those who shared rooms felt the lack of privacy. Alcohol consumption was a major factor in social life in the Antarctic, and several women mentioned that they drank more in the Antarctic than they ever had before. Life in a small community was conducive to

the spread of rumors, and women were affected by (or contributed to) this atmosphere.

It is interesting that, despite the small numbers of women in the Antarctic, some women felt closer to women in general than they ever had before. Some women (particularly those in the Navy) had never worked with other women until they got to the Antarctic. Generally, the women performed jobs traditionally done by men and were used to being "one of the boys." Other women felt that in the Antarctic, women were classified immediately as either "whores" (if they were seen interacting with men) or "dykes" (if they didn't interact with men); either way, they were stigmatized. Sexual harassment was common for some women, and they found ways of coping with this harassment. Sometimes, women supported each other in this predominantly male environment, forming close bonds that persisted after they left the ice.

Recent reviews of Antarctic research mention the importance of studying women for future microsocieties in outer space. Yet women's presence in the Antarctic has been so recent that those included in this book still represent the first generation of women in the Antarctic. The women who are considered U.S. "pioneers" went to the Antarctic in the early 1970s.

The interviews were recorded, transcribed, and coded for major themes related to our research questions. We have included our list of interview questions in the appendix. Upon completing the research portion of the grant, we felt that the women's words themselves shouldn't be lost. We invited a number of women to be part of this book project and all but two agreed with enthusiasm (one woman had moved and could not be located; one agreed but expressed reservations so we recommended she not be included). This overwhelmingly positive response reflects the general attitude of women who have been to the Antarctic to engage in new ventures.

For this book, we decided to focus primarily on the women's voices. We eliminated our questions from the interviews and the women edited their own transcripts. They added more details, eliminated the repetitions that come with colloquial speech, and sent us photographs, entries from their diaries, and letters received while they were on the ice. We then included two women "pioneers," the four women connected with the American Women's Trans-Antarctic

Expedition (AWE), and their female research psychologist. Except for this brief introduction, some commentaries, and the discussion chapters, this book reflects the voices of women in the Antarctic. We will now let them speak for themselves.

REFERENCES

Chipman, E. (1986). *Women on the ice.* Melbourne, Australia: Melbourne University Press.

Darlington, J. as told to McIlvane, J. (1956). *My Antarctic honeymoon: A year at the bottom of the world.* New York: Doubleday.

Solomon, L.J., and Rothblum, E.D. (1986). Stress, coping, and social support in women. *The Behavior Therapist, 9,* 199-204.

Wethington, E., McLeod, J.D., and Kessler, R.C. (1987). The importance of life events in explaining sex differences in psychological distress. In R.C. Barnett, L. Biener, and G.K. Baruch (Eds.), *Gender and stress.* New York: The Free Press.

WOMEN PIONEERS

With the exception of Jackie Ronne and Jenny Darlington's presence during the Ronne Antarctic Expedition, women were not part of the Antarctic "heroic age" of discovery in the first half of this century. Beginning in the 1950s, private expeditions ceased and governments took over in mapping and researching the Antarctic. Once again, women were virtually absent. According to Chipman's (1986) book, *Women on the Ice,* if a woman came to the Antarctic, even for a few hours (e.g., on a commercial flight), the media were wont to say "women invade Antarctica." It was not until 1970 that Dr. Irene Peden became the first American woman to work in the Antarctic interior, and 1974 that Sister Mary Odile Cahoon was one of two women to spend the winter at an Antarctic station as part of the U.S. Antarctic Program. Here are their accounts of being female, Antarctic "pioneers."

If You Fail, There Won't Be Another Woman on the Antarctic Continent for a Generation

Irene C. Peden

First U.S. woman in the Antarctic interior

In the late sixties, *Irene Peden* was an associate professor of engineering, conducting research on the polar upper atmosphere. The National Science Foundation required people who had polar science grants to travel to the Antarctic to conduct research. The justification for the policy was that it allowed the researchers to experience the conditions under which experiments were conducted. However, no woman had worked before in the Antarctic interior. Consequently, Irene faced a number of barriers from the Navy commander—including the stipulation that another woman accompany her. Breaking through these barriers, Irene became the first woman to work in the Antarctic interior in 1970.

I was an associate professor who was doing research with partners senior to me in my department who already had an Antarctic research grant with the Polar Upper Atmosphere Program at the National Science Foundation. They were conducting very low frequency experiments to try to understand the lower ionosphere over Antarctica, which is a very interesting and complex region that has quite an influence on communications—long-distance communications and navigation.

I had worked on the Antarctic grant for several years already. It was NSF policy that principal investigators and co-principal investigators of research projects were supposed to go. They were supposed to go because the belief was—and it's a correct belief in my opinion—you couldn't really design experiments or other kinds of

17

research for the Antarctic unless you understood the region, the extreme difficulties of doing anything there, and the nature of the constraints that you work under. You could design very complicated, delicate experiments and couldn't perform them if you didn't understand the environment in which they would be done. So that was policy, except that no women had worked in the Antarctic as principal investigators.

There were three of us who were partners, plus the advanced graduate students, one of whom had wintered-over in the Antarctic. Both the senior partners had gone for summer seasons already so, according to the policy, I was overdue to go. But they couldn't take me because I was a woman. I must have been on that grant at least four years before I actually got to go. By that time I was really carrying a lot of the work of the grant. One of the senior partners had become an administrator and was barely involved anymore. I had most of the graduate students at that time, including two who had wintered-over already, and I still couldn't go.

We were working in the interior of the Antarctic but women hadn't even been allowed to go to the coast yet. The NSF program director was very sympathetic to the situation, and he felt there was no way I was going to be able to go until women got to the coast first. He told me of a team of four women co-investigators—geochemists from one of the Big Ten schools—who were going to the coast in the summer season of 1969. He predicted that after that, he'd be able to get me in.

That's the way it happened. I went during the austral summer of 1970. For whatever reason, probably because there had been so much foot-dragging about and resentment of the first women going there, a mythology had been created about the women who'd gone to the coast—that they had been a problem. I heard that their presence had been a problem, and they had not been productive because they hadn't published anything yet. Well, given the lead times it takes to get your research results out and to get anything into print, it's not really surprising that less than a year later nothing was public. They were heavily criticized because of this, and I think it was used partially as a reason to try to prevent me from going.

The problem was not NSF, however. The problem was the Navy, which controlled the transportation. So NSF suggested that I stay

completely out of the picture, that I write a proposal. I don't believe most principal investigators had to do this to get their trip, but I did. I had to write a proposal for a specific, short-range project that could be carried out down there and only there, which fed into the overall research. It had to be sent out for peer review; it had to be approved—the whole ball of wax. The reason for that, they told me later, was that if the Navy turned me down after my project had been reviewed and approved by the scientific community, it would be precedent-setting, since they had never refused to support a legitimized scientific project before. They'd have to decide if they wanted to go out on a limb in order to turn me down, which was pretty good thinking.

So I went through that whole rigmarole and, sure enough, they kept dragging their feet. It was a particular admiral, commander of the South Pacific fleet at the time, who didn't want to take women. All kinds of bathroom problems were mentioned—no ladies' room on the military flight, no ladies' room in the Antarctic—those kinds of ridiculous things. I was just staggered to find that years and years later the first woman astronaut, Sally Ride, had to put up with the same stuff. When I read that in the newspapers I thought, "Oh my God, they're still doing it."

One resistance argument after another came to the fore. I even had to give a briefing at an orientation meeting on the science that my whole group was doing. I had to do the whole briefing for everybody on VLF (very low frequency) lower ionospheric research, which was unusual too! NSF told me they would see to it that the admiral heard it—so he could see how totally scientific and professional I was. Then he would realize that I was not some adventuress just trying to get down there where all the men were, which is the kind of thing they were saying, you see.

I gave my briefing, but the admiral didn't come. Nevertheless, NSF said, "We're going to make the assumption that you're going to the ice." And so I went through the beginning stages of getting ready to go.

Then the admiral insisted that I must have a female traveling companion because I was not allowed to go alone. NSF agreed, and they lined up a woman geophysicist in Christchurch, New Zealand—I suppose, from Canterbury University—to go. Okay, that

was fine with me. I was a bit dismayed about the whole thing, but this was 1970 and there really wasn't any women's movement to tie into.

Then the other woman failed the physical. The flight was scheduled to leave on October 28th, and by this time it was probably October 26th. The program director said to just go ahead and get on the plane and go to Christchurch. They would keep trying to find someone in Christchurch to go with me. If I got stopped, at least I'd be closer to the Antarctic. I did go to Christchurch, and when I arrived, they had found a young woman, Julia, who was a member of the Alpine Climbing Club in Christchurch. Her husband had wintered-over in the Antarctic several years before. NSF had asked for volunteers at the climbing club. They figured, by God, anybody at the climbing club was not going to fail the physical. When I arrived, she was waiting for me, along with the NSF Christchurch people. She was charming. I really liked her a lot, and so the two of us were going to go together.

When I went to the Antarctic, I was forty-five years old, and happily married. All I wanted to do was my project, my research. My university was very supportive. The other partners had gone, and arrangements had been made for that. They simply arranged to have my teaching load taken until the end of a quarter. I started the quarter, and then somebody else took over my classes. It was no problem for the institution because they were used to it. They were used to me by that time too, I guess. At that time, I was the only woman in the department until probably the early 1970s.

I was in the Antarctic for six weeks. It was late October when we got there. Julia and I got outfitted with our polar gear in Christchurch. One of my partner's graduate students was with us too. He had wintered over the year before so he knew where everything was and how to get all the equipment together. I also had a technician with me. Our small station in the interior was about twelve miles from Byrd Station, and it was called Byrd VLF (Very Low Frequency) substation. At that time, Byrd was a station; now it is just a field camp.

The Navy took care of the transportation. Unfortunately, the Air Force pilot who flew us in had never landed in the Antarctic before. It was a wild landing. God, the flights are not terribly comfortable to begin with. We were down there in the hold, in hard little seats,

facing backwards, and not able to see out of the window. When we were coming in for a landing, Al, the graduate student, was sitting next to me and he said, "Now, this is going to be a very rough landing. We're going to land on ice, outside McMurdo. It will be very rough, so just don't get upset." Well, it really was. I've never experienced anything like it. The plane went back and forth and bumped, and we went a long, long way. When it was over I looked at Al and he was green. I was calm, because I had been warned, but he said, "My God, I've never been through anything like that before." Well, the Air Force pilot had never landed on the ice. Apparently, there are tricks to it he hadn't learned.

We drove into McMurdo and had to stay there for four or five days because it was early in the Antarctic season and we had to wait until Byrd opened up. Then we had to wait until the admiral went in first. Protocol in the military is terrific. He had to go first. I had met him—grudgingly, on his part, he was very obviously disdainful, but we did meet.

While we were in McMurdo, we went over and spent a day at Scott Base. The difference between McMurdo and Scott Base was amazing. In those days, there was no environmental concern in the United States. I remember being shocked and appalled at the casual attitudes in U.S. bases. For example, when a piece of equipment stopped running, they just abandoned it wherever it was—left it for the snow to drift over. The Antarctic has a very harsh climate. It's very, very dry. It's a desert—a very cold desert—and you're just parched with thirst all the time. People would constantly consume beer and soft drinks, and they'd just toss the cans anywhere. Toss it and leave it. Garbage in bags just tossed anywhere. And the Americans overheated the buildings to the point where you could hardly tear your outdoor clothing off fast enough; your tongue was hanging out. They had a nuclear power plant at McMurdo then too, and the pipes were lying around on the surface melting the snow. At Scott Base it was a totally different story. They kept the interiors in the mid-50s, so you could just unzip your parka, throw the hood back, and be comfortable. They didn't waste water and there was no garbage lying around, and no abandoned vehicles. They fixed everything, and if they couldn't fix it, they cannibalized it for parts and used the parts. I do understand that now members of the U.S.

Antarctic Program are very careful and are picking up the trash from previous generations whenever they find it. But not in those days.

Julia and I, of course, were roommates wherever we went, which was fine. She was terrific. I really enjoyed being with her, and she was wonderful backup. She was very strong, very well-balanced, and just a charming companion. She went out of her way to take the stress off me. She was an expert librarian. She could have been anybody, could have been awful, but she was fantastic.

What I remember about our arrival is that it was the end of the season and there were a bunch of kids who were ready to come home, some of whom were *more* than ready to come home. The civilians had volunteered; the Navy guys really hadn't, and some of them had had problems. Many of them just needed somebody to talk to, and they were just kids—twenty-two years old. I was a mother figure to them, and some of them just wanted to talk to me. With Julia it might have been a different matter, but she handled herself like a pro in that situation. They just wanted to get acquainted with us; they just wanted to talk. Certainly some thought they'd finally found a place where they wouldn't have to put up with the intrusion of women, but I think a lot of them who had been there all winter were just happy to see a woman.

After Byrd opened, we took off for there about half an hour after the admiral did. We were the first people into Byrd. Now that was quite a flight. It's a long distance and we were on cargo planes— prop planes. They were equipped with survival gear, tents, food supplies, snowshoes, and all kinds of stuff. The weather can change very, very suddenly in the Antarctic, and if you can't land, where are you going to go?

Byrd was an old station then, and it had sunk deep under the surface. The plane was gone and then we were in this vehicle driving down, and a huge black hole appeared. There was a steep snow-packed driveway going down, and as we drove down it we noticed black everywhere from the soot and smoke. I felt like I was descending into hell. It was cold, and everything was sort of slippery and icy. The station was composed of quonset huts that had been lined up in various configurations with board walkways in between, and they were all at a tilt. This is because the glacial ice is

moving all the time, so that the ice is really sliding out from under the station. It's very slow, but it does distort the shapes of the buildings and pop walls out and twist and skew the floors. Overall, it was a very grim sort of a station. It was very spare and sparse and grimy with simply no amenities.

We were only at the Byrd Station for the day before we headed out to our substation. We were really treated as curiosities. But while we were there, we were told these wild stories about the misbehavior of the women who'd been there the year before. I continued to be admonished that it was up to me to make it all good, which I thought was an inordinate burden to put on me. I had enough on my shoulders.

We had dinner with everyone at Byrd; the chef had baked a special cake in our honor, so that was kind of fun. We headed out to our substation after dinner since it was still daylight. There's no darkness at that time of year. It could be any time of the day or night. I even experienced a strange phenomenon of not knowing when I was tired.

That night we went on to our substation. The sky was very milky, and they were afraid it was going to close down into a white-out, but we went anyway. We went along, driving very close to the flags on the path, which are placed there so that people won't get lost, because there are no other markers at all. There is nothing on the terrain at Byrd—it's absolutely blank.

Anyway, that first night we were afraid of a white-out. Fortunately, it didn't happen and we got there. It was kind of a strange sight because there was nothing on the horizon at all. There was an American flag flying in this murky sort of semi-light situation, an antenna tower, and a little hill of snow and the top of the ladder. That was it. The ladder went down twenty-five feet because the station had partially sunk from its own heat load and was partially buried by the blowing snow. It doesn't actually snow often, but the wind blows all the time and the snow keeps getting redistributed, so that the station had been buried over time. It was perhaps five years old—that's all—and buried twenty-five feet in that length of time. The rungs on the ladder were widely spaced because the people who built it were young adult males with long legs. I had a hard time climbing in and out of the snowcat, climbing up and down that

ladder. You had to get your footing on this slippery snow slope as best you could, swing one foot onto the platform of the ladder and climb. That was a bit of a challenge.

I did it, but I wasn't comfortable with it. I got down all right, but then I realized I was terrified of having to do that again. In the middle of the first night—whatever passes for night—when everybody else was asleep, I got out of bed, got dressed, and went up the ladder, climbed out, and then climbed back in and went back down, just to prove to myself I could do it. I was afraid if I put it off I'd become more frightened, and it would get to be a real problem. I'm like that. That's what I do. If you have an automobile accident, you get back in the car and drive.

The substation was tiny. It was made up of three trailer vans shaped in a U, with the part that would otherwise be open serving as our living room, with a floor and a ceiling over it. One of the trailer vans was a laboratory, one an electronics lab, and one contained the bathroom, the kitchen—such as it was—and the generator room. There were also two tiny bunk rooms—you had to go outside to turn around. Ours had a double bunk in it, and Julia, bless her heart, took the upper and I took the lower. She was younger and had longer legs.

Then there was a little ham radio shack; everybody keeps in touch that way in the Antarctic, or did then. You have schedules. You have to check in on your schedule with McMurdo so they know that you're okay. If you fail to check in, they will try to contact you, and if they try and try and can't, then somebody has to come out and see what's happened. The radio is on all the time, crackling with static. You hear a lot of voice traffic, various stations checking in with each other to talk with each other. Part of the loneliness is alleviated by that.

Our graduate student was a radio ham. One thing we discovered was that it's not easy to find graduate students who can winter-over. If you make a mistake, you can be in real trouble and so can the student. My group had already learned that the best kind of young person to winter-over with is a radio ham. These individuals are very competent and autonomous in tinkering with electronic equipment. Part of the winter-over job is just to keep things running. No new science was really done in the wintertime, but you have to

change the chart paper and fix the equipment. These kids can fix anything in that category. The other reason is that they tend to be rather introverted, and they don't want a lot of people around. They seem to get what they need from others by talking on the ham radio to people all over the world.

When we got there we realized that some of our equipment had been lost along the way. We had been concerned earlier, but they kept telling us, "It's on another plane, and it'll arrive right behind you." Well, it didn't. Finally, after we got to Byrd substation we had a finite amount of time to do our job because all the equipment was scheduled. We had a snowcat that we had to radio-equip in order to run our experiment. We had to drive up and down the baseline, taking measurements, to conduct the experiment that I had proposed and received approval to do. And there's no resupply. When you get into the interior you'd better have everything with you, and spares, because there's no way you can get anything more. This equipment box had not stayed with us, and it was vital to our experiment. It was a small box, and was supposed to have been hand-carried by our technician. There were a number of people who knew more about what was going on in the background than I did, and some were absolutely convinced that it was sabotage. In retrospect, I think it probably was. Anyway, for whatever reason, it had been taken off our plane. The technician was told he couldn't carry it in the cabin; it had to go into the hold. Then they took it off in Hawaii and put it on the other plane, which then didn't come in. We later learned it came in on the flight that arrived as we were leaving the Antarctic.

Now, what were we going to do? We had a certain amount of time—no more—and then the equipment and vehicles would go to somebody else. We were scheduled to leave, and we had to go when we were scheduled. We couldn't do the experiment without it, so they kept saying, "It's going to come any day; it's going to come any day. We're checking the route." We went ahead and modified everything we could in the electronics lab. We did everything possible, and still we didn't have the needed equipment.

By now the NSF station chief in McMurdo and the one at Christchurch, too, by radio, were saying to me, "We're doing everything we can; we haven't located your equipment. You must do your

experiment on time, and if you fail, there won't be another woman on the Antarctic Continent for a generation." It was getting pretty tense. Then a Stanford graduate student who was the chief scientist (they tend to be young down there) over at Byrd station came to visit us at a very crucial time. In the course of talking with him, we described our problem. He immediately knew that he had some equipment at Byrd that we could modify. It wouldn't do the job we needed done as it stood, but he knew that we could modify it to make it work for us. Al, the graduate student with me, was an electronic wizard and radio ham, and he knew exactly what to do. We finally were ready to go. We loaded up the van and started to work. By then, we had to work twelve-hour days to complete the work in time.

Meanwhile, Julia took the load off me by assuming my duties. All the jobs in a small station are rotated—cooking, cleaning, doing dishes, and shoveling snow for water. I gave up my snow-shoveling duty immediately upon arrival because my nose was bleeding, and I had a splitting headache from the altitude. By that time I was really exhausted, and I was forty-five. I just said, "I really can't do it. I might have a heart attack here if I start shoveling snow, the way I am." They immediately revised the schedule and I was relieved of snow-shoveling; they divided that up among themselves. The only way to get water is by shoveling snow into a melter. Because the snow is so dry, it takes a great deal of it to make water.

Cooking was a major activity. We made our own bread from a mix. The Navy provided the mix, but the Navy didn't man this little station. We had to do all the work. Up on the top of the van, but under the quonset hut, there was a lot of space. It was extremely cold, but it was protected, and that's where they stored the food, which was all canned, frozen, or dried. So we had all these industrial-size cans. A can of peaches was huge, and it was all up there. menus had to be planned the day before; the cook would go up there, get what was needed, bring it down, and try to thaw it out so it could be cooked. I did some of the cooking, but when we were actually running the experiment, I didn't; Julia cooked then.

We worked in twelve-hour shifts, day after day, to use the remaining time. We knew we had good data that I could take back with me to Seattle. Each day we would load up the van with food

because there could be a white-out while we were out collecting data, and we had to be able to sustain ourselves. We always had a tin can for melting snow for water, food supplies on board, and sleeping bags. We never experienced a white-out while we were out collecting data, but we were close to it at times. We worked in very borderline conditions, and we were running out of time. There were several mornings when we'd pop up and find it was a total white-out, and we couldn't go out at all. But every day that we could, we went out to collect data.

We took turns driving. I didn't do much of it because my legs were too short. I had to lift my bottom off the seat in order to reach the clutch. Julia did a lot of the driving; she was a long-legged girl. Sometimes, Al or the technician did the driving, but at times the technician stayed back at the station. Al and I mostly did the measurements.

My husband Leo had bought me a port-a-potty before we left, and I took it along. When you spend twelve-hour days, you have to deal with these things. I made everybody else get out of the van, and I stayed in it so as not to be uncomfortable. I'd then take my little plastic bag and just toss it; there wasn't anything else you could do out there. Julia, on the other hand, made everybody stay in, and she brought the port-a-potty out. Of course, the young men would just go out.

We had a lot of visitors. It was quite a unique little substation and was often shown off. People would appear unexpectedly and we'd have to provide food. One day Julia and several of the men walked the distance to Byrd—twelve miles. They were not supposed to do that because of frostbite. A certain amount of grumping and complaining was going on about our use of the vehicle. We were resented because other people wanted to do their experiments, too. The vehicle had to go to somebody else as soon as we were through, and of course the people assumed they would have had it if we hadn't. A lot of complaining went on in the background. We just ignored it. And I don't doubt that there always is that kind of stuff. I think some of these things get exacerbated when women are involved, but they happen to men, too.

My subordinates had more Antarctic experience than I did, but that wasn't a problem. I just said, "You know the environment; I don't." When I needed to act like the senior scientific leader for

some reason, I did. Sometimes I did need to exert my influence, when there was tension between people or something similar. If we had to make a decision, I made it.

After we finished collecting our data, we went back to McMurdo to wait for the flight out. The admiral was there by then, and he was determined we weren't going to get any internal flights. If you're at McMurdo and there's a plane going somewhere, you can go (or could then). Anybody who is not scheduled to do something, can get on. But we couldn't. The admiral issued an order about that. In the past, everybody got a ride to the Pole, but the admiral made very sure that we did not. When he was asked by the NSF senior representative there, who tried to get us a ride, the admiral said, "I'm not going to take any damn foreign women to the Pole" (Julia was from New Zealand). That was a terrible insult to her. My God, the Pole has been besieged by people from various countries who've gotten rides on American planes. It was a nasty thing to say. Still, we didn't get to go there, didn't get to go anywhere.

We just hung out, actually, in McMurdo until there finally was a flight back. I think we must have been there at least five days. We flew back to New Zealand, and it was terribly hot. It was in the nineties when we landed—in our polar gear. They were playing Christmas carols in the airport in this blistering heat. They're so English in New Zealand. In this heat, there were plum puddings in the bakery windows and all the traditional Christmas trappings of the northern hemisphere.

I remember being so exhausted the first night back in the hotel. Our flight back was not in the plane that we went down in but in the cargo plane, and it had taken twice as long. It had little canvas seats all around the edges. The admiral was on that flight, and he was up in the flight deck. He didn't speak to us. He was so rude that the Navy captain who was the mayor of McMurdo at the time actually apologized to us, and I'm sure that's against the rules. Anyhow, we never saw the admiral again. We just perched on our little canvas seats for perhaps ten hours; then we arrived in New Zealand. We were terribly tired, but I made myself stay up until it got dark because it hadn't been dark all the time we were in the Antarctic. Then I went out to a fruit stand, bought quantities of fruit, took it back to my room, and just ate as much fresh fruit as I could.

I had to wait quite a while in New Zealand for a military flight back. The NSF program director had said to me before I left, "Please, whatever you do, go along with all the arrangements. Don't make any separate arrangements. Don't get a commercial flight home because the timing is better; please just do everything the way they've scheduled it." So I became a tourist. I went over to Queensland and spent a couple of days sightseeing, and then I went over to Milford Sound and took the boat trip around the harbor, and I went up to Wellington. Julia actually lives in Wellington now. I spent some time with Julia and her husband in Christchurch. The technician and the graduate student did their own sightseeing independently in New Zealand. We didn't hang together after we got out of the Antarctic.

I finally caught a flight and got off at Hawaii where Leo met me. We spent Christmas together there. By that time, I'd been gone two months.

Overall, I received positive reactions. There were several people who said to me, "You really did a great job." One of them, a Stanford senior guy who was at McMurdo, said, "Irene, you were standing ten feet tall in the Antarctic. You really did it. Congratulations." This really wasn't fair to the women who went to the coast the year before and it put too much pressure on me as well. It doesn't make any sense to think it was up to me to make up for all of that. I published my results as rapidly as I could because so much lead time is required for publication.

The trip was a miracle. It was my compulsiveness, my anxieties, and my determination that got me there and through—whatever it is that made me go up and down that ladder until I was sure I could do it. Now there's a place in the Antarctic named for me—the Peden Cliffs. The location is 74 degrees 57' South, 136 degrees 28' West. I've since met a geologist who has climbed the cliffs.

If Women Are in Science and Science Is in the Antarctic, Then Women Belong There

Sister Mary Odile Cahoon

Member, first women's team to winter-over

Sister Mary Odile Cahoon **had a PhD in biology and was teaching at a college when she was asked by Mary Alice McWhinnie to accompany her in wintering-over in the Antarctic in 1974. She was extremely excited to go and received support from her religious community and most of her friends and family, except her mother who was very worried. Being an adventuresome person she was not too concerned with the risk. Her team was the first team of women scientists to winter-over in the Antarctic.**

I completed my master's degree in biology at De Paul University under Mary Alice McWhinnie and did my doctorate at the University of Toronto. When I finished, I taught biology at the College of St. Scholastica during the year but went back to De Paul as a research associate for three summers, working on crayfish. By this time, Mary Alice had become interested in the Antarctic. In fact, she became the first woman to go on an NSF research ship, the *Eltanin*, which went down to the Antarctic in the Antarctic summers.

Starting in 1970, I went in the summers to do research work in trace metals at Argonne National Lab, just southwest of Chicago. Then one day in 1972, Mary Alice called the lab and asked if I wanted to go to the Antarctic. She was applying to NSF to winter-over the next year. Since she'd been the first woman on the research ship and had become a world authority on krill, the head of the polar science division of the National Science Foundation was pushing her to be the first woman to winter-over. Mary Alice had always

taken young graduate assistants with her on the ship. She had never said it, but I felt that what she or the National Science Foundation was looking for this time was a more mature person to go for the winter-over. NSF and the Navy were uptight about how it would work to have women in the Antarctic during the long winter period of isolation.

When Mary Alice called, the idea sounded wonderful. It was hot in Chicago during the summer, and the labs at Argonne were very crowded and busy. Doing research in peace with relatively few people and definitely cool weather seemed great to me. I had grown up in upper Michigan and spent most of my life in Duluth so the cool weather was particularly attractive.

I am basically an adventuresome person so I was not fearful of the expedition. Others had gone to the Antarctic, and this was sponsored research so it seemed reasonably safe—risky maybe, but not fool-hardy. However, when I went to the library and then to a bookstore for material on the Antarctic, the only thing I could find was *The Worst Journey in the World,* the description of one of the worst Antarctic winters endured by members of Scott's team in 1911.

My friends and family shared my excitement. The people at Argonne thought the opportunity was great, and my family and Benedictine sisters back in Duluth supported my going. My mother had grave reservations. She was in her late seventies at the time, and she wasn't sure that she would ever see me again. I was never sure whether she thought something was going to happen to me or to her! She didn't put up a real fuss, but she expressed concern.

On January 1, 1974, I left Duluth, Minnesota, and was down in the Antarctic until early September—for part of a summer and then a winter. The last plane flew out of McMurdo Station on February 22nd, and the next one came in on September 2nd. We flew by military aircraft because of the NSF grant. To do this, I needed to fly from Duluth to the East Coast to join the military flight, then on to the West Coast and then across the Pacific. We stopped for a couple of hours in Hawaii and one hour in Pago Pago, Samoa, and then landed in New Zealand. We were there for a few days to get out-fitted and then flew to Antarctica.

There were five people on our team: Mary Alice McWhinnie as principal investigator, two young fellows who were lab assistants

from De Paul University, a Polish biologist, Dr. Stanislaus Rakusa-Suszczewski, and myself. I had met the two young fellows the summer before at DePaul.

McMurdo Station was like a dusty frontier town. Early January was midsummer down there, and since the town was in a bowl-shaped area, it caught the sunlight twenty-four hours a day. The ice and snow had either melted or just sublimated. Outside of town the ground remained snow covered. There was only one road, leading from the airport to town. At McMurdo there were buildings—some of them large, like the Navy barracks that had a lot of other facilities in it, and the administration building. Before moving into the Navy barracks for the winter, we lived in the senior science quarters, which had six or eight double bedrooms about the size of train bedrooms in a metal pre-fab building. We were very cramped in there.

Mary Alice was my roommate the whole time. The one difficult part of the experience was that since Mary Alice and I were the only two women "wintering-over" and we were part of the same team, we shared the same lab, the same office, and the same bedroom. In inviting us anyplace, either the men invited both because we were always together or else had the awkward situation of inviting one without the other. It was a good thing we were friends. That closeness was more than most people would have now; women are more common in the Antarctic so one wouldn't have quite that same situation. During the winter we did move into a large bedroom which had wardrobe closets built into the middle of the room so that we did have some sense of privacy.

Our research in the Antarctic was on temperature adaptation. While Mary Alice had been working on the ship, she studied krill and expected to continue that work during the winter, so that she could do some work on their life cycles in the winter. But when we got down to McMurdo, we realized there were few krill there, so we expanded the study to include any invertebrates we could get hold of, plus fish. It really made a better study than if we were limited to one species.

The Antarctic Continent is barren of life. The part sticking up toward South America has some of the lower forms, but down at McMurdo and for most of the continent, it is absolutely barren. Yet,

the waters are richer per unit volume in living mass than tropical waters. We were trying to learn through metabolic studies how the marine life adapted so well. We did find that all of the animals we used had very high fat content. They shipped most of their nutrients into fat synthesis rather than into energy production, resulting in slow-moving and sluggish animals. The high fat content served two purposes, really: they had stored fat to live off as a reserve if they didn't have nutrients, but also, I felt that the fat protected the cell membranes from frost damage if they started to freeze. We had some creatures with which we were doing some super-cooling experiments. We saw crystals forming under the transparent shells and suddenly they were solid ice. Yet, when they gradually thawed, they swam around and looked just fine. Something was protecting the cell membranes and it seemed to be the high lipid content.

The two young fellows went out to a fish house over a hole in the ice to get the samples. There they would put down the nets, dredge or set a trap, and then bring the samples back to the lab, sorting the animals into refrigerated aquaria. Most of their work was outside so we didn't have them do the glassware and other equipment. When I suggested this—that we needed to wash our own glassware because the two young fellows were doing the very heavy work outside all day and should not be expected to come home and dig into washing glassware—it came as a surprise to the Polish scientist, who was a senior scientist, too, but he accepted it in good spirit.

In the summer we would work all day and go over to the barracks for supper. Then it was still broad daylight, so we would go back to the lab and work perhaps until midnight. Then we'd think that this was nonsense, there was still tomorrow, and we would go home to the little senior science quarters. Everybody there would be sitting around in the lounge since it was daylight. We would join them for an hour or two, and then finally I would go to bed.

Breakfast was served between 5:00 and 7:00 a.m. Mary Alice was a night person; I was a day person. I would roll out for breakfast and get going; she might sleep in, but then she might have gone to bed much later, too. In the summer, I was always tired because we kept working on and on. When winter came, it became dark part of the time and then finally all of the time, and when we moved into the barracks, I was a much more regular sleeper. Our room was

inside a huge building with interior halls. I would get up in the morning and have breakfast and be going out of the door to the lab before I would be reminded that it was still dark out. We would stop for lunch and stop for dinner and then, since it was dark, it was perfectly all right to relax. The old work ethic of working in the daylight had been strong. It was certainly all right not to go back to the lab when it was dark.

So the winter meant a much more regular life for me. In the evening, I might read or watch a movie, go out and look at the stars—I'd brought a star chart down for the southern hemisphere—or similar activities. Mary Alice had a regular day, too, but it was different from mine. She would sleep in late and then appear in the lab between 10:00 and 11:00 a.m. She would go to lunch and dinner, but since she hadn't been working all that long, she would go back to the lab at night and work a long time. I was usually sound asleep by the time she got back. In that way, we both did find some privacy, too.

The reason we specify that we were the first two women scientists to winter-over is that a couple of women wintered-over with their husbands back in 1947. That was not a happy situation, apparently, and one of them said Antarctica is no place for a woman. Someone quoted that to me and asked, "What do you feel?" I responded, "Well, if women are in science and science is in the Antarctic, then women belong there."

Before we went down, women had spent summers in the Antarctic. In fact, a couple of them were very resentful that they had to leave at the end of the summer, while we were staying. They called Mary Alice some very uncomplimentary names in venting their resentment. Yet, both the Navy and NSF were concerned about having young females down there. They have done it since 1974, but they were really nervous about it that first time when we went.

People in the Antarctic were very friendly and welcoming to us. The commanding officer felt that it made a real difference to the Navy personnel to have us there. He felt that people were neater, and he was pleased at how our inclusion turned out. In the winter there were twelve civilians and 117 Navy personnel. In the summer there had been considerably more of both—perhaps several hundred scientists and support staff and quite a few more Navy personnel.

Communication with home was limited while I was in the Antarctic. The mail was great as long as the planes flew. Up until February 22nd, mail was arriving in less than a week, even every three or four days at some times. After that, there wasn't any mail until the New Zealand Air Force flew a training flight and did a mail drop in early August. It was exciting to see planes—remembering that there was a world outside of the Antarctic.

We didn't do anything that seemed particularly risky. I did go out to a crevasse area and down into ice caves. A number of times since I've come back I would be showing slides and somebody would say, "Weren't you scared?" But we felt pretty secure at the time. The person leading us seemed to know what he was doing, was skilled in search and rescue, and capable on the ice—and he wasn't nervous. I would have hard time admitting there were dangers.

Mary Alice and I came out at win-fly (winter fly-in), the first flights off the continent. Mary Alice went out on the first plane in order to take care of arrangements to have a body flown back to the States. One fine young fellow, Greg Nicholls, was killed in an accident. He went out in a truck in the dark. It was evening but dark all of the time anyway; it was winter and very blustery. Apparently he missed a turn and went down an embankment. We knew the next day that he was missing. Finally they found the truck; Greg had been thrown out of it and apparently was killed immediately. The body was kept frozen down there until there was a plane in, and then Mary Alice went out with the body to do the paperwork in New Zealand. I stayed for two more days and came out on the second flight. After flying for about an hour they announced that we should put on our parkas and our seatbelts. I had never heard about putting on a parka before. We sat this way for several hours and then finally we were told that one motor was out and they had never flown with only three engines all the way back. They considered going back to McMurdo but knew there wasn't going to be another plane in for a month, so they thought, "What's the use of going back?" and decided to go on to New Zealand. Apparently the airport tried to divert the plane from Christchurch because they expected some dignitary there on another flight, and they didn't want a crash on their hands. We were told to go farther on but the

pilot said, "We don't have enough fuel." The incident made the headlines the next day: "A plane limped in from the Antarctic."

While I was there, I kept a diary of sorts—more of a listing of events rather than feelings. There were some, for instance, the awareness of tension at times. When Greg died I wrote more about feelings since it was strange. The sadness was so overwhelming; we had gotten to know each other, the whole group, so well, so fast. And yet there seemed to be so much we didn't know about Greg. I remember writing that there was no real ending. There was a service but no burial; there wasn't any resurrection joy. It was just solemn and sad and no way of escaping it because all of us, the whole community of 129, were affected by it. I think the isolation added to the sadness. You couldn't walk down the street and talk to somebody else that didn't have the same thing in mind, too. I had written in the diary that the body was left frozen, placed in a coffin, and secured in an unheated building. Then it suddenly occurred to me, "I didn't know they had coffins down there." Someone must have felt that there was some risk.

Men came to talk to us quite readily. Once I remember describing us to somebody as "maiden aunts." Even on the way into the Antarctic I had an added responsibility, if one calls it that, of being a Sister. Sometime after we had left Hawaii, one of the officers came up to me and said that there was a young Navy fellow who wanted to talk to me in Pago Pago, Samoa, because he had started instructions to become a Catholic but then was shipped out. Now he had some questions and wanted to continue his instruction, so my hour in Pago Pago was spent sitting with this young man discussing the questions he had about being a Catholic. He was baptized and received communion down on the ice shortly after we had arrived by an Australian priest who was down there at the time. The young fellow came around a time or two after. A number of other fellows did come to talk too, various ones that were concerned about their wives, usually. That was the hardest thing for them, being away and not knowing what was happening, especially if they did not have a stable home life. I am sure they talked to Mary Alice, too, some being attracted to one or to the other of us.

Coming home felt strange. We flew all the way back by a Hercules Navy transport plane, which meant a slow trip and no real

seats. We did stop in Christchurch for a night or two and then flew on to Hawaii, arriving in early morning. We went into town and sat on a patio at a hotel on Waikiki Beach—for the whole day. We had been in such a sameness of environment that the barrage of sounds and scents and of seeing trees, flowers, and people in the water was amazing. We had no interest in sightseeing, although neither Stan nor I had done any in Hawaii.

One change the experience made in my life was that I became a public speaker, certainly a change I had not expected. People started asking me to talk at Rotary and Kiwanis meetings, schools, church groups, and other occasions. I got so I really enjoyed that sort of thing, and the people seemed to as well. Even now, if ever I am out of a topic of conversation, I can just mention the Antarctic and that will be good for a couple of hours. The trip was a very special occasion and a great satisfaction, certainly. Pushing for continued peace in the Antarctic when I talk to people seems to be a little contribution I can make for that great experience.

My mother did survive my time in Antarctica. In fact, she lived to be almost ninety-five years old, dying a couple of years ago. In 1974, when she was so concerned about my going, I felt that I could not live my life, setting everything I wanted to do aside until she died. That seemed like a horrible frame of mind. I just went ahead and have done this consistently. It worked out well, and I was with my mother when she needed me.

In 1976, I became Academic Dean at the College of St. Scholastica, and I've been in administration ever since. When I came back from the Antarctic that September, I returned to teaching, but I really felt I had peaked in teaching and in research opportunities. I was ready for a change and jumped at the chance of becoming Dean.

Here at the College, I feel that women are more adventuresome than men. I direct the study abroad program in Ireland, and I always have far more women applicants than men. People around here say, "Well, you know women are more adventuresome." Maybe this says something about the heritage of the pioneer women in northern Minnesota!

After Mary Alice died, the National Science Foundation named a lab at Palmer Station after her. She certainly was a key figure in the early days of women in the Antarctic. Mary Alice has been likened to Jackie Robinson of baseball fame. I don't think they had more

women wintering-over in the Antarctic immediately after us, but they did soon after and it continues now.

People frequently ask if I would go back to the Antarctic, and my immediate response is, "I would go in a minute." In 1981, I did submit a proposal to the National Science Foundation. It was after Mary Alice had died and I wanted to go back to my own research, using bacterial cells. So I sent in a proposal and they reviewed it. They said I was too far removed from bench work and from publications, did not give any indication of continuing the research work afterward, and I wanted to do too much in too short a time, since I was trying to go down there for three months in the summer. So I sat down with all the referees' comments and figured out what I would need to do to return to Antarctica. It would have meant working in someone's lab for a year, getting some publications going, and then planning to spend a year down there with follow-up afterward. Obviously, I could not take that kind of leave from the Dean's office. I admitted, after considerable thought, that I didn't want to return for a driving desire to get back into research; I really wanted to go back for the adventure. I decided that I would remember that I had had the chance of a lifetime and be happy with that. I did not pursue the idea of returning any further.

WOMEN EXPLORERS

The first men to reach the geographic South Pole were members of Roald Amundsen's expedition in 1911. The first women arrived at the South Pole in 1969, as a public relations event, while they were conducting research at an Antarctic field station (Chipman, 1986). In 1982, Ursula LeGuin wrote the short story "Sur" that was published in the *New Yorker* (February 1, pp. 16-24). In this story which takes place in 1929, a woman wants her grandchildren to know that she and two other women reached the South Pole. They stayed at the Pole for an hour, had a cup of tea, and left no marker in order not to break the hearts of future men who would struggle to find the Pole.

Despite discouragement and barriers by governments who have a presence in the Antarctic, private expeditions to the Antarctic have continued. The *National Geographic* has published several articles about expeditions to the Antarctic. U.S. television covered the Will Steger expedition across Antarctica by dogsled in 1989-1990. Recently, four women skied to the South Pole as part of the American Women's Trans-Antarctic Expedition, headed by Ann Bancroft. Here are the separate accounts of these four women, as well as that of Dr. Gloria Leon, the psychologist who collected data on this all-woman team.

The American Women's Trans-Antarctic Expedition is still fund-raising to meet the costs of its trip. To make a donation, contact AWE, 16560 220th St., N., Scandia, MN 55073.

We Persevered in a World That Did Not Want Us to Succeed, and We Did, and We Did It Together

Ann Bancroft

Expedition leader

A veteran of many expeditions, including a well-publicized one to the North Pole, *Ann Bancroft* conceived of the idea of leading an all-woman trip to the Antarctic. With that, the American Women's Trans-Antarctic Expedition (AWE) was born. Still, Ann had neither led an expedition before nor participated in one with only women. To make this a reality, Ann gave over five years of her life in single-minded devotion to the expedition, as well as personally pledging her own finances. She took her role as leader very seriously, and she put great effort into developing her leadership skills, which were strongly challenged during the course of the preparations and the actual expedition.

When I first got back from the North Pole trip, everybody said, "What's next—the South Pole or Everest?" What struck me at the time was how ridiculous it was to think that you had to go off and do something, in the public's eye, that was big. I made sure that I did some soul-searching on my own to avoid that trap of always trying to top a previous accomplishment, ready or not.

However, Antarctica had been something I'd been thinking about since high school, when I'd read old accounts of explorers. There was always something that was out there—the dream. People's inquiries nudged my mind toward formally doing something. I thought about what might be the appropriate next step for me. Was I ready for Antarctica merely because I went to the North Pole? Was I ready to lead a group?—that kind of thing. I did a lot of talking with friends and family and just chewing on it for about a year.

I knew that Antarctica would stretch me, but what I needed to come to grips with was—did I have enough skills to put together a trip of this magnitude as a leader, and just for myself? What I did during that year of soul-searching was not only talk to family and friends quietly about what I was thinking but also to read as much as I could about this place and to talk to people who had been there. I needed to determine, really, how much would be involved, to the best of my ability, before making the decision.

At the same time, I wanted to do something that could be called a calculated risk. I wanted to mount an expedition that would also have a very high percentage of success. I took a year to gather some information—enough information so that I could make a decision about whether or not I was really ready. Then I just sort of closed my eyes tightly and took the plunge. My desire to see that continent only grew as I started to uncover information, and then I started to feel somewhat confident that I had enough ability and accumulated experiences to be able to do this, particularly if I put together the right team.

It's been five years since we really began the project to put together the team. We went on training exercises; we started gathering the necessary gear, equipment, and knowledge. That process that went on the first year, undertaken quietly by myself, continued for four and a half years as we trained. The main objective was to uncover as many stones as we could possibly turn over, to find out as much as we could find out before we went. Again, trying to achieve that feeling of knowing that we had done our homework so that our success was going to be due, in part, to our planning and preparation. We wanted to go down there and leave what I would call our margin of error open to Mother Nature—the force that we would not be able to control; we could just be as ready as possible for it.

That's what the next four years of our lives would entail—raising money and getting ready. We became a nonprofit organization. We had satellite programs off of the expedition, one of which would be research. The research for us was, more than anything, just an opportunity to give back and share our experience and the fact that we were a unique vehicle for them to gather a small bit of data. We also had an educational program that grew to be bigger—in my mind—than the entire expedition, where we had 250,000 kids fol-

lowing across the country with us as we went across Antarctica, learning about geography and the political issues that surround that continent, the environment, and women's issues. As a former teacher, this was a real vehicle to continue teaching, sort of sharing both of my loves—kids and the out-of-doors—and bringing those two experiences and skills together. The educational program launched several years ago, with the help of teachers creating this curriculum and distributing it across the country, and has continued well beyond the expedition; it's going on now.

We also had 150 volunteers in the Twin Cities area who would help make the engine move. This huge beast that we had created needed worker bees, and of course, we had no money to supply them so we had a huge driving force of volunteers. They were our grassroots movement that would allow for us to actually go to these places, to both train and actually do the trip. So we became a huge organization—a wee bit bigger than I ever had imagined in those earlier years of formulating the idea and the dream.

Then, we would finally, after many training exercises, go on the final trip in Antarctica itself. The trip was meant to be a traverse. We wanted to start from Hercules Inlet, where the ice shelf meets the continent, go toward the Pole, with a resupply in the middle after thirty-two days, and then go down from the Pole to McMurdo. We were hoping to hitch a ride on a cruise ship that would give us free passage off the continent on February 17th. The big hitch is that you've got to be there; it won't wait for you.

And that ended up, in a sense, costing us the traverse, because we needed more time. We got waylaid for ten days in Punta Arenas, Chile, with three other expeditions all doing different trips with different objectives. We were all stuck under that same time line of needing to get to Antarctica as quickly as possible—the beginning of the season, which is November 1st—so that we could try to fulfill our objectives before the summer was over. Two expeditions—ours and another expedition—were both trying for the traverse. Neither one of us made it, primarily because of those ten days lost in Punta. Still, we all set out on different routes with different objectives.

We would be skiing, pulling a 200-pound sled each, as a group of four. There were two team members from Colorado, one from California, and myself from Minnesota. We set out—I think it was

the 9th of November—and headed toward the Pole. We reached the Pole on January 14th of 1993.

The entire group had had experience leading groups. I would say that Sue Giller, who was our oldest member at forty-six years old, had had the most experience with both leading and following major expeditions. She had just been on more. We had all been on mountaineering expeditions. This was my first major expedition as the leader. We had all worked for outdoor organizations, from Outward Bound to the others, and had acquired that kind of leadership experience.

In the beginning it was pretty intimidating. Looking back on one of our first month-long training trips, I realize that I failed miserably, I think, as a leader. I had three other people in the group who were extremely experienced, had been leaders in their own right, were all older than me, and I felt that I wasn't sure how to lead a group of such experienced people. I sort of balked; we all froze, no one really knowing what kind of leadership we all wanted. I didn't know how to deliver it and really didn't know what kind of style to fall into at that time. They didn't know what they wanted either; it was just a bizarre experience.

I also realized that there has to be a leader. The leadership role doesn't mean that you have to snuff out people's voices and think that you're the one to make all the decisions. But there is always a time in an outdoor trip where somebody has to gather the information and then say, "Okay, this is what we're going to do." Still, create an atmosphere where people can voice their opinions, however different they might be or difficult to listen to.

I knew I had to listen. I also knew I wanted to succeed, and that if I didn't listen and be honest with, first, my own shortcomings and recognize those and then also the shortcomings of the group, we stood to lose a lot in terms of not succeeding or possibly making a very dire mistake out on the trail. We were going to an area that has very little margin of error and it demanded honesty.

I think one of the driving forces for me was the school kids. They never lost enthusiasm. They weren't influenced by a budget and the lack of funding support that we faced, a good portion of the time. They just had a tremendous amount of enthusiasm for what we were doing, and I would go into the schools and they would basically tell

me to go. It looked as if there was going to be defeat at every turn before we would ever get a chance to ski. Most of it centered around costs, and the kids didn't see that stuff. To them, everything was possible, and it was somewhat contagious. When you go into the schools and there's that jazz about what you're doing, and they're having school fairs to help raise money, it's pretty hard to stop at that point.

And the mail that we got—our grassroots movement—we had hundreds of thousands of people partaking in this adventure. They would reenergize us from time to time. We would get very heart-warming letters from people of all ages, encouraging us to hang on.

The fact that we had no corporate sponsorship, in my mind, is a direct relationship to being a women's project, particularly as I watch my peers—my male peers—continue to get funded. Seeing that, it's very hard for me to totally believe the line from corporations that it's hard times when they are turning around and funding my buddies. So I think that there is a direct correlation just in that area alone. We were primarily propelled by women and girls all over the country who wanted to see us do this. They're not people who have an interest in Antarctica, necessarily, nor in the outdoors; they're women who want to see women achieve. There is a real hunger for that because we've not always had the chance or the social climate to achieve a lot of things that perhaps we've wanted to. I think we represented a lot of different emotions, for women particularly. It struck a chord—and so it was an easy sell. We didn't have to justify it; we would just say, "This is what we are doing," and they'd come on board.

That really changed our direction and result. There has been no other expedition that I know of throughout history that has been funded solely by a grassroots movement. There have always been grassroots movements attached to expeditions, but the bulk of expedition support has come from corporations, governments, and patrons, from extremely wealthy individuals who kick in a huge chunk. We didn't have any of those, so we've done the unheard of.

To me, that is extremely typical of a women's project. We are very efficient; we have a tidy little budget—it's an astounding budget for a five-year period. No other nonprofit group that I know of works that tightly; it's a classic women's project. Women are used

to working on a shoestring; they're used to not getting a whole lot of support, except at the grassroots level; and they're used to banding together to accomplish goals, to overcome struggles that really shouldn't be there, that sets our gender apart. I think that gender has a whole lot to do with it.

We didn't just have the objective of getting across the continent through the Pole; we also set objectives that I think male expeditions tend not to articulate—to bond as friends and to have fun. Those objectives were written down. I think it is typical of females to state objectives and to stay committed to them throughout the course of the experience. I think it played out for us in making our decision, at the bottom of the world, not to continue, for a variety of reasons, and to make it to the Pole as a group of four when it looked as if it might, first, jeopardize the traverse and second, be a more expedient process to evacuate one or two people in order to reach our goal. We kept examining the whole picture and returning to the basis of our objective.

Finally, after the twelve-day delay, we were able to board the plane and take the nine-hour flight. When we got there, it all took a second. The two pilots dropped us off and they looked at us like, "You're out of your mind for doing this." We were the first group of women to really do this, so we were a somewhat novel group down there. Everybody knew about us—the science bases, the pilots, the Navy, the Air Force—they all were keeping tabs on what they called "the girls." These two guys dropped us off, and I don't think they thought we knew what we were doing at all. They gave us a look that said, "Oh God, we really shouldn't be leaving them." You know they wouldn't be giving that look to other groups they're dropping off. So we sort of waved, so busy that we didn't realize at the moment that we were standing there, just the four of us, all by ourselves.

So we arrived. The wind was blowing about sixty miles per hour, and we turned around and we worked as hard as we could. Our food had been sitting in the belly of the plane for twelve days and got a little warm. They wouldn't let us touch it in Punta. We had to separate some cheese and meat that had gone bad and try to replace it with some of our extra butter. We worked feverishly to try to get things in order, during all of this wind, and then we boarded another

plane, a Twin Otter, that took us actually to the edge of Antarctica where we would start our journey. We were there for about five hours and then flew again.

It was a crummy couple of days. We were extremely tired. I hadn't been sleeping, just trying to get things ready, and was very aware that if we didn't start right, with our feet on the ground, we could make a major mistake. We were going to either forget something, or in our rushed state and our fatigue, just make a wrong move. When it's blowing great guns, there is great opportunity to lose a tent or sleeping bag or have something major go wrong. It was a little bit tense.

The continent sort of knocks your socks off. It's so enormous and so gorgeous, and you've been planning for it for so long that you have to just stand there for a second and center yourself mentally before you get behind your sled and start going. I was really excited. I was feeling extremely relieved to finally be at our starting point, without any more delays. Forget the rotten cheese and meat; let's just do it.

Then, the very first night, the stoves went bad, and the pit of my stomach just turned when that happened. The stoves were brand new but the fittings weren't quite right. You're so dependent on your stoves for water and food, for your existence, for everything. We were cold, thirsty, and hungry; we needed a hot drink to revive us, and it would be some time before we would we able to repair the stoves. That was the time when I thought, as a leader, "I've blown it." We should have checked the stoves one more time. We have hundreds of thousands of people that are watching our expedition, and we're going to blow it on the first day.

We built on our mileage, worked on it bit by bit, depending on the overall group feeling. Occasionally we would have major disagreements. I'm trying to think exactly how they were resolved, but usually we talked about it. Sometimes we were in the tent, and sometimes we were outside. The advantage to being outside is you've got to make your point quickly—it's cold. One of us would express a thought and say, "I don't have that point of view; I don't agree with that, and this is why." Generally it wasn't the kind of disagreement that really fostered a lot of bad feelings. We had worked in the training portion of the expedition to be able to resolve

those issues fairly early and to deal with them so nothing was harbored. That worked very successfully.

I think one of the greatest achievements of our trip was the way in which we interacted. We're all extremely different people with very different approaches, but we got through that. I think it was, again, the commitment to come together as a group and to create an atmosphere in which it was safe to talk.

The traverse was an issue from the beginning, because we started ten days late. It was an issue for everybody, to a certain degree. There were times during the second week of the trip when I felt that some members of the group did not believe that the traverse was possible. I felt that it was my job to knock that out of their heads; let them have their moment of doubt, in a sense, but continue with the strategy. I had to keep stressing that the traverse was still a possibility because they believed in it; we could not let defeatism interfere. In fact, one pessimistic group member worked on the other two team members. She had never really come to me with it, but in her discussions with the other two, she would start to convince them that maybe it's really not possible, and that really what we were doing was going to the Pole. Then I would work on them from the other end of the spectrum. I really did trust that this pessimistic team member, who's very precise with numbers, would come around. We were actually blended very well with each other.

Once we got to the Pole, we would have to make a decision within twenty-four hours, as to whether or not we would continue and, if so, who was ready to continue at that juncture. Because the Pole was a place where we could resupply our sleds, it was also a place where, because of that resupply, we could get people out. The plane came there, so it was be a natural place for a decision such as this.

What really precipitated broaching the subject was that the flight company knew that we were under a slow time line—knew that we were in trouble. The plane's crew was on the radio with me and said, "You know, we really don't want to bring you your entire cache at the Pole if you're not going to need it. If you are anticipating having someone come out at the Pole—one or two or four people—we need to know that and what your thoughts are at this

point because that affects what's on the plane, and what we're able to do, logistically." It forced the issue out into the open. I had been thinking about this for a long time, since I had been monitoring the group from the start.

We had one individual who had been plagued with injuries and illnesses the entire trip. It was my opinion that she would not be able to go on, because Antarctica's a place where you don't really heal; you just maintain. Although she was able to keep the pace to the Pole, to a certain degree, I couldn't jeopardize the next 900 miles, which would be even more arduous because of the time frame. We'd really have to put a lot of fourteen-hour days under our belts, with the prospect of absolutely no days off.

I had tried to prepare them to a certain degree. Before the radio call came in, I knew I was coming to terms with some of this, and it was clear that the injured person had to be evacuated. I also felt that it was going to be easier to say this to her, because she had an injury. An injury is easy to explain to the public and to the press. The second person was going to be tougher because I didn't think, emotionally, that she had another 900 miles in her. That is not something that the public understands; that is not something that we, as individuals, are proud of. A bit of shame tends to be associated with not having another 900 miles in you, although there shouldn't be, after a very arduous 700 miles under your belt. It was really all about telling those two women that the goal for them now would be the Pole, not the traverse. They had worked so hard for the same thing. I was very worried at that point so I was discussing it with them bit by bit, before the radio call, just feeling them out and getting them used to the idea that maybe they needed to look at some things very selflessly, for the betterment of the group. Then when the radio call came in, I had to broach it that night because the plane crew wanted a response the following day.

I called a meeting at 10:00 at night; that's normally when people knock off. It was pretty tense. I didn't have a whole lot of time to think about it. They knew something big was up. I was living with the injured person at the time in my tent, and she suspected from the conversation on the radio even though she couldn't hear it all. I presented some of the issues, and then I went from one group

member to the next and discussed my perception of her readiness and the reasons for my thinking.

It was very hard. It was the beginning of a series of the most difficult things I ever had to do. How do you keep compassion and make these first remarks and then judgments and then lay it out exactly? For the injured person, there was no question. Everybody spoke one by one. Fortunately, most everyone agreed, to a great degree, about what I was saying and why. It's a genuine tribute to the people that I traveled with to be able to have that presence of mind and that openness, particularly the ones that weren't going on—particularly the one who was being considered to go out at the Pole because I didn't think she was emotionally ready to do the rest. She was able to sit there and listen to that, keep her ears open, take it in, and digest it. I talked to her afterward and I said, "You're going to be furious with me. Tomorrow morning you're going to be absolutely furious with me, I just know this." I said, "And I think it's a good thing. I want you to be. I want you to churn this up and be angry and to be honest with it. And at the same time, I'm going to demand of you that you go toward the Pole as you have been going; this is really where the team effort is going to come into play."

At this time, the traverse was just a flicker of hope that I was clinging to. It would have been much easier to deal with all of the difficult decision time if the traverse were a solid thing. But here we were, trying to keep our morale up, trying to keep going, and the traverse was such an "if." Yet we had to treat it as a possibility and broach all of these very painful issues with that in mind. For the next couple of weeks it was difficult for them to stay focused on the team effort. If two of them did continue the traverse, the two left behind had to deal with their own despair about not meeting all of their objectives. The one individual who would be going out, because of the emotional reasons, was extremely concerned about how that would be perceived publicly because she wouldn't be limping off the ice; she'd look just fine. How do you articulate that to an ignorant public?

From the very next day on, talk increased and fears surfaced, including some very tender times and also some very tough times, with considerable anger and frustration surfacing with the pressures that we were under. It was the crux of the trip, in a sense—what our

trip was all about. It was not about the dangers that we faced; it was really about what happened to us as a group.

So two people were going out at that point. The question was—could the remaining two make the traverse? Up until that point, you're always monitoring both yourself and the group because a lot can happen in two weeks. You can talk about this two weeks before the Pole as if two would go on, but either one of us could fall. We could use up a lot of energy, both emotional and physical, trying to get the other two weaker ones to the Pole. That factor weighed heavily in our calculations.

The woman who was sick developed bronchitis in addition to her badly sprained ankle, and the bronchitis worsened as we approached the Pole because of the increase in altitude. The Pole is close to 10,000 feet, so the air is thin and the temperature is extremely cold. A couple of times I seriously considered evacuating her. When I was considering the evacuation, of course, the other woman who was not continuing was concerned about whether or not I would evacuate her, too, because it would then be cost effective to do that.

I didn't know she was concerned about this. I was focusing on the injured person and the very thin line that we were pulling—should she continue on or get out. A couple of places were inaccessible to a plane, so we would have had to carry her out on a sled. How do you weigh out her desire and what she's really telling you about how she feels when you're so close to the Pole? Is she pulling at it with all her strength or is she pushing it too far? She was also the youngest and the most inexperienced member, so I trusted her the least in terms of her judgment about her own physical and emotional condition and about her understanding of the group aspect as opposed to her individual objectives.

At the same time I was dealing with all of this, I was also dealing with my own personal desires for the traverse. I had been in this longer than anybody, and I think the leader has a higher commitment to the overall objective and a bigger desire to accomplish these things. I had to separate my own personal desire from my desire for the group success. If we evacuated her, would we be able to make the traverse? Every day was a pivotal day. Would this be the day that would make it or break it? It was just horrible.

Finally, I decided that this woman could make it to the Pole. It might jeopardize what little hope was left for the traverse, but it was most important that we get there as a group of four, that she was physically able to do it. We had enough food, I thought, with which to do it; we should do it as a group. This overall experience, not only for ourselves as a group but also for the whole organization, needed us to come to the Pole as a group. Once I had determined that and accepted the concept of four to the Pole, I was able to lift some of that burden that I had been feeling, although I was devastated. I cried every day under my face mask.

I pronounced it to the group saying, "We are going to the Pole as a group of four, so wipe out those past discussions. Get them out of your head; they just don't matter. All I want you all to do is focus on getting the four of us to the Pole. We have enough food left to do it safely, and that's what our objective will be."

I think it was great for the group. I think they felt relieved; I think they once again had one focus, rather than a fractured focus. They didn't have to worry about whether or not somebody had sabotaged my thinking about going on. There was nothing else to think about. We were once again a group. I think it made a big difference for them but it took me quite a while to get used to it.

In making the decision, I looked at the facts, I looked at the situation, and I talked to the team member that would be going on with me. I looked at all the scribbles that I had made on the backside of my journal: the logistics of a group of four, of a group of three, two, and even a solo option. I looked at all of our options over and over and over again: the miles, the time frame, the money angle, the legacy—all the different aspects to the decision, and it just kept coming out the same way. You have to have insurance to make a trip like this, and the insurance is for a rescue. One of the options we could have chosen was to have been dishonest. At the very end of our trip, wherever we were when we finally had to stop because of winter, once the trip was no longer an option, we could have utilized our insurance at that time. Actually, sad to say, it's somewhat common practice on expeditions such as this, but who's to know? By that point you're going to be pretty rough-looking anyway. You could, in a sense, create a rescue to get most of that plane paid for. We looked at that, and we felt that we just couldn't do it. It just

didn't jibe with the way we felt. We couldn't live with that kind of decision, that dishonesty, particularly after being on a trip where so much depended on honesty. And part of that is leaving a legacy for others, because it could jeopardize the next expedition. It just wasn't an option for us. In trying to make the decision, the frustrating part was that I tried to radio my connections to get a feeling for what the mood was back in the United States, how the expedition was being perceived, what their feelings were, and what was the present money situation. I couldn't get through so I had to once again make that decision by myself with the facts I had. I kept falling back on the bigger picture. I kept saying, "I've got to look at everything." Because I have physically never been in better shape and never more emotionally ready to take on a challenge in my life, that moment was very frustrating and very difficult. It has been a long process for me to come to grips with not being able to finish what I set out to do and feel triumphant about what we have achieved.

I think if we had made the traverse, we never would have caught the boat. Being at the Pole January 14th, the boat was not a possibility as it would only be at the coast on February 17th. There was a 900-mile trip remaining; we had forty-five days to do it in, basically, a little over a month. No one had ever done that by pulling sleds and using wind canopies to try to aid in sailing. It was just impossible. The boat wasn't a reality for us. What would that mean if we continued on? Well, it meant a lot of different things for our organization. It meant putting a tremendous financial burden on our already in-debt operation. To be picked up at the other end of the continent meant $350,000 more for one flight for the four of us or the ones who went on. That was, in my mind, an irresponsible decision.

As it turned out, I'd been vindicated, because when we came home we were already $400,000 in debt. We're having a dickens of a time paying it back, even after being successful at reaching the Pole, which is what most people identify with on a trip such as this. They don't really get into the traverse so much; they're into the Pole. We're still struggling. So in regard to that one aspect of the decision, I feel that it was right on the money. We never would have been able to pay back $800,000 on teachers' salaries and Outward Bound salaries, and that would have been horrible for the people—

the crew back here that was working. What kind of message would that send if we were to continue and something were to happen—either to the pilots who would have to make that dangerous flight or getting picked up and having that incredible monetary burden? Would that have detracted from the actual success of the trip? What would that do to the Pole experience, having the four of us reach the Pole?

We were also looking at the consequences for folks who came after us, who wanted to make other expeditions. You do have a responsibility, when you take these kinds of trips, to the folks who will probably come after you. Your behavior is extremely important to the reputation created, whether that's cleaning up your garbage or getting injured and having to be rescued. Those are all legacies that you will leave for others, which will affect others whom you'll probably never meet. So it always came back to looking at the entire picture.

I continue to give slide shows and share the story with groups around the country. I think that's been a very cathartic experience for me because when I talk about the part of the story where we made the decision, often we'll get a standing ovation for just the process and the difference in the way people perceive this group—a women's group making decisions about what they perceive has been done in the past. We have been told that we made a very wise decision.

We decided to get to the Pole as a group of four, and the Pole was actually anticlimatic. It's the same old adage; it's really the journey. The Pole itself, being a research base, was very bittersweet. Sue talks about it very eloquently about how we loved seeing all of those people, in a sense, but how we also hated it and felt intruded upon. After sixty-seven days of isolation, you want to say, "Get out of here." But they live there, and McMurdo at the end of the traverse would have been worse. There's a certain amount of those folks who help you to realize that you are finally finished. It's a difficult concept to grasp. I remember being at the North Pole and there was nobody there and no Pole; there was nothing, and you have nothing to bounce that reality off of so it doesn't sink in at all; it's not until people come and congratulate you or something, that you realize, "Oh, yeah."

When I look at the sheet that we used to hand out to people about our mission and our objectives, I notice we hit them all except for the traverse. We made it to the Pole; we made history; we maintained as a group of four; and we did have fun throughout all that hardship. We laughed a lot, to the point where people from *National Geographic* complained that we were smiling too much in the pictures—we're not grizzly enough, like our male counterparts.

I still want to make other trips. I keep going back and playing those facts over and over in my mind and asking myself, "Would you do it again today?" The answer is always "yes."

Survival Mode

Sue Giller

Expedition member

At forty-six years old, *Sue Giller* was the oldest member of the American Women's Trans-Antarctic Expedition. She was also the most experienced, having participated in numerous mountain-climbing expeditions and having over twenty years of experience with skiing. Despite her concerns that her age would be detrimental, she was well able to meet the demanding and challenging physical needs of the expedition. Her previous experience made her better able to deal with the physical and social isolation of the trip.

I got called out of the blue, after I'd just returned from a climb in the Himalayas, by this woman who was thinking about putting an Antarctic trip together. She said, "I'm trying to get together a team of women to go ski across Antarctica. Are you interested?" I thought, "Good God, no." She said that they were having a meeting in a couple of weeks, in a place I was going to be flying through, so I said, "Well, sure, I'll go to the meeting."

When I went to the meeting, I was convinced, sort of, about the romance of a trip to Antarctica. I also liked the concept of such a large-scale trip of a whole traverse with just four women—at that time we were planning on five—and doing something a little different than mountaineering. It was also a good time for me to change venues, having done seven expeditions to the Himalayas.

I'd been skiing since I was about twenty-three years old. I'm forty-six years old now. I've been a Nordic ski instructor for three years in Yosemite. I do a lot of back-country skiing there. I learned my winter camping skills about the same time, back in my early twenties, and have climbed and done trips in cold weather in the Himalayas, in South America, and in Alaska. I had never done a ski

trip, though, that was longer than three or four days. However, I had done climbing trips that were three to four months and one snow-shoe trip that was about thirty-five days.

I had some concerns. I had a very deep concern about my being able to get along with the woman who put together the trip to the Antarctic, as it was originally conceived. So for about eight months I worried: Can I contribute to the team effort, feeling as I do about her? But we basically threw her off the team, and so that issue went away. What also grew out of that was self-concern about my feet, whether they could deal with the cold. I was imagining very cold conditions. Could I physically, at my age, do my share? That was a very big issue for me because I'm not used to being the weakest person on the team, and I was anticipating that being the case, since I was at least seven years older than anyone else going.

I have a hard time using the word "adventure" to describe this experience. I think I would use the word "challenge." Somewhere I read that "adventure is what happens when you make a mistake." I don't go for adventure so much as I go for the personal challenge of what I have to learn to do for the trip, whether I can do it, and what I'll learn about myself—those types of challenges. It's not an adventure in the sense that people think of risk-taking, being in an extremely cold place and surviving, and dying if you fall in a crevasse or whatever. I don't go looking to get as close to the edge as possible; I go looking to be as much in control as possible.

The first three weeks were, for me, very difficult to connect with what I was doing. It usually takes about a week to cut the tie to where you've come from, to let go of the expectations that you've brought in from civilization, and to really get yourself into where you currently are. But after I got in shape I was able, to some extent, to get outside of myself and start seeing where I was. Somebody heard me talk about this and said, "Well, it sounds like you almost hit a meditative state," and I think, in retrospect, she's right. You do such a repetitive motion, and you're looking for ways to diffuse yourself so that you aren't really conscious of time passing.

Despite the feeling of no time, we lived by the clock. We would get up usually at six in the morning, fairly rigidly, in terms of getting up as soon as the alarm went off. One person would cook and the other would do personal things. Sometimes you'd get to

sleep in; sometimes you'd be patching your feet or something. We had agreed to be out of the tent at 8:00 a.m., two hours later. You'd cook breakfast, get your water ready, pack your gear, and then everybody would be out of the tent at the same time. Then it took us thirty to forty minutes to take down camp and pack up our sleds, and we would basically pull for two to two and a half hours and then take a twenty- to forty-minute break for a nibble and something to drink, and then repeat that all day long. We would stop anywhere from 6:30 to 8:00 p.m., depending on how many miles we were trying to make and how heavy the sleds were. It usually took twenty minutes to put up the camp. The person whose turn it was to cook that night would get in the tent as soon as possible, and the other person would finish the outside chores for that tent. Then she would crawl in and that person would have a long evening off while the other person cooked and prepared all the water. That's when we did all of our sewing and preparations—a lot of first aid. That was sort of a social hour when you had a little spare time to really talk about how you were feeling and anything else you wanted to talk about as two people in a tent. During the day you can't really talk at lunch or when you're pulling. You're in a line, pulling, and at lunch you're just trying to shovel stuff in as fast as you can. Evening chores would usually take about three hours, and you would try to be in bed as soon as you possibly could because you needed all the sleep you could get. The hardest thing about the twenty-four-hour daylight was that you never felt like going to bed. I found it very energizing.

I found that the group dynamics were very good, that we were all able to talk to each other very well, that we took good care of each other, and that we were free to say what we wanted if we were having trouble with ourselves or with what somebody else was doing. It was a very supportive atmosphere—it was not confrontational or judgmental.

We started out choosing tentmates by drawing straws, and then we rotated every eight days through the group, and then started over repeating that rotation. Our food and cooking fuel were packaged in eight-day units, so we deliberately set out to do this rotation from the very beginning. We felt it was very important. Even in eight days you would get a feeling of "them and us." Not in a negative way, but you would be asking, "Oh, I wonder what they're doing

next door?" You know, "We're having this for dinner," "Our tent is cleaner than your tent," or something like that.

You couldn't talk during the day, so talking in the tent was the only way you could connect with those other people. During the day, talk would be very much focused on the necessities of life: "Are you getting enough to eat? Are you tired? Do you need help putting up the tent? Here, I've got some extra snow blocks," stuff like that. You don't really sit down and say, "Hi, how'd your day go? Tell me about your childhood."

When things were really bad, it would be not that I couldn't do it, but that I didn't want to do it. I didn't want to expend the effort to suffer this much. Yeah, I'll go out at the resupply. I never was at the point of "bring the plane in here"—maybe one or two days when I really believed that.

We had questionnaires that we had to fill out every night. They were designed to assess how we were feeling physically and emotionally. Physical and emotional factors were rated on a scale to determine elements of stress in these areas, as well as dynamics. Then there was a list to determine how you coped with this—you cried or you played, or you talked to somebody, or you wrote in your journal, or you kept quiet. We all, I think, found that having that list of coping mechanisms actually gave us ways to deal with difficulties. I would think, oh well, I'm kind of mad at somebody; what am I going to check off for coping with this? So you might choose to go talk to the person, have an internal dialogue, or something. I think, to some extent, that by having that checklist, it helped diffuse some of the stress that might have otherwise built up.

The questionnaire didn't ask if it was stressful to fill out the questionnaire! The other thing it never asked—they had us spitting in these stupid tubes—was whether it was stressful to do all of the science. It *was* stressful. There was a place where you could write comments, but I don't think anybody wrote that in. That's the uncertainty principle: you can't observe something without imparting a change to it, in science, and that's exactly the same thing— they can't study us without somehow having the study itself affect something.

In terms of group dynamics, three of us had been on two training trips together, and the one in Greenland that we'd done in April just

prior to that fall was an extremely difficult trip for me, much more so than the Antarctic trip. We ran out of food; we were on half rations for ten days, which, with my metabolism, was very difficult for me. We were under heavy time-line issues. One of the women got sick so we had to deal with all kinds of issues. I think that the three of us who went on that trip came out feeling, even though we had some fights, that we could deal with this new expedition. We felt that we basically liked each other and the style in which we wanted to travel. We had worked deliberately on being nonconfrontational, where we could bring up issues and not be judgmental. That was our priority during the Great Slave Lake trip in Canada.

So I think it didn't just happen; we had made it a priority to try to be open and nonconfrontational, and we had discovered that we could get along. The biggest issue was more the poor fourth person, Sunniva. She joined us at the last moment and had none of this background and had to try to work into the group, both from the physical part of how we handled all of our camping routines as well as the emotional part of it. We were just extremely lucky that she fit our style very well and also fit in well when we had confrontational issues that had to be dealt with. We didn't have a regularly scheduled group meeting. That's one thing I fault a little bit. We should have tried to meet once a week or every ten days to just sit down and see how everybody's doing, to make sure what our goals are for the next ten days, and make sure we're all still on the same time line. That's one of things I think we could have done differently because that's what probably caused the most group stress. We would gradually drift apart in terms of what our goals were. When we finally did have the meeting, we'd realize that were all slightly apart but still in the same ball park; we got reconnected with everybody else's thoughts. Then it would be really good.

I've been on numerous trips where I was the only woman, and my general perception is that women are more willing to make communications—good communications—a goal and to work for this. Guys tend to be a little bit more closed and a little less willing to work on the issues about communication. They seem to believe that everybody is sort of on the same wavelength without needing to have discussions, which I think is a mistake. Again, this is not true of all men nor of all women that I've been with.

We had a big discussion when we were about ten days away from the South Pole. The day after the big meeting, Anne Dal Vera was pretty upset. We were skiing along in a white-out, and we were expecting the resupply plane to fly over us. It was going to pick up a Norwegian fellow from another expedition, and dump out some mail and some food for us. We were running a little low, and we didn't want to risk getting caught without, so the plane was going to dump out four more days of food. We were expecting the plane, but we didn't know exactly when. We were skiing along and all of a sudden Anne saw this little dot on the horizon. We finally realized it was a plane, and we at first thought it was the Twin Otter for us, but it was coming from the Pole. Soon we could see the hatch was open and a little dot fell out about a quarter mile away. When we opened it, we found the plane crew on their own had included a little letter saying, "We want to wish you the best," and signed all their names. Inside were all these goodies, homemade cookies and candy and lollipops, Tootsie-Roll pops and Goldfish and stuff, and then there was a rose—a fresh rose. The first thing I noticed when we opened the package was how much we could smell that rose. It was amazing. You just hadn't smelled anything much at all until then. Just the thoughtfulness behind being in the middle of nowhere, almost to the Pole and at the end of the earth, and here came this plane with these people who'd been following us by our radio communications and chucked out this little package. It was great. That was actually a very good boost to Anne Dal Vera; I think that perked her up quite a bit. I still have the petals from that flower in my little box. I don't usually collect things, but it was just that connection with all these people who had been following us, sort of unbeknownst to us, was like, "Wow, look at this."

Approaching the Pole is interesting because normally when you travel, you get to wherever you're going at 8:00 p.m. and you put up your tent. It's not like you're going to a certain spot. But as we started to get closer to the Pole, there was a defined spot we were now headed for. In my mind, I always had visualized that little red- and white-striped barber pole. The last day, we knew we were only twelve miles out, fourteen miles out, and we could actually see it all day, although we thought at first it was a field camp. We had this "going toward the barn" effect, and I think all of us hadn't really

thought about what it would be like to get there; we just knew we were going to get there. The Pole was our goal all this time. I don't think it was until we started skiing up and seeing it that we started thinking, "What's this going to be like? "

I was flabbergasted to have people come out and meet us. We were about a mile away when the first group came out. We said, "Well, we're all going to ski up to the Pole," and because I was the navigator I was thinking, "Where in heck is the barber pole? I've got to find it." So I was looking around as we got closer, trying to figure out where, in this maze of flags and buildings and all of this stuff, was this barber pole. All of a sudden, we noticed about fifty people—a little wave coming out to meet us. So we all stopped, and they came up and they were kissing us and hugging us and shaking our hands and saying, "This is so great! We're so glad you're here!" At first you wanted it to be a private time, in a sense, just the four of you, and you wanted to be alone and just go over there and celebrate it alone and this attention was intrusive. But this changed as we started. They told us where the Pole was, fortunately, so they all walked over with us, and about twenty-five or thirty more people came out. So about two-thirds of the group that was there in the summer came out with us—this herd of people. We skied over to this Pole, and I was actually feeling embarrassed because "Gosh, why are all these people out here cheering us? Big deal. We just skied to the Pole. So what?"

In one way it was rather embarrassing, but in another way it got to be pretty empowering because all these people *did* care about what we were doing, and it helped, I think, for all of us to get a feeling that this was an achievement, in a sense. I still have a hard time perceiving this as an achievement, beyond just a personal trip, and yet so many people have come up and said, "Wow, what a great, significant, neat, wonderful thing you've done."

I think, to a large extent, that being an all-woman trip made it more exceptional. I think because we were Americans, and we were the only American group there, and we were a women's group, that a tremendous amount of doubt existed that we could make the trip. But for the people at the Pole, I think they've spent so much time there that they have a better feeling for the conditions, and therefore, they know what we've had to travel in and what it's been like.

So that makes their acknowledgment of our achievement more powerful because it's, in a sense, our peers—people who've been there and really know what the weather and the terrain is like. Their view was, "Oh, this is the neatest thing since sliced bread."

If I ever do this with a traverse, I will never stop at the Pole. I will come in, I will spend an hour, and I will go on, if it's only an hour beyond there. Because it's very difficult to get refocused again. There's all this new stimulus and stuff to go see, indoors, where you suddenly realize it's warm. You can take your clothes off and stand up and walk around. You get reminded of all those nice things, of sit-down toilets, of the nice things of civilization, and I think you really lose your focus.

We never, as a group, discussed what we felt about the trip, about the decisions, or anything like that. There was a lot of debriefing, in a sense, by having to talk to so many people there and tell them what the trip was like. We talked about the trip to the whole group in the gym. They asked questions and we were there for show-and-tell. It was a very public forum, and I did weed out a little bit—I filtered what I said. Usually it's with good friends when I get home that I'll start telling about the trip, and I'll realize what I'm saying about the inside part of it. But I think, for all of us, just having to talk to so many people about our experiences actually helped us do some of that debriefing before we got back home.

We were at the Pole, I think, about five days; we were getting very antsy. We had communication difficulties; we couldn't get a great deal of news out to our headquarters. First, we were waiting for the plane, and then the plane arrived, and we flew back with a group of Japanese who had skied partway in doing science. We stuffed the plane. When we landed at Patriot Hills, we discovered they'd had very bad weather there so we were not only ones stranded there. We were stuck there almost two weeks. There were about forty people in a camp designed for no more than about twenty-five, including climbers. It was just awful. People were on top of each other; it was impossible to get away or sit down as a group and do anything. We were on weird time lines. Some of us had switched over to Pole time, but some were still on Chilean time. The Norwegians would get drunk every night and come and harass us because we were among the only women in camp. There were a few in that climbing group,

and these women were harassed too. They thought women should be played with and not taken seriously so there were all these comments about, well, "Why did you take this gear? You can get this, that, and the other free." We thought, "Look, you can get this free because you're a hero in Norway. They don't even tell us this stuff exists in the States. How are we supposed to get it?" They were very condescending. The biggest thing was the guys would get drunk and one night they came over, trying to get in the tent, and they were half-assed teasing, but the teasing had very sexual overtones. So there was a lot of sexual harassment. They did that to the other women, too. There was one woman there who they were continually making comments about. She had very big breasts and was very good-looking, had a lot of money, dressed well, and there were all these side comments in Norwegian, which Sunniva would tell us about later (she spoke Norwegian).

I gave up about two-thirds of my life's savings, which I don't anticipate getting back. I gave up three years of my life, but I don't perceive that as giving up; I may have relinquished opportunities to do other trips or to get a job. I was unemployed part of that time, and I couldn't really look for a job. I couldn't tell them, "Well, I've got to go for six weeks to do this training trip and then three months to do this trip, etc." So, in a sense, I put my life on hold for that time.

I certainly gained a lot in terms of personal growth. I learned a lot skill-wise: navigation, winter travel, and this sled/ski business, really extended long-trip mechanics. The growth is more, I think, in self-knowledge of how I function in these scenarios, how I deal with these things. A reinforced commitment to communications, which has been an ongoing chore for me since my thirties, the task that I have undertaken in terms of self-improvement. It used to be a very, very, low priority for me, and I've been trying hard to work on that as an area of personal growth, to be more willing to communicate and share emotions. Certainly, because I performed so much better than I anticipated for myself, I have been able to renew my self-respect and self-esteem and rededicate myself to staying in shape, and to believe that maybe I can go on another trip. This experience has helped me not think of retirement quite yet and to wait to see what else can come down the line.

Skiing with the Big Girls:
An Intense Experience of Relationships
in an Incredible Environment

Anne Dal Vera

Expedition member

Anne Dal Vera **was one of the four members of the American Women's Trans-Antarctic Expedition. She is an accomplished skier with a strong background in women's outdoor trips. Originally chosen as an alternate for the AWE, she became a member of the expedition when another woman was hurt. Anne became involved in the project from 1990 on, going on four training trips. She is a lesbian, and left behind her partner of eight years to go to Antarctica.**

I had first heard about the AWE from Sue Giller. We had been skiing together occasionally over quite a few years, since 1986 when I first met Sue. She told me that she was meeting with Ann Bancroft and some of the other women who were involved with the expedition at the time.

In February 1990, when Sue came to ski with me in the mountains, I had a dream that she asked me to look for a piece of equipment for an expedition. When she asked me that, I had the strong feeling that I was a member of the expedition. I told Sue about this dream and she said, "Oh, you should apply. You'd fit right in." And I thought, "Oh, really?" She said, "Oh yeah, you have the experience and the qualifications for it."

I wrote up my résumé of outdoor experience and sent it off to Ann Bancroft and some of the other women who were involved in AWE at the time. In November 1990, they asked me to become a part of the expedition as an alternate team member. I would then

69

train with the team, and if someone else couldn't go, I would be a part of the team that went to Antarctica.

At first, I was frustrated because of the uncertainty of not knowing whether I would go or not. I also knew that I would learn a lot just from being associated with this group of strong women, so I felt that it would be very valuable to have that experience. Also, I had the kind of personality that could deal with the uncertainty well and be able to take each opportunity to learn and grow. I would be able to contribute what I could to the expedition and to feel that I was still getting a lot out of it, even though I might not go to Antarctica.

We did a training trip in Yellowstone where I got to meet Kelly Erwin Rhodes, an AWE team member. The other team members at that time were Lucy Smith, Sue Giller, and Ann Bancroft. We skied together and tested food and equipment in Yellowstone in November 1990. In January 1991, we got together in Colorado for a training trip in Keystone.

When we got together in March 1991, I told the rest of the group that I needed to be a regular team member. At that time we still wanted to have five women on the expedition, but we only had four. Everyone agreed to that. I think that worked out well because then I knew that I was going along with everyone else. It still took time for me to adjust to the idea that I was "one of the big girls," so to speak. It did feel a bit risky, for sure. I was saying, "Hey, I'm good enough to be considered an equal with all of you." It was also risky because I was saying, "This is what I need. I would like to make a commitment to this effort, and I need to have some reassurance."

One of my closest friends, Martha, was very supportive of my going. She also likes to make long expeditions, and she's my life partner. It has been very important to me to be able to figure out how to balance AWE with our relationship. We've always felt it was important for us—either one of us or both of us—to be able to go on expeditions. Although she's also a good cross-country skier, she knew that the AWE wasn't the kind of trip that she wanted to undertake. It was a challenge throughout the whole time that I was involved with the AWE, to try to determine how we could be supportive of each other and what it meant to our relationship to be apart for so long.

Other people's reactions ranged from being very excited about it to saying, "You've got to be crazy to go there." Most of the people that I associate with at work are very excited about personal expeditions. I work in experiential education for National Outdoor Leadership School and Outward Bound, where personal expeditions are seen as a way to hone skills and develop judgment. Some people were envious when I'd talk to them about doing this. I also worked at a rubber stamp factory in Fort Collins, Colorado, and the owner of that company was extremely excited about the expedition. He gave me time off to go on training trips and to go on the expedition and still be able to come back to my job. That was very good support. He also helped me buy some liners for my boots as a contribution to the expedition.

A difficulty for Martha and me was that I needed to spend a great deal of time getting ready for the expedition. Fortunately, we were able to do a lot of the training together. That was a high point of the whole process. We were able to share time together outside, doing what we really love to do.

I spent most of my free time arranging to get donations from various food companies for the expedition. That involvement along with the work that I had to do with getting some equipment arranged and raising money for the expedition was time consuming. At times I think Martha felt that I was not always present with her and not involved in our life together. That put a lot of stress on our relationship. Being apart for four months was stressful also. We had had some times when we were apart before—because we've been together for eight years now—but in those times when we were apart before, we were both doing work in the outdoors in beautiful places. When we were apart during the AWE, she was here in Fort Collins in civilization, working as a scientist, and I was off in the Antarctic. That was harder for us. It was particularly hard for the person who was at home.

That's something that doesn't really get addressed in past expedition reports that you read. The men who went off to do those explorations, such as Scott and Amundsen, often left a wife behind. What was her life like, waiting years and years for her husband to come back and not knowing anything about how he was doing? At least during this expedition we could send reports back about our progress and what risks we were encountering.

In March 1991, Ann, Sue, Lucy, and I went on a training trip skiing on Great Slave Lake in the Northwest Territories of Canada. In January, Kelly had injured her knee badly in a skiing accident, so she was not able to go with us on that training trip in Canada. We tested our tents and sleeping bags and every item of equipment that we were going to use, and we also tried to develop our systems of camping and skiing. We were very task-oriented on that particular training trip, and it was a difficult one, emotionally, for all of us.

I remember watching Ann Bancroft when she was leading in low-light conditions and being impressed with how she could be so patient with herself about it. She would get her compass to settle down, then she'd sight off into the rolling mist and find something and trudge off toward it. If somebody would correct her course, she would just correct herself and keep on going. She took that very matter of factly. That was helpful to me, to have an example of how to accept criticism that I could emulate.

I took care of the details about the food for the expedition's 120 days, making sure we had the right numbers of calories per day and the right balance of different kinds of foods, so that we had good nutrition and enough variety to not get bored with the food.

One of the biggest risks that I've taken in my life was the financial risk of AWE. We knew that we didn't have the money to pay Adventure Network International (ANI) in order to get on the plane to the Antarctic Continent. According to our contract with them, we were supposed to bring down $168,000, and we didn't have it. We were asking them to join us in taking a financial risk. We said, "We don't have the money, but take us anyway." If we didn't go to Antarctica, there was no way we were going to be able to raise the money to pay ANI. It was an incredible thing for Ann to have the courage to do that, to bring us all down there and stand on their doorstep and say, "Okay, here we are."

But we did it, and we ended up having to sign a new contract with Adventure Network. They said, "Okay, this is how much the American Women's Trans-Antarctic Expedition owes to Adventure Network, and there must be a $50,000 payment at the first of every month." If Adventure Network didn't receive a $50,000 payment on the date, they would fly in and take us off the ice and take us home, no matter where we were. It was an incredibly risky thing to

have to sign that contract, agreeing that not only would they bring us off the ice but that we would still be held legally liable for all the money that we owed them. Every time one of those dates would come up, we would have a big celebration on the ice and cheer our fundraisers back home saying, "Well, we're still here!" They must have sent the check, so hooray!

On November 9, 1992, we finally flew from Punta Arenas, Chile. Flying over the ocean between South America and the Antarctic and looking down at the icebergs and seeing the mountains of the Antarctic Peninsula, I began to realize that we really were going there, and it really *was* going to happen. I felt so incredibly lucky to be able to go to the continent. We'd been waiting and preparing and planning for so long, and finally it was happening.

Fear, excitement, and a deep longing for the earth engulfed me as we landed on a blue ice runway. The plane was gradually getting closer and closer and closer to the earth, and you could look out the window and see the rippled blue ice. At one point the plane hovered over the ice in a thirty-knot crosswind. I had talked to the pilot a couple of days earlier, and he said that we were not able to go on that particular day because there were forty-knot crosswinds. He said that he had landed there in a forty-knot crosswind once before, but he said he wouldn't do it again because it's so dangerous. Finally, the plane hit the ice and slowed down quickly, a very smooth landing, considering how bumpy the ice surface really is. When we skidded to a stop, everybody in the whole plane cheered.

The next morning we woke up, had breakfast, loaded up the plane, and flew off. People took a lot of pictures of us as we were leaving. We had a twenty-minute plane flight to the edge of the continent, near Hercules Inlet. It was an impressive landing. The Twin Otter plane with all of our stuff and us in it landed on about a fifty-foot runway.

Now that I've had some time to reflect on it, this experience was incredibly intense—to be out for sixty-seven days in an environment where the only sensory stimulation that you receive, really, is from looking at the scenery and the tactile stimulation comes from the environment, in terms of the cold and the wind; basically, most everything else you get from the other people in the group. It was a very intense experience having to interact with the same three people

for sixty-seven days. For me, it was a big challenge in all realms: mental, physical, spiritual, emotional, and financial.

Ann and Sue and I had all trained together on three trips before the Antarctic trip. Sunniva joined us three weeks before the Antarctic expedition. Ann has said that she thinks it was important that we didn't know each other very well before we got together to work on the expedition, and that in the process of that work, we became closer. She states that ours was a working relationship with one another and not necessarily close friendships.

As we skied toward the South Pole, we knew we were behind schedule and felt that the winter was approaching. Ann felt that I had had a difficult time emotionally and physically. Although we all wanted to continue from the South Pole to McMurdo, she was not sure how I would manage, given that going from the Pole out to McMurdo would be quite a bit more stressful because of the time crunch that we were under. Sue also expressed that she felt that there wouldn't be the opportunity to give each other emotional support because of the extreme push that would be necessary. I tried to imagine what that experience would be like.

Although at that time my tendonitis had healed and I was feeling much better, I knew that my body was starting to wear down. I was concerned about that because I was pushing very hard, and I was worried about doing some more serious injury. Sue also expressed that she was concerned for herself physically. She had been losing a significant amount of weight. She wasn't sure, because of pushing herself so hard, that she would still have the resources to continue, particularly once we got down onto the Ross Ice Shelf where we might have to pull through some deep snow. She knew that she had the mental and emotional ability to focus and to continue, despite whatever happened, but physically she wasn't as confident. Due to her bronchitis, Sunniva felt that, although she really wanted to continue on past the Pole—in an incredible way, she just did not want to give up on the traverse—she was beginning to realize that it just wasn't responsible for her to go on. So she agreed that she should go out at the Pole.

At our meeting on January sixth, I said that I would think about it overnight and let everybody know what I'd decided in the morning. The next day I realized that I had decided to leave at the Pole, and I

told the rest of them. That was a very difficult decision for me. I felt extremely sad to have to come to that decision, but I also felt that it was the right thing to do.

I felt very alone. I felt I was taking a big risk; I didn't know if other people would understand my decision because I wasn't physically injured. I was especially afraid that people would feel that I had wimped out or that I had lost courage or had lost my desire to do it. That wasn't the case at all, really. My decision was partly motivated by logistics because it would be easier for two people to continue than for three.

I also thought that if Ann had so many reservations about my ability to do it, I wouldn't be a good contribution to the effort. She would have doubt and a lack of belief in my ability. To me, it's so important if two people continue on together, that they be able to trust each other wholeheartedly.

I thought a lot about Martha and about times that we had worked together and how much we trusted each other that, should anything come up, we would be able to deal with it together. In the back of my mind, I used that as a ruler. It is very important to have that knowledge about each other and that trust and be able to say that we can rely on each other, which I had experienced before with Martha. I didn't feel that Ann had that belief in me. It was extremely difficult for me to make that decision alone and not be able to call up people that I rely on, such as Martha, and be able to say, "Help me assess the situation here."

I also had been looking forward to that part of the journey where we would be able to use the Up-Ski wind canopies and make a great deal of distance. I wanted to see the country and experience what it was like on that side of the continent. I felt that I was a strong skier and that physically I could have done the traverse.

Because I had made the decision on January 6th not to continue, I went through the whole grieving process between the 6th and the 14th, when we arrived at the South Pole. I went through my feelings of denial, anger, depression, and all those extremely strong emotions during the time that we were still skiing toward the Pole.

By the time we got to the Pole, I had realized that it was a good decision, that I felt comfortable with it, and that I knew what I was doing. Ann and Sue didn't share with me the process of their deci-

sion to end the expedition at the Pole. For me, it was a very lonely time because I didn't know what they were thinking and feeling.

The day before we got to the Pole, I had pulled hard and gotten completely exhausted. When we did get to the Pole, I was skiing along fairly slowly, still feeling pretty wiped out from the previous day. Ann was starting to slow down, and she had slipped back pretty far with Sunniva. Sue and I were way out in the front and Sue was just motoring for the Pole. She could see it; she was going; nothing could stop her. About 6:30 p.m., Sue and I had stopped for a break, and we saw some lights approaching us. People on snowmobiles rode out to greet us—three construction workers, one woman named Sparky and two men. They were so excited for what we were doing and what we'd accomplished.

The energy that came from them was very rejuvenating, very uplifting. Sunniva and Ann caught up with us. As we continued going to the Pole, wave after wave of scientists and support workers kept walking out to us, greeting us, and chatting with us for a little bit, snapping pictures of us.

When we got to the pole, about 100 people came out to the ceremonial pole and stood with us there. We were greeted by the National Science Foundation representative who was at the South Pole that day. He introduced us to the base manager and the doctor and some other people who were in charge of various aspects of the station. It felt very formal and very welcoming and warm at the same time, to feel the wonderful energy from all these people who'd come out to greet us because it was obviously something that was important to them.

I looked over at one part of the crowd and I saw a friend of mine who was working at the South Pole. She just very calmly said, "Oh hi, Anne." And I said, "Hi B.K.! Come over here and let me give you a hug!" I gave her a hug and we said we were going to talk later, when we had time. I had a wonderful time visiting with different people who were working there. I think of going back and someday working on the ice, too.

It was such a unique opportunity to be on the continent. I really missed the people back home, especially Martha. I'd been away from her for so long. Yet, at the same time, I felt a very strong connection with the land and the continent, and I didn't really want

to leave that either. I had mixed feelings. When we got home, many people were so excited about what we had accomplished and so generous with their energy and their congratulations. It was overwhelming to us. While we recognized that it had been a significant accomplishment to ski to the South Pole, we still felt that we had not accomplished our original goal, which was to ski all the way across the continent. We felt some dissatisfaction and disappointment in ourselves for not being able to accomplish that.

It was quite challenging going back to a normal routine. We came back a month or so earlier than we had originally planned. That threw a kink into Martha's plans because she had been psyched up for finding ways to deal with me being gone for that long. She figures out everything ahead of time and doesn't like sudden changes in plans. While I was gone, she was offered a position to go to Russia and work there establishing a university and teaching experiential education for the Association of Experiential Education. After I got back from Antarctica, I was in Colorado for two days and then she left to go to Russia for a month. We had a short time together, and then she was gone. That was really difficult for me. Fortunately, I have some other very close friends here, and I was able to get some of that closeness and intimacy with them while she was gone. It took me some time to get settled back in. I went to a therapist for a while, to help sort through some of the things that I was dealing with. I learned more about myself and what this amazingly intense experience meant to me.

I give slide shows about AWE to different audiences. Sometimes, I give a talk to a predominantly lesbian audience, and they usually ask questions such as, "Did you leave a significant other behind, and what was that like?" I do talk about what that was like for me. When I was at the Pole, I met two different scientists who worked there every summer. Both of them asked me if any of us were married, and at that time I chose to answer the question, "No, but each of us have people who are important to us whom we've left behind." Then I talked about what that was like and tried to figure out what their understanding was, and how risky it would be to come out to that particular individual.

It's something that I have actually dealt with for a long time in my life—people asking me, "Are you married?"—and trying to

figure out, now, what did they really want to know? There are so many things that someone could want to know from asking that question. For many heterosexual, married women, it's a very simple answer—Yes, I'm married. But for me that's not quite so simple. So it's something that, living in Colorado with Amendment Two, I have to think about because there certainly are very conservative people who would just as soon not see me around. But then there are also people who are very interested in what my life is like as an explorer and what that means to leave somebody who is really significant behind and how difficult that is. They're curious and interested and concerned, too. It is a worthwhile challenge to try to figure out how to answer these questions. I certainly don't have all the answers yet, but I'm learning.

One of the resources that I've found to be very helpful is a book titled, *Homophobia: A Weapon of Sexism*. It gives people insight into how homophobia is a tool to restrict their behavior. That's the power behind homophobia. One of the local newspapers here in Fort Collins was interviewing me before the expedition, and the reporter said to me at the end of the interview, "I'm not sure if this is germane to the article that I'm going to write, but as a reporter I have to ask some of these hard questions. Are you all lesbians on this expedition?" I said, "Well, I have mixed feelings about that question." I pointed out to him that, on the one hand, I felt that people who think that we are all lesbians may have some difficulty dealing with the idea that women can do challenging things. It's a way of saying, "Oh well, they're different; they're not like other women." When people say that a woman is a lesbian, it's a way of trying to control her behavior and getting her to do things that are more traditional because it's a scare tactic. On the other hand, I felt that it was important that people know that lesbians are doing things that are exciting and nontraditional, and that we do exist in the world in many different places. I answered the question for myself. I said, "Yes, I'm a lesbian." He said he didn't know if that was going to be important to the article or not. He didn't put anything in the paper about it. I think a lot of people have looked at us as a group of women, and have either assumed that we are all lesbians or at least wondered about it. I think homophobia does motivate people to say things that they wouldn't if there was just general

acceptance of people's lifestyles. That's part of the "interesting" times that we live in, I suppose.

We did run up against homophobia and sexism in our corporate fundraising attempts. Comments were not made directly to us, but we found out about it through other people who were doing some of the contacts for us.

The grassroots support that we received has always been and continues to be a source of inspiration for the hard work of skiing uphill against the wind or finding creative ways to retire the debt and continue to pursue our dreams. I will always feel humbly grateful for the widespread support we have received from the "everyday heroes and heroines" who cheered us on.

I Really Felt That There Were Spirits on the Continent That Were Taking Care of Us

Sunniva Sorby
Expedition member

Sunniva Sorby joined the American Women's Trans-Antarctic Expedition only two months before it began. Those two months were a whirlwind of activity and preparation. She was concerned about the physical aspects of the expedition because she had not trained with the others. She was also concerned about fitting in with the other women, who had all known each other for a much longer time. As this book goes to press, Sunniva is currently planning a traverse in 1999 to 2000. She has been lecturing onboard icebreakers in the Arctic and the Antarctic.

I phoned Ann Bancroft when I heard that one of the team members had dropped out. We talked for about an hour and a half on the telephone, and she gave me the phone numbers of the other two team members. I called them and the next day booked a flight to Minnesota, met with Anne Dal Vera and Ann Bancroft for about three days while they were packing food and doing all kinds of expedition-related things. It was after the three-day period, during which I met them, that it was decided that I was going to be the fourth team member. I'd spent three rather intense days with them in Minnesota, getting to know them individually, and they were doing the same with me. I took a list of questions to ask them, and I was happy with the answers, and things just started rolling.

It was two months before the expedition planned to leave, so they were at a critical point about whether they should even take a fourth person. If it was going to happen, it had to happen quickly. I'm just glad it worked out smoothly.

I had concerns about the physical aspect of the trip. I was also concerned about how I was going to fit in because I was clearly the "new kid on the block." The others had already gone on training trips together; they had honed and refined their gear. Everything was just fine-tuned, as far as the system goes. It was pretty interesting because, given that everything was already established, I had to fit into that system.

It was really important for me to be able to contribute as much as possible and as much as I was capable of. The physical part did concern me because I'd never pulled a sled before. I'd been training quite a bit before I even met them. I do a lot of running—a lot of marathons—and I was in very good shape, but I still hadn't pulled a sled. I don't think there's any substitute for that, having come back now. I don't think my body will ever be the same.

Those two months were life in hell. It was unbelievable. I wouldn't go through that again. I had to get the gear and everything. I was managing an Adventure 16 store—it's an outdoor/travel outfitter. I had to find and train somebody to fill my position, write out my will, contact my family members, everything, as you can imagine. There was a lot to do, but it was very clear that I should go, so everything fell into place. I had so many people at work that helped me get stuff together. Still, it was very stressful. I ended up losing weight, and that wasn't good. I was trying to put on extra pounds.

When we got to the Antarctic, it was both overwhelming and exciting. I felt extremely proud to be there because of all the hard work that it had taken, specifically by Ann Bancroft, to get to the ice. So I thought okay, now it's our chance to do it, to kind of "walk our talk." It was a very exciting moment. The reality of everything hit me—with a bang—when we landed at the Hercules Inlet.

I was nervous about how things would go. Despite the fact that we were flying over this incredible continent, it was very peaceful. It wasn't a feeling like "you're stranded here," or something like that, or "what a morbid place." I found the place extremely beautiful and was absorbed in that for a while. There's a curiosity that stirs, and you wonder, "How is this place formed?" The beauty of the continent comes from knowing it's virtually uninhabited and that the wind and the weather are the predominant factors. The terrain clearly indicates that forces move through there with great

power. It's wild. The constant daylight was something that kept me very stimulated.

Coming from a city and the busyness that surrounds it, I didn't have to use my mind because so much was done for me; I was overstimulated. Everything that I needed to survive was at my fingertips. I knew that I would need to use my mind as a survival tool in the Antarctic. I spend a fair amount of time alone or doing things alone, so I'm used to kicking into that gear, and I think I was prepared for that; it didn't bother me. I was looking forward to the mental challenge. I was expecting that I would need to be imaginative and creative in my thoughts. And I admit, I hallucinated a couple times. I saw things that clearly weren't there; I saw mirages. I also just tried to think of things. Sometimes the sastrugi (the ice waves) would turn into animals. It was just a wonderful way of entertaining myself. The slate was clean in the mind, and you just went for it. Sometimes I saw people. I imagined Amundsen—imagined what it would be like for early explorers to be there. At times I would picture these men, way back when, just trudging through this area with little information. It was pretty interesting. I haven't reread all my journals, but I wonder if I recorded much of that.

The days really varied. Every hour seemed to be a little bit different. Sometimes I would just think of songs or I would think of people; I would compose a lot of letters. I would build things in my mind—I work a lot with wood. I always seemed to be constructing something in my mind, and that seemed to keep me busy because I could focus on details that I wouldn't otherwise be absorbed with in my mind.

Forcing thoughts didn't always work, though. Sometimes I had a hard time thinking of anything, and that was very frustrating. I just couldn't think of a thing except, "Can't you think of a thing?" That was really odd, to feel so frozen—emotionless. My mind really numbed out sometimes. When that happened, I would simply think of nothing and focus on my breathing or focus on something that was there, that I was doing, whether it was my next step, or planting my ski pole, or what was ahead of me.

I really felt that there were spirits on the continent that were taking care of us, and I think that's one of the reasons why I didn't feel daunted by the magnitude or the vastness of the place. I felt at peace there. That was my time alone in my head—it was what it

took to get me through. I don't think, for the most part, we shared much of that. Most of what was shared were more personal things, tangible things.

Even though you're out there as a team, you're totally on your own—doing your thing alone. It's your breath; it's your step. Whatever you think, whatever you need to do to get you through, you do it. I went through periods of excruciating pain, and I didn't want everybody to know what I was doing to get me through. I just did what I had to do. I didn't want anybody to feel sorry for me or make concessions for me. It was as if this card in the deck had been specifically dealt to me, and I had to accept it; I couldn't fight it. So I just dealt with it.

Our thoughts were the only things that were entirely ours because in a tent, you're in each other's face.

I came to realize, after a few days, that each of us had a fair amount of experience in the outdoors, some more than others. I didn't want to be intimidated by that. It hit me one day, that *none* of us had been here before. We were *all* going to have this experience together. This is where we are, and I should take where we are now as my starting point. That helped me a lot, just to realize that what we were doing now was being done for the first time, for the others as well as for me. Even though they had gone through the motions of the physical tasks, they were doing them here for the first time so they were also having new experiences. That helped me to realize that I wasn't the only one having such high emotions.

The most difficult time for me was when I couldn't walk because of my ankles. I could ski, but I couldn't walk, not to speak of. I started to get worried about when this pain would leave. I trusted that it would, but I wanted to know when because it was taking a lot of my energy dealing with the pain. I was in a horrible amount of pain. I was consumed by it, and I couldn't help but not be consumed by the pain because it was there, and it was so intense it often prevented me from moving. I was on massive doses of drugs just to get through the day. Instead of dwelling on the pain, I tried to work on ways—even though the pain was discomforting—to get to a comfortable level of discomfort so I could maintain and move forward. That was a very spiritual experience for me, actually, because I sort of bottomed out emotionally and then got to another level that I wouldn't have imag-

ined possible. It was a very liberating experience. However, I was worried about how the others were perceiving my pain because I was the weak link.

I'm sure my injuries were perceived as a weak link because it was preventing me from giving 100 percent. But I was giving 100 percent based on my pain, based on where I was. So in my mind, I was doing the best—if not pushing myself to do more than that. It's hard to stay positive in such a situation, but it was important for me to do. I tried not to indicate that I was experiencing pain, except they knew that I was because of how I was moving. I was concerned about how they were feeling about that and worked on ways to get them to help me, as opposed to feeling sorry for me. I did that just by communicating, saying, "Look, this is where I'm at. I'm not doing great, but I need to keep moving, and I don't need anybody to feel sorry for me or worry about me."

I had to make this explicit because I needed help. I didn't have all the tools to get me through this thing on my own. I don't think any of us did, and we sought different ways of getting that. Because my difficulty was apparent—the physical injuries in my legs—I had to let them know that I might not have all the right answers or any answers for how I'm going to get through this, but I'm going to do it.

I was really blown away by being at the South Pole, but I also felt as if I wanted to leave. I wanted to go on and do the traverse, but it would have been an unwise decision. But at that point I almost didn't care about that. I really wanted us to complete the trip. Unfortunately, the odds in so many other ways were against us, and we simply couldn't continue. I was trying to process all of that. There were parts of me that really wanted to go on. I had more in me, and I wanted to keep going. Up to that point I'd been through so much, and I'd developed a very different kind of strength in me. My level of reference changed; I started to realize that I was capable of more than I thought possible. I just felt as if we were not done yet.

Trying to process the fact that there were all these people around all of a sudden felt very strange. All of the conversation was overwhelming, the noise level, the smells, looking at things, and being in stuffy rooms. Once in a while, when I got out of the galley or the dome, I would walk outside and just take a look out at "nothing" and feel comforted by that. I didn't want to go away from this place that I had

come to know so well. It became imprinted in my mind. Everything I'd experienced up until that point was inside; it was very psychological.

By the time I got home, I was in a new frame of mind. "We're home; we're off the ice." But I was extremely concerned about the money aspect, as I am still. I wondered what information people had received. It was important to me how the information that we did send out was interpreted.

I had trouble walking for the first few weeks. The pain started to subside because I wasn't using my feet, but I still had badly swollen ankles for quite a while. Still, they're weaker. I'm working on trying to strengthen them now because I can't stay off my feet completely. For the most part, they started to heal rather quickly—a natural process, I suppose. I just finally gave my feet a chance to rest.

After talking with people, I started to realize what we had done. I hadn't realized—it hadn't hit me. It didn't hit me until we got home. I felt very proud that we got to the Pole together, and I felt very lucky that I got to know the team the way I did because we developed some strong bonds. I was enormously proud to be at the Pole but still hadn't accepted the fact that it was an accomplishment because I had really programmed myself to do the traverse when I signed on. I did not want to go home at that point; I wasn't ready. That's probably why I can't stop thinking about the place.

Studying Polar Women

Gloria Leon

Polar expedition psychologist

Gloria Leon has an interesting history of doing research with polar expeditions. As a professor of psychology at the University of Minnesota, she is interested in studying people's stress and coping, especially among those who engage in challenging, demanding activities with some component of risk. When she found out about the American Women's Trans-Antarctic Expedition, she was excited about having an opportunity to study women explorers for the first time. She conducted studies before, during, and after the expedition, including interviews on stress and coping, personality assessment, and group processes.

I've had a general interest in studying stress and coping over quite a few years. I became interested in one particular North Pole expedition (before AWE) that Ann Bancroft was on. It just sounded like a fun kind of project to evaluate with respect to stress and coping. I was interested in looking at the personality characteristics of persons going on expeditions such as this, to see whether these persons are really high-risk-taker, danger-seeker types of individuals or what other characteristics might be predominant.

So I approached the expedition leaders. I wanted to give them some personality measures and other measures that they could take with them on the ice and fill out on a weekly basis. I arranged for an interview with the leaders when they came back to Minnesota. That's how all of this research started.

The group was, surprisingly, highly motivated to cooperate so it was extremely easy to work with them. As I said, Ann Bancroft was on that particular expedition; she was the only woman in the initial

group of eight people. It was very interesting to study her performance and reactions to being part of that group and also to analyze, from the perspective of the male group members, how the group might have been changed by including a woman.

Ann's presence definitely changed the composition of the group. There's no question about that. The males all said that having a woman on the expedition made them feel less competitive with each other. Somehow they perceived that with a woman as part of the group, they didn't have to act so macho all the time and always be performing exceptionally well or feeling that they had to be holding their emotions in check. Actually, that had a negative impact on Ann because she began to feel overburdened, in that other people kept coming to her with their problems. She felt that trying to cope and to perform well on her own was a hard enough task. She began to be annoyed that she was being, in a sense, bothered by other people's personal problems or physical problems. Some of it was just because she was in charge of the first aid; people would come to her with aches and pains, and that was part of her job. She definitely was put in a nurturing role, and again, it got to be burdensome after a while. So she had to set limits and distance herself a little bit.

Well, after Ann got back from the North Pole expedition, she started talking and thinking right away about having an all-woman expedition because it was something she wanted to do. Also, she did find it difficult coping with that many men on such an intense basis over such a prolonged period of time. Her feeling and her hope was that with an all-woman group, there would be different types of group processes that people would, in general, as a group, be more sensitive to each other's needs. For example, she thought they might be tuned in to each other's feelings, and there would be more of a general sense of cooperation and group cohesion. She thought that she as leader, in terms of her leadership decisions, could operate in a way in which she was the final authority, but at least the group could feel that they had more input in the decisions that had to be made.

My role with AWE then became one where I again looked at personality characteristics and so on. At this point, I was really more interested in looking at various aspects of the group process, to see if there really were any gender differences. I was interested first to just simply describe how this group functioned. Second, to see if there

were any differences from findings with mixed-sex groups or all-male groups.

With a previous expedition, the Soviet-American Bering Bridge Expedition, I had already looked more carefully and more systematically at group processes. It was because of that information that some of the daily ratings for this expedition revolved around the setting up of the camp in the evening, the breaking down of the camp the next morning, and so on. My work with the previous expedition indicated that this is always the kind of situation where teamwork is really needed and a key daily occurrence that changes the mood of the group, depending on whether it is performed efficiently or not.

I really didn't get into the polar research to study women; it just happened. The first study was with the North Pole team, and there happened to be one woman as part of the team. That made it very exciting, but that was not the primary reason for studying that group. My other study, the Soviet-American Bering Bridge expedition team consisted of nine men and three women. That expedition went across the Bering Straits, from Siberia to Alaska. They went by dogsled. It was extremely interesting to explore the issue of both the national—the Soviet versus American—and the gender differences.

My department has been very supportive of my polar research. Everyone is very excited. It's just a fun kind of thing to do. People are interested in the findings, I think. The findings have all been published in good journals—they're substantive findings gathered by taking a very close look at a very small group of people in a particular type of situation.

The American Women's Trans-Antarctic Expedition had a very strong commitment to research and science. The aspect of our studying them was an important part of their view of their group, and they always mention our research in any discussions about their expedition. They really considered this to be very important and made a tremendous commitment to be cooperative. In fact, not one of them missed a day, in terms of doing the daily questionnaires and so on. That was just part of their daily routine. It was part of their job, just like setting up the tent and eating their food. That was part of what they had to do; that was their view of it. The men I've worked with weren't so compliant.

Incidentally, the women's group had a difficult time getting financial sponsorship. They never really did get a large corporation to sponsor them, and it was the primary reason why they stopped at the South Pole, rather than going on—because of the finances. They said it was a very bitter experience to see a group of men from Britain go whizzing by with all of these endorsement patches on all of their clothes, while they simply could not get the sponsorship.

WOMEN SCIENTISTS

More typically than expeditions and discoveries, life in the Antarctic today is spent in research stations or field camps. Although the percentage of women varies widely from year to year, from summer to winter, and from station to station, about one-quarter of the people who are part of the United States Antarctic Program (USAP) are women. There are three groups of people in the USAP today: scientists, Navy personnel, and civilian support workers.

The first group, scientists, apply to the National Science Foundation (NSF) for research funding. Researchers who apply to go to the Antarctic are interested in studying meteorology, geology, oceanography, marine biology, astrophysics, atmospheric chemistry, etc., as well as the psychology and health of the people who go to the Antarctic. People who receive grants to conduct research are called principal investigators or PIs; their grant often includes funding for other research team members such as research assistants, laboratory technicians, and graduate students.

The number of women who go to the Antarctic as PI's or members of research teams has increased dramatically over the past decade. These women usually go the Antarctic in order to set up their equipment (e.g., a telescope to monitor the stars) or to collect their data (e.g., testing for radioactivity in penguins to study the effect of the ozone hole). Sometimes they are based at one of the three U.S. Antarctic stations, at other times their research (e.g., collecting rock samples at a glacier) necessitates setting up a temporary field camp. Sometimes their research is conducted aboard a ship in the oceans near the Antarctic, and they do not set foot on the continent. Scientific research teams often come to the Antarctic for short periods of weeks or months during the summer season when travel to the Antarctic is possible and the constant daylight makes data collection easiest.

You Just Get to Stand There
and See How Nature Reacts to You

Paige Martin

Field biology researcher

Paige Martin **is an experienced field biology researcher with a specialty in bird behavior. She went to the Antarctic to study skuas, a kind of bird related to gulls. The behavioral study required that the birds be watched constantly—the researchers worked three shifts around the clock. The research was conducted at Cape Byrd, a small field camp in the Antarctic that is run by the New Zealand Antarctic Program. Field camps are isolated—very few people are there at any one time, and they must share rather tight quarters.**

I was at Cape Byrd as a research assistant; we were looking at demography and some behavioral aspects of the skuas there. Both Adelie penguins and South Polar skuas live within the Antarctic Circle. The skuas don't breed in as large numbers as the penguins do. They eat penguin eggs and chicks in addition to their more usual diet of fish, so they usually nest near penguin breeding colonies (rookeries). Skuas are in the same family as gulls, but they are a little more aggressive.

For this study, the PI (principal investigator) on our project would have been able to do the demography with one assistant. He hired three assistants because a large part of the study dealt with studying behavior. We monitored all of the skuas in the immediate vicinity of the northern penguin rookery at Cape Byrd. We made behavioral observations of as many birds as we could, particularly banded birds. Many of our birds were banded, and most were readily recognized as individuals (these birds had three to four bands in unique combination). They had color names: red, silver, blue, for example. We knew all of our birds as individuals. For a demography project, there would

93

only be one or two people monitoring the birds—when the birds arrive, make their nests, lay their eggs, when the chicks are hatched, who survives, that type of thing.

A female skua lays two eggs. Both eggs usually hatch, so the pair starts off with two chicks. Often only one chick survives, and generally, it is the older chick (the eggs are laid and hatch two days apart). I assisted with data collection in the third year of this project—data which confirmed siblicide. As it turns out, the older chick either kills the younger chick or intimidates the younger chick with brutal aggression, preventing the younger chick from eating and causing it to stray farther from the center of the parent's territory. The parents bring food to the nest site and often don't defend the edges of the territory as aggressively. A wandering chick is an easy meal for a neighbor.

We did behavior watches, which had to occur around the clock in order to know what happened to every egg and chick. Since it was summer, we had twenty-four-hour daylight. We also determined how much time the parents spent sleeping, loafing, defending the territory, incubating eggs, brooding chicks, and feeding chicks. We did our twenty-four-hour watches with the three of us switching off every four hours. Three assistants were required because of the sheer number of stiff, cold hours sitting in a blind.

Cape Byrd is a Kiwi (New Zealand) field camp, so we were the guests of two Kiwis. Altogether there were six of us living in our site. The Kiwis were studying penguins. There was a woman and her assistant doing some research on the penguins. That project ended at Christmas, but the assistant stayed and sort of helped out with our work. She didn't do behavior watches but assisted us by monitoring a number of the nests for demographical information. The skuarie at Cape Byrd is very large, about 500 or 600 birds. There were 175 breeding pairs, which is a large number of sites to be visited every day.

I was well-qualified for the position. After I graduated from my university with a bachelor's degree in zoology, I began working in field biology as an assistant. I worked at a research station in south central Florida for four years. I got to the point where I just wanted a break—a vacation. It ended up being a working vacation. I went to an island off the coast of San Francisco, Southeast Farallon Island, to work on elephant seals. I really got into the island life

there. There are western gulls and other seabirds nesting there. I was so taken by them I stayed to work the seabird season.

Immediately after returning to Florida, I saw the advertisement to work on skuas, and I submitted a résumé right away. I ended up in the Antarctic because it was a position to study the behavior of seabirds and I have always been interested in behavior. It was ideal for me.

It was much later that I started thinking, oh, the Antarctic. Then you start thinking, this is dangerous and this is really remote; this is truly unique. I was worried about traveling by helicopter. Our PI mentioned to us that you have to travel by Navy helicopter to and from the site and I was afraid of the helicopter crashing into a crevasse. I felt nervous the entire time I was there. Although, as soon as we were traveling with Navy pilots, I felt very comfortable with them, but still there was a shadow of fear.

There's a point when you realize the risk involved. For me it was when they told me to go to the dentist and ask him to make a full set of dental x-rays. You start thinking, hmm, I wonder why they want those? It occurs to you that this is a little tag which says there is risk involved. I wasn't as concerned about the weather risk. Going to the Farallones from Florida was a great big change in climate for me. I thought I was going to freeze to death then, and I didn't. The weather was something else, for me, that had already been battled. Cape Byrd is actually warmer than other parts of the Antarctic. I knew it was going to be cold, but I had seen the gear that they issued and figured I could probably survive. As far as the helicopters are concerned, that was something I had always wanted to do—fly in a helicopter—so I was able to make a little tick mark on my life list of things I've done.

We spent about three or four days in New Zealand. We were on the frequently bumped plan. Once we finally arrived at McMurdo, the helicopters had been grounded because of some accidents elsewhere in the world with the Hueys. We stayed in McMurdo for about two weeks. I got a bad cold as soon as I got to the ice. I think there was a New Zealand cold that everyone was getting, and it was very bad, so I was not in the spirit of trying to get things together. We took our ice safety course. My attitude at that point was that I should be in bed, resting. That's how you feel when you get sick.

I don't think of myself as an adventuresome person, but as I look back on the different things I've done, they certainly seem like adventures. I don't like to downhill ski all that much; I like things to be relatively controlled, even though putting yourself in the hands of the Navy might not be a good way to keep control of your life. So I don't think of myself as very adventuresome, although I have a very close friend who I call and say, "This is what I'm doing next," and he's commented, "Oh, it's always neat to hear what adventure you're going on." Right now I'm working on bald eagles in Montana. That's certainly an adventure. The adventures sort of seek me out, I suppose. I don't seek them, although the jobs I seek are challenging. I need to be challenged in some way.

In my job I look for intriguing things to watch, and it was wonderful to be able to watch the penguins. They don't have a genetic memory to be afraid of man or anything large. They come to look at you to see what you are. You're sitting there watching beings that don't know that you could hurt them. You just get to stand there and see how nature reacts to you. That's a wonderful feeling. The skuas, of course, they're dive-bombing you, and hitting you, and sitting on your head because they don't know that you could hurt them either.

I was mostly isolated from the social aspect of McMurdo, but we did make a couple of trips back, and that was neat. Go into town, grab some crackers or something to stuff in your bags so that you can have a treat one day, and then get out of town again. At McMurdo, you could see the morale level change, from the beginning to the middle to the end of the season. It was different at Cape Byrd. I think we had a higher morale at the end of the season than we did at the beginning or middle, as things worked out. At the beginning of the season, McMurdo was very crowded. They had a lot of construction projects. When we went through town, we were supposed to be there for just a couple of days, and we ended up being in a room with two other women. So there were four women in a very small room, and there was a lot of that going on. There was a lot of grumbling, but everybody seemed to take it in stride. In the middle of the season, at Christmas, we went back, and it was very, very relaxed because most of the beakers, as they call us, were out in the field and there were fewer people around. But when we returned at the end of the season, right before we were leaving, I

thought the morale at McMurdo was very poor. People had just had it. Most of the people had been there for two or three months and they were ready to go home. Once you start thinking in that direction, there's no stopping. It was fifty miles into town for us. That's approximately forty-five minutes by helicopter.

We were near Shackleton's hut and Scott's hut. We were able to go see them, and it suddenly occurred to me how neat that was—that I could go and see something that you only read about in books—and to really think about what it was like for them to be in the Antarctic. Now *they* had it hard; it was really rough. That also pertains to the morale question at McMurdo because a lot of the people that go through town don't get to do much exploring; they're stuck in town.

I had two kinds of typical days, depending on whether or not we were doing observations. We did observations for two twenty-four-hour periods, back to back. So a typical day for me, if I were doing observations, would start with relaxing a little bit after dinner, playing Scrabble—we played Scrabble every night—and then I would try to take a nap. Then my day would start at two a.m. I'd be in the blind for four hours, come out of the blind for eight hours, and then go back in for four hours, then be out for eight and back in for four, until we went through a complete forty-eight-hour cycle.

The observations were intense and also, at the same time, it could be quite boring because the skuas sleep a lot. They could be doing nothing, and so every minute you'd be making sure that no one had moved and marking that down, too. Yeah, it required some concentration, but in between every minute beep, if it was three in the morning, you probably had your head down in a half-meditative state, waiting for the beep to go off. You were trying to keep from falling asleep, but sometimes it was really hard.

When I finished at six in the evening, I got to have my drink. I'd have my gin and tonic or something like that. You got an incredible liquor ration while you were there. It was absurd, if you really looked at it. I drink, but I don't drink a lot. Still, I like to always have some on hand for just relaxing after work or something. Not that I drink every day after work, but that's an option. One of the other guys drank three beers a day, regardless of whether he was in the blind or not. In fact, I did feel that it was a contradiction to say,

"Alcoholism will not be tolerated on the ice," but you can drink if you want. I think you can have the ration of one case a week, but that doesn't include what you can get if you go to a bar. So that was a contradiction that I saw—because alcohol really was quite available if someone were prone to an alcohol problem. But I appreciated the fact that I wasn't restricted in the amount for my own personal consumption.

For Christmas and New Year's, of course, we had planned ahead, so we had pretty big blow-outs for those. Officially we had Christmas Day and New Year's Day off, so we had big parties then too. It was pretty neat to have a huge party for only five people; the sixth person had left before Christmas. We had a big dance both days and drank a lot of alcohol, cut loose. It was my first Christmas away from home, so that was hard. I have a very small family, and basically, it's my parents and my sister and my two grandmothers—we spend Christmas together. I've never thought I put a lot of importance on Christmas, but subconsciously I always have, I think, in that it is a tradition with my family.

There wasn't much risk being in the Antarctic. We actually were chased by a leopard seal, so I can't say that nothing was risky. But even that wasn't a close call. He just happened to see us and thought we were penguins or something. Then going out to the blinds, there was one day we did have a storm, and I did feel happy that we were very close to the hut when we needed to switch over because it was basically a white-out. That was the only time when I thought that it was dangerous, given certain situations. It wasn't; I had a little valley to follow straight to the hut, so it wasn't a big deal. But I do remember thinking that if I had to walk a long distance, I'd be really lost.

Cape Byrd felt very safe, very cozy, probably, although there were certainly hardships about it. We didn't have running water; we didn't have toilets or showers. It didn't seem to bother the men very much, but having a toilet was probably the thing we missed the most. That was the thing that the women seemed to agree upon. Although the shower ranked pretty high, I think, and we in fact got a shower the second half of the season. A Kiwi gentleman was able to hook up a shower in the hut, and if you boiled your water you could take a really quick shower, which was great. After that, what more could you want? We had a pretty nice little house; we had

food—they supplied us with food, and we cooked it so it tasted good. We had two menial tasks that we had to perform every day, but it wasn't hard to live at all. It was quite comfortable.

The Kiwi people read the newspaper over the radio. I guess that's another outside contact. We had communications with the Kiwis twice a day, and if somebody really needed to be chatty, we could either chat with them or they would be chatting with us or something like that. We asked them to call McMurdo and find out who won the Superbowl. Actually, we had a hard time getting them to tell us who was even playing, because the New Zealanders don't know anything about football, so they got the teams all screwed up. That was kind of funny.

Right from the outset I felt as if there was a problem because I felt intimidated by the PI. Everyone at the hut agreed that he did single me out or he picked on me about certain things. I discussed it with him, and things did seem to work out, for the most part. But then, close to the end of the season, I thought that he needed to be more supportive of us and our work. I could work for him again because I know him now. But I certainly could never be a graduate student of his. Part of it was just me reaching the point at which I'll say, no, I'm not going to take this anymore, and letting him know that. He's a good guy, but I wouldn't say he's a very good supervisor. Of course, we had one of those field-station romances going on (two people were having an affair), and that's also something that was building the tension, I think, between him and the other two people.

The PI knew all the important aspects of working together in a group and the need to communicate with him, but we never really felt comfortable with that. He wasn't quite as interactive as he thought. He was in some ways more self-centered, so that as long as things weren't affecting him very much, it wasn't a big deal. Sometimes, when I try to explain something, I'll screw up the way I'm saying something and not really realize it. But instead of asking, "Oh, do you mean this?" or something similar, or working toward what I'm really saying, he would respond in more of a direct manner, more of an attack, and I didn't like it. Other people in the hut could see it, and they didn't like it either, but nobody could really say anything. But I did receive some support from them privately.

And I think the PI did sort of get to know me a little bit after a while, and I tried to stop taking it so personally. It was a personal attack, whether he meant it to be or not, and I was just really taken way off guard by it.

The other woman didn't have any problems with the way the PI ran things; she didn't think he was unsupportive. Much later on, after we traveled around in New Zealand some, she actually confessed to having some weird feelings about him. When we were on the ice, at one point I was pointing out things to her right before we left, and she seemed really surprised that people felt that way and that things hadn't gone quite as well as she had thought. A lot of that is the isolating circumstance.

One of the Kiwi women was going through a divorce at the time. While she was on the ice her husband wrote her to say he wanted a divorce. She left before Christmas. After she left, things at the whole hut, in general, became much more relaxed. I think she had an effect on the hut atmosphere. I felt the New Zealanders were very aloof. You can get to know them, but it's on their own terms, and this individual was definitely a very reserved person. She wasn't very receptive to us when we first got there. It was quite obvious that she wasn't entirely happy with our presence. She wasn't unhappy, but she wasn't receptive, and I think we all felt that.

There was a woman who came down to write books, and she, perhaps, was the very first person I was able to talk to. Before this woman came, during that first week, none of us spoke to each other during dinner. Never. Out of six people, no one would ever say anything. That was very hard for me. But the hut atmosphere definitely changed after the Kiwi woman left, which was just a few days before Christmas. Everybody was afraid to say anything because you're just meeting these people, and you don't know how they are. You're never really sure when you should say something or not. After this woman who came to write showed up—I think it was maybe the second day she was there—she and I happened to be sitting around after everyone went to bed and some very insignificant comment was made. I think I must have made a comment, and she remarked that people didn't talk to each other at dinner, and I thought, "Oh, thank God!" I was so happy. I said, "Will you talk to me?" We sat up till about 5 a.m.

I personally am an up-and-down kind of person. I think back and a lot of the time I felt like I was being really down, and I know that there were times when I was thinking I really shouldn't be that way. It was quite a unique experience, and I should not have been so worried about the way people were interacting. However, it was very hard for me because I was so far away from home, and there was something way deep inside that recognized that there was no way out of it until the end. Perhaps because of the lack of sleep, my mood was a little bit more erratic. Then, I was much more likely to get cranky and just feel angry toward somebody. But with me, the mood either changed and I wasn't down anymore, for no particular reason, or I got a letter and that changed the mood, or I found an outlet. Whether or not the person wanted to listen, I talked to them. I think I kept a lot inside. In fact, I know I kept a lot inside. You're there; it's a beautiful place. There's no need to be pissed off at everybody. On the other hand, you've got thousands of miles of space to be in, right? This is my corner of the world. I don't need to be in your space; get away from me. So I think I just shelved it and had my normal up-and-down mood swings, the same as always. Again, that's a way of life for me because I've been living this field technician thing for about five or six years now.

What I learned from the Antarctic is that even if you shelve it, eventually it's going to come out. It just depends on when. And I hope I can convey that I think I had a good time at Cape Byrd, overall. I would tell a newcomer to be perceptive and aware of the other people and how they feel or what they're doing. At the same time you can't be totally accommodating to them. The hardest part is either being perceptive of other people or having them be perceptive of you, so that accommodations can be made, I think. That's the most important thing in a group situation.

It seems as if groups usually work out better if the sex ratios are half and half, so that things are kept even; there's an equal voice between the men and the women—all sides are equally represented. We had more of an age problem than a sex ratio problem because one woman was the mother of high school and college-age children. Gary, the PI, intentionally hired two women and one man so it would be basically even for our team. If you get too many females together or too many males together, you either get a female attitude

or a male attitude dominating the group, and those in the minority sometimes feel outnumbered, which they are. For us, though, since the gender ratio was even, this wasn't a big problem.

One member of our team ended up pretty much having an affair with a Kiwi woman. They're getting married now. It was hard at the end because they were island-fevering together, so they were separating themselves out. Of course, they were trying to spend as much time as possible together, so that left the other three of us to support each other, which we did in our own way.

I had left my job at a field station and had basically moved all of my things to my parents' house in order to go on this trip. When I returned home, things had been shuffled around because in the interim my sister had also moved home. There was not a space for me to be. I had a bed to sleep in, but there were many things that people had just moved back into the house. There was no personal space. I did not deal with that very well. When that happened, it was very harsh, and I was pretty uptight.

I just wasn't very talkative. I'm not very close to my family, so I was frustrated about this lack of personal space. My father was laid off from his construction job the same week that I got home, so then he was always home, and I couldn't just hang out in the house because there was someone else there. All I really wanted to do after three months of working was to do nothing. I sort of felt guilty about that though. And there actually was a little bit of pressure about finding another job, you know: What are you going to do next? I just wanted to sit around for a couple of weeks and maybe watch a lot of TV. I find that I usually watch about a week's worth of TV after I've been isolated.

I have sort of kept in touch with my group. I heard, once I got to the next job, because it was on the Farallons, that the wife of the guy who had the affair had committed suicide. It just added to the bizarre quality of our group. I've been in contact with him a couple of times, and I visited with the woman who was also on our team. I stayed at her house for a few days and have written and phoned her once or twice since then. I talked to the PI a couple of times, I think, but it's a waning thing; it's probably not something that will keep going.

I gave up a job to go to the Antarctic. There was no reason for me to leave it, other than to go to the Antarctic. I actually was moving in the direction that I liked, which was seabirds. I've continued working on seabirds. This bald eagle project is just a little flirt with fun, and in a couple of months, I'll be starting a new job, and that will be a permanent seabird job. I've moved in the direction that I wanted to, so I never felt like I gave up that much. I gained the obvious—I gained more seabird experience, which was very beneficial. I put another little notch on my confidence belt, as far as doing certain field work.

I Was Amazed at How Much
I Was Affected by Antarctica

Kerry-Anne Mammone

College student

Kerry-Anne Mammone, a marine geology student at Hamilton College, was asked by her research advisor to go to the Antarctic to do field work on her thesis. Kerry was very excited but was a bit worried about the reaction of her family and friends to her newly planned trip. Having never been out to sea before, Kerry was also a bit nervous about crossing the Drake Passage and cruising through ice-laden waters. She spent five weeks on a research vessel doing geologic sampling and reconnaissance along the Antarctic Peninsula. She enjoys working outdoors and is always seeking new adventures on land or at sea. Kerry plans to continue her research of the polar regions in graduate school.

Journal entry, April 17, 1992, 5:12 p.m.

There is no place on earth like Antarctica! I hope that I can return again some day. I would be disappointed, for I cannot relive this trip. Maybe my wanting to return to Antarctica is to try to relive the experience I now am leaving behind.

I can understand, now, why going to Antarctica is so addictive. It is the friendships, the special bonds which cannot be formed anywhere else on earth, that keep you coming back. The solitude, the scenery, a continent almost free of human intervention and exploitation. I will miss Antarctica and everything and everyone associated with it forever. This experience lies deeply imbedded in my mind, heart, and soul. Thank you, everyone, for all of the memories that you have given me.

I went to the Antarctic to do some geologic sampling, take cores, grab samples, and pick up sediment moorings that were already

105

there. They had been put there in October by my professor, Gene Domack. We were sampling all day and night, a twenty-four-hour period.

The way I got to go to the Antarctic was that my professor pulled another student, Matt, and me aside one day and asked, "Hey, do you want to go to Antarctica?" I said sure. I had helped him do some research, analyzing some of his samples he had taken in previous years, hoping that maybe I could go to the Antarctic sometime. When my professor invited me to go, I was happy. I thought, "Yay!" When he asked me, I said, "Sure, I'll go." I never even thought to see if it was okay with my folks or anyone. I didn't ask anyone. I just said yes.

I wanted to go because so few people have been there. It's so barren, so isolated, so remote from civilization, which makes it so much better—no everyday distractions, no everyday stress. There's nothing to worry about when you're there. It's so peaceful. There is no noise pollution or any pollution, in general. It's so clean compared to the United States.

There were financial worries though. I wasn't sure if I'd be able to afford the cost. Then there were other considerations such as, are my parents going to say, "No, you can't go"? They weren't too thrilled about it when I first told them. They didn't really like the idea of my going someplace so far away, where they really couldn't get in touch with me. That was another thing; you can't really contact anyone at all. You're isolated, which is nice, but after a period of time you think, all right, I need to talk to somebody or at least receive a letter or something. I found out, when I got there, that there's much more communication than I realized, but initially it was a worry. Also, I was worried about missing school. I had to catch up within two weeks because we got back two weeks before the semester ended. I had to make up work like crazy, and that was a concern. I was afraid I would never be able to make it up.

But in general, I felt it was a great opportunity; how many people get the chance to go? I decided I wanted to go, and I figured my friends, my boyfriend, my parents, would just have to deal with it. I knew that none of them would like me going away for that amount of time, when they couldn't speak to me, but I wanted to go. Every-

one said, "Well, why do you want to do that?" I guess my parents were supportive, but I think it scared them.

My friends said, "Wow, that's great. I wish I could do that." Then they were upset because most of my friends were all seniors that year and were all graduating. I was leaving the very end of the semester, and they were leaving after that. Initially, my boyfriend wasn't too enthusiastic—"You're going away for a month?" Although he complained, he was very supportive because he wanted me to have the opportunity; still, he didn't like the separation.

I was very hesitant the week before I left. I looked up all my old friends I hadn't talked to because I didn't think I was coming back, at one point. I don't know why. I really got scared because I've never been out to sea. The Drake Passage is one of the roughest waterways, especially at the time of year we were traveling. I was nervous about that, and there were so many other things that could go wrong. I thought, we could hit an iceberg, and then we would sink. I know that everyone else has come back, but there's always that chance. When we got there, the first thing we did was run over sea ice and icebergs, and it scrapes the hull. I didn't know what it was. I thought we hit something. I thought we were going down. I was in bed; all of a sudden—crash—and the whole ship rocked. Scared me. People said, "Oh, don't worry about it. We'll hit bigger ones later."

I don't go on lots of adventures. Maybe if I had a car I'd do more traveling. I haven't traveled all that much. The summer before, I went to Colorado to do geologic mapping. I decided I was going to go, in advance, and I went. I don't usually just take off and do things. Usually things are fairly planned and calculated, although I tend to do very strange things occasionally. I try to be unpredictable. I will do things on a whim, but a fairly large adventure is a little bit out of the ordinary.

On our team there was the chief scientist; he was from Colgate. Then there were two students from Hamilton, four from Colgate, one from Middlebury, and a professor from Middlebury, also, and then one graduate student from Rice joined us.

We went away for five weeks in the southern hemisphere fall. We were the last research group to go down. We brought people with us and dropped them off, and we brought people back, but everyone who was there after we left was there for the winter.

It started getting very dark. It got dark early, and it started getting stormy. There was a lot more ice than we had anticipated, so we couldn't do some of our research because the ice prevented us. A lot of people were surprised that we went down there that late. I didn't think it was that late, but I guess most people go in the Antarctic summer—January, February, December. But it was nice. Not too much sunshine, though.

It was probably the best month of my life. I enjoyed it so much that I never wanted to leave. It was incredible. Sure, we were there for sampling and things such as that, but I think I spent more time learning about myself and others than doing actual sampling. The actual scientific work was a small part of it. I found that most people agreed with me about that. If it'd just been me, I would have thought, "Well, maybe I'm weird." But most people agree because you're all alone a lot of the time. You're sitting out on deck, and all around you, everywhere you look, it's snow and ice. You're out on the ocean, and you can't help but sit there and think. It's amazing. It's beautiful, too.

We had shifts we had to work. It would change every week, the shift you were on, which made it extremely difficult. You got used to one sleeping schedule, and then your shift would change. Instead of being up all night, you were up all day, and that changed every week. By the time you got adjusted to it, it changed again. I must have slept about three hours a day. I didn't want to miss anything, and I was so busy doing other things. You might work all night, and then breakfast would be at around eight, so you'd go to breakfast. Next, you might hang out for a while or go to bed for a while, then get up around noon to go to lunch, then hang out for a while. People tend to play cards, write in their journals, read books, watch movies on the VCR on board, or go up onto the bridge and chat with the captain and the first mate. They let me steer the boat, which was fun. Dinner is around six p.m. A lot of people would use the sauna or use the bike downstairs before dinner. There was even a sun lamp, although I don't think anyone used it.

Many times after dinner, if you weren't working, people would sit in what they call the dayroom. The crew was all Norwegian, and a lot of them didn't speak English well. They'd be speaking Norwegian, and you'd know they were saying something about you, and

you didn't know what it was. You'd sit and just get to know the crew a bit, although it got very smoky because they all smoked. I spent my free time hanging out with the crew, getting to know them, because they were a lot of fun. The crew members were so unique and had many stories to tell.

I would sit out on deck if it wasn't too cold or windy and enjoy the environment. I might write in my journal. I wrote ten to fifteen pages a day. I spent a couple of hours writing a day. I've never quite had a journal like this. Everyone said, "Oh, keep a journal. You'll want to." I usually get lazy and do it for two days, and that's it. But I wrote consistently, at least once a day, at least ten pages a day. For the most part, I wrote what happened in my day, just discoveries I'd made and insights I'd learned about myself, and about other people, and just human nature in general. It was really philosophical, which is weird, because that's not like me. I look back through it now, and some of it I laugh at, and some of it I can't believe I wrote. I ended up filling two journals. I actually quoted one, in a paper, the other day.

We were on land once or twice. We stopped on one of the islands, at one of the U.S. stations, and it was incredible. The people there have a common bond because they were all there together, and nobody else was going to be around, and you definitely had to work together; otherwise it wasn't going to work. It was pretty incredible.

I was amazed at how much I was affected by Antarctica. I was excited to go, but I didn't expect to have the strong reaction that I did have to the place. It was strange. The first time we'd actually seen Antarctica was when we stopped at Palmer Station because most of us slept because we were so seasick on the Drake Passage. Three days—I've never been so sick in my life. It was so bad that I couldn't even get up to get a drink of water.

We stopped at Palmer that first day, and then on the way back, we stopped again. It was like seeing old friends. We'd only been on the ship with these people for three or four days when we dropped them off, but yet we were all excited to see each other. When we got back there, they had an annual festival; they planned it so we could be there for that day. We had a big party, until about 4:00 in the morning. It was pretty amazing because they have a hot tub outside. At 2:00 a.m., we were all in the hot tub. The stars were just amazing. You'd get out and you'd immediately freeze, but it was incred-

ible. Then we got to climb up one of the glaciers nearby, and that was an incredible experience. The morning of the day we left, one of the girls, whom I was particularly close to, and I went up the glacier because everyone else had gone the day before. We had gone to a penguin rookery that day instead, so we did get to see the penguins and an elephant seal colony, too. And then, the following day, my friend and I climbed up this glacier. When we got to the top, we just stopped and turned around, and it was amazing. It was so quiet. I've never seen so many shades of blue and gray in my life.

I didn't take many risks, really, except once when we got off on one of the ice shelves. We had to watch out because if there were crevices, you could have fallen right in. But it wasn't that dangerous because we checked. Everyone else went before me so I just watched to see where they went. If they fell in, I wasn't going to follow.

I can't think of much that was dangerous, except for those icebergs we kept hitting. That just worried me because the ship would run over some huge ones. Every time we hit ice, I'd lie in bed thinking, "Oh my God." We encountered a couple of storms and we were just tossed all over the place. I thought, "We are going to go over." You were literally tossed out of your bunk, just flying and slamming into walls. It's so funny because you're walking along, and all of a sudden, we would hit a huge iceberg or there was a storm or something, and you'd go flying across the room. You'd start walking and you couldn't walk a straight line. You'd end up on the other side of the room. At one point, the waves were coming right over the bow. Then we got into quieter waters because we were in the fjords, which are similar to lakes.

I thought the research team members were very supportive. They were always there to help if you had any questions. I thought they were great. It was tough in the beginning because there were four students from Colgate and only two from Hamilton. Of the four females, three were from Colgate; I was the only one that wasn't. So they all knew each other well before we went, and they were all good friends, and I was kind of left out. The only other person that came from Hamilton wasn't around much. They would talk about things I didn't know, or they'd go running to each other's rooms. But in the end, it worked out better. You kept changing your shifts, and as you changed

your shifts, you were with different people. Then a lot of times you just ran into people, hanging out. So it definitely got better with time.

If I were having a problem, I'd definitely write it down, and once I got to know the people better, I'd talk to the other people, and they usually were helpful. I think you could perceive when somebody was having a bad day. You lived in such close quarters, you couldn't help but do that. For me, a bad day was when I couldn't exercise; that's something I need to do on a daily basis, or I get in a bad mood. I'm not a happy person until I go running. Also, if something went wrong when I was on my shift and I screwed up something, I'd be kind of upset.

I was extremely upset in the very beginning because when we went to pick up the sediment traps, they were all gone. The moorings were to be my thesis as an undergraduate at Hamilton College. We lost three of the four moorings; they took off with the icebergs. So I thought, "What am I supposed to do now?" I'd already written a thesis proposal. I knew what I was going to be doing with these, and now I no longer had them. So I thought, "Wow, I have to just throw out all the work I've done so far." I had done so much research. I'd written a twenty-page proposal for this. I was immensely upset, and people didn't realize how much it meant to me. They just said, "Oh, don't worry about it." I said, "No, this is *my thesis*." I had been so excited about it. I barely slept those three days that we were waiting for the sediment traps to come up. But then only one came up. I don't think people quite understood how I felt because they weren't doing their research on the samples we collected. They were using samples from previous cruises. That was a good part of why we went down there, just to pick up the sediment traps. Unfortunately, we lost them.

The crew was entirely male, and they did have a problem with female scientists. The crew seemed to think if you were aggressive in any way or you were trying to do some work, you were outspoken and you were for women's rights. They had a problem with me because I felt, "I can do this just as well as you can." They said, "No, the place for the woman is in the home." I said, "Maybe your country is still a bit backward." A crew member said, "That's what my wife does." And I answered, "Well, it's not what I'm going to do."

It was horrible, though, coming home from the Antarctic. First of all, I didn't want to leave. I had become close to most of the people on the ship, and it was hard to break those ties, knowing that I would probably never see any of them again—at least the crew. And I had to go back and make up all my work. It was a long trip home. Once we finally left the peninsula, we spent three days on the ship and then another day just sitting around in port getting all the business for the airlines worked out. It was so anticlimactic after experiencing the Antarctic.

When I came back to school I had one bad experience after another, basically. My friends were great; they were all excited to see me. Welcome back signs were all over, but they were all so busy. My boyfriend had a lot of problems, and I felt as if I should have stayed in Antarctica. Making up classwork was especially difficult. I thought, "I have to get all this work done?" Nobody was sympathetic to my cause. "Oh, you've been gone five weeks? It's all right. You'll get it done when everyone else gets it done." I didn't sleep; I was so busy. I kept telling myself the trip was definitely worth the troubles.

There are times, even now, that I wonder if maybe it was a wrong choice to go. But I just have to remember, "The trip was definitely worth the stress." My grades dropped a little bit, and I didn't take on a full load of courses, so it didn't look good on my record. But I keep looking back and saying, "It was worth it." One of the crew members used to play a particular tape after dinner every night in the dayroom, and I made a copy of it. It's a bad copy, and I'm sad about that, but the other night I played it. I hadn't heard it for quite a few months. It took me back—it was so sad because I knew I wasn't going back.

Culture shock—you come back and there are people everywhere. I just couldn't deal with the crowds. I'd go out at times, when there weren't too many people. I slowly got used to having people around. Everywhere I went, people asked, "Oh, Kerry, how was it?" I wanted to say, "Well, I had the best time of my life, but I'm going through one of the worst times now, so just leave me alone."

I've never been so relaxed in my life as when I was there. I'm probably one of the most stress-prone people I know. And there, I *could* just relax and just sit back and enjoy life. And here, I got back and, "Oh yeah, I've got to start running again. Here I go." It was

pretty tough. All this lasted about a week, I think, and then I was right back in. It was almost as if I hadn't gone anywhere. I had to be reminded that I actually went to the Antarctic.

I almost gave up my relationship with my boyfriend. It is an awful thing to say, but if I had known going to the Antarctic meant losing my boyfriend, I would still have gone without a second thought. I didn't think at all about it. I just figured I'd come back and he'd be so excited to see me and I'd be so excited to see him, but it wasn't either, really. It was difficult.

I gained self-awareness. I did more thinking about life and myself than anything else while I was there. I thought about people in general, and how people interact. I became a philosopher, very unlike myself. I definitely gained experience, scientific and personal, such as skills in communicating with all these people from all these other places. I learned a lot on the ship because I'd never been on a ship out to sea, and every little thing was totally new to me. Coming back, even, was a learning experience. My thesis ended up being based on samples from the cruise. It was a 100-page thesis, based on three samples. I've sent out an abstract to the Geologic Society of America, to be able to present my thesis. I've been accepted, so now I'm going out to Cincinnati to present it. I think that's going to be incredible. I don't know if it would have been accepted if it hadn't come from the Antarctic. They're publishing my abstract, and they'll probably publish part of the paper, which is kind of exciting. I don't think I'd have the chance to do this if it wasn't Antarctic related, just because people are so interested in the Antarctic now. It's great, because if I hadn't gone, I would not be going to Cincinnati. Now I have someone to room with that went with me, so I've got connections. Going there will hopefully get me more connections. And I think, applying to graduate school, it's going to look really good. It's great, especially since I want to continue in the marine sciences. Having had ship experience, it might be easier for me to get an internship next semester.

Hopefully I'll go back again sometime. I'd really like to stay on land. We were supposed to go to Deception Island, which is a volcanic island. We were supposed to go and then—it never fails—the equipment broke down. So we got behind schedule, and we ended up not going. That would have been incredible; I've seen

pictures. I'd really love to go back there. I'd like to spend a longer period of time there, on land, at one of the bases.

Journal entry, March 23, 1992, 4:45 p.m.

Here I sit looking all around me. I am surrounded by the most beautiful, the most magnificent and natural continent on earth—Antarctica! I never believed that I could feel this way. I am in awe! I feel this uncontrollable urge to cry. Why? Maybe it is for all those who will never get to experience the beauty and magnificence of Antarctica. Maybe it is because I know what I am seeing can never be captured on film or be put into words, yet in vain I keep snapping pictures of what is around me, hopelessly. I need to take a piece of it back for my parents, sister, brother, and friends to enjoy. I will cry, but later! I have finally found a place where I can exist peacefully with myself and others, and with nature.

Everyone here is so different, yet we all have in common a certain respect for our surroundings, Antarctica, and each other.

I Get a High from the Antarctic

Sarah

Research technician

Sarah **was finishing a master's degree, focusing on phytoplankton, minute plant life that floats in the ocean, when she was hired to be a technician in the Antarctic. The project she worked on involved drilling samples from ice in frozen lakes. She was stationed at a small field camp in Lake Fryxell in the beautiful but remote Dry Valley area on the Antarctic Continent. She wanted to go because she enjoys outdoor work, especially under harsh conditions.**

[*Editors' Note:* Interspersed throughout Sarah's interview are excerpts from Sarah's journal entries and from letters she wrote to her husband while in the Antarctic.]

I was finishing a master's degree; I had worked on phytoplankton communities—what species of algae are present and how they fluctuate through time. I worked on a lake in Rocky Mountain National Park, so I had a lot of experience drilling holes in the ice. I like to be outside, and I get a charge out of working in harsh conditions. I was hired on a contract basis to be a technician and help out on a research project the first year. It was a collaborative project at Lake Fryxell in the Dry Valleys of the Antarctic Continent. My role was to collect lake water for analyses, maintain a weather station, and measure glacial melt.

Dear Steve: Flying into the Antarctic, it was white. Endless white. As my eyes adjusted, I could see mountain ranges and the paths of the glaciers, and the regions of huge crevasses and ice falls. It was stunning.

I thought of the Antarctic as a cold, isolated, difficult place to be. I thought the experience would be exciting and adventurous, not

knowing what would happen next. It appealed to me, and I was completely jazzed about going.

I got married right before I left, and people at my wedding were horrified, saying, "You're going to leave your husband and go to the Antarctic?!"

My family doesn't like what I do, and it scares them. My mother was worried about me going to the Antarctic. She came and visited because she thought it would be the last time she would see me. At the same time, I think she thought I was bold to go. My husband was supportive because he knew how excited I was, but he felt that he wouldn't want to do it. Most of my friends were pretty excited and supportive and wanted to know what I was doing.

My first trip to the ice was for little over two and a half months, and the second time I was there for three months. I'm a technical rock climber, and this sort of challenge—outdoor physical thing—really appeals to me. The concerns I had were social ones. I thought it was a bit scary, thinking of being with seven people in a small camp. That was what I anticipated as being difficult, not anything about the environment.

We flew into McMurdo, gathered our supplies together, and then flew by helicopter to our camp. Our camp was located about sixty miles from McMurdo. I came back once during the season to run some samples into McMurdo, but that was the only time that I had a break from being at the field camp.

I knew my boss a little but didn't know any of the other people. I was worried about that because they knew each other and had been working together for years. The first year there were about seven or eight of us. People came and went, so it wasn't the same group there the whole time.

I thought going to the Antarctic seemed adventurous but not risky or dangerous. My perception may be different because I do a lot of things that other people consider risky. The rock climbing on long-exposed rock walls that I do is pretty extreme. I see climbing as challenging, but I don't think that I am very bold, and I do things that are actually very safe. I like to be in control of what I do, and I love to challenge myself with outdoor, physical activities.

In the field, I could leave and hike all night by myself. People probably thought that was a risk-taking aspect, too, because rarely

would someone join me. I sensed that people in the group were fearful of leaving camp to wander the Taylor Valley. But that is what appealed to me and made it great for me. If I had been somewhere in McMurdo where I couldn't leave a small area, I would have been miserable. I hiked up some nearby mountain peaks and explored other valleys, the other side of valleys, and some of the different ridges. We worked most all the time, so I'd have to hike at night when I was already exhausted.

> I decide to climb Mt. Falconer. Incredible windblown rocks have arms like Joshua trees. Solid-looking rocks turn out to be hollowed on the inside and only an inch or two thick. Shatter like dinner plates beneath my feet and hands. I climb up a couple thousand feet. Incredible views of the glaciers and surrounding mountains. But then the clouds close in on me at the summit. I keep going along the ridge toward the Commonwealth Glacier. Keep going, going. I'm not sure I can get down. The clouds have closed in. Weird, weird. It looked like Mars. I wouldn't have been surprised if I saw a spaceship. So I sit down to mellow out, eat something, collect my thoughts, drink some hot coffee. Sit there for the next hour in meditation and singing a sort of mantra in nothing short of an intense religious experience. Got some undescribable feelings. There is no comfort here. I carry truth and life gently within myself.

Being in the Antarctic was the closest feeling I will ever have to being on another planet. It was so hostile and so remote. It was so hard for people to be there, it took such organization for planes to fly in and bring all the supplies. It was such an incredible effort for people to be there, that it was clear that they really didn't belong there. Because of the adventure and the twenty-four hours of light and the freedom from any kind of twentieth-century life, I was incredibly high being there, just a real rush, for a long time. It wasn't like anything else I'd ever done. I got a buzz out of it—a complete charge.

At our camp we had a Jamesway, which is a common area where we cook and have a table and sort of meeting area. We each had our own tent for sleeping and privacy. Early in the season, both years, I didn't know how I would be able to last because I was so cold. I put my tent far away, up on a hill. It seemed warmer up there, or maybe

I just got used to the cold. The disadvantage of having a tent far away was that no one could see me. We had an incredible windstorm. A big experiment had been canceled because of the wind, so we were just hanging out. I went to my tent to rest, just in a T-shirt in my sleeping bag. I heard a pop, and the edge of my tent lifted up. Even though the tent was staked on the outside with rocks, and I had all of my bags full of clothes and boots and gear and me on the inside, the tent rolled. The whole thing pulled up and ripped, and it started rolling, flapping, and making incredible noise. I was terrified thinking, "All my stuff is going to blow away, and I don't have any clothes on, and what am I going to do, and how am I going to get out of this collapsed and shredded tent?" I couldn't tell which way was up, and it took me about an hour to orient myself and stuff things into bags so they wouldn't blow away. Because I was out of sight of camp, nobody even knew my tent was blowing away. I finally got all my gear crammed in bags, so I didn't lose anything, but the tent was ruined. Later, people came up and helped me drag all my stuff to the Jamesway. It was just a few days before I left, and I had to share a tent with someone else. And I sure wouldn't want to have to do that for very long.

A typical day's work was sampling for various blocks of time. We'd prepare for an experiment that would take a couple of days to complete, or do routine sample collection around Lake Fryxell. I would get up around 8:00 a.m. and be up working until midnight or 1:00 a.m. After work, I would either talk with people in camp or on the radio to McMurdo. During the day, we had visitors fairly often. Helicopters might stop by, and the crew would have coffee, and we'd get the news of the world.

In our work, there had to be coordination between people because rarely was there any task that anyone could do by themselves. We did a lot of work in the center of the lake, and it was about a quarter-mile from the camp. We had to put all our collecting gear on a sled and pull it across the ice. A lot of times you just needed somebody to help you, either to get the sled across the ice, or it might be a three-person job to drill a hole or to move some crates. Almost all the work was like that. You couldn't work on it independently; you needed somebody to help. It took incredibly long to get equipment and have adequate tools, clothing, and food. Inevitably,

something would go wrong with equipment or conditions. We had to move from plan A to plan B, all the way to plan G. The work depended on a lot of support, and each person had different priorities, since each had a different focus to the research. Everyone wanted help for what they were interested in, but they had to give help to other people or they weren't going to get any help. The first year, I think it worked pretty well. There were always grumblings and things, like "I spent all night doing this for you," or "you weren't even ready" or "you weren't even set up," and that sort of thing.

Although I had some of the highest times I've ever had there, I had some of the lowest lows ever. The second year, I really had a pull to return to Antarctica, but, at the same time, I was worried about being stuck with people whom I disliked. The last year was one of the worst experiences I've ever had, and it was almost all attributable to the social composition.

We were divided in the second year. I worked with one guy most of the time. We had common goals, but I couldn't stand the guy, and it was almost unbearable to work with him. But we were both strong in our opposition to the group of people in camp. One guy in that group would violently object to something that we wanted to do, even if it wouldn't impact him or his work directly. He just didn't like the idea of our work. It was a bad situation because I was put in a situation where I had the most experience, and I had to deal with this unsavory character, but I didn't have any authority. I don't have a PhD; I had nothing behind me at all, so he could really bully me around, and that was the major problem. He was the type of person who wanted to maximize his authority. He really didn't want to help anybody else out; he wanted our group to help him, but never would he help us. It wasn't amicable at all; there was yelling and screaming, as to who was going to be able to get things done and how it was going to happen.

It really is interesting being stuck working, sleeping, eating with the same people all the time. . . . I expected some weird stuff being isolated with a small group and it is definitely happening. Power struggles between Ted and David. Henry is really depressed and says this is the worst trip he has been on . . . We

have all gotten sucked into some sort of isolation syndrome and I
can't even realize it. . . . The tension is getting so tight with Ted.
He is driving everyone crazy. John almost punched him out on
the lake today. He won't listen to anyone. He has a huge ego. He
treats everyone like they are a grad student working for him. He
is in this hurry time compulsiveness . . . What fun it is staying up
for 30 hours straight then sleeping 5 then trying to control myself
dealing with Ted.

The first year I was so high most of the time, I can't think of a
time where sad feelings would last. I had some down times then,
too, but they were fleeting. The second year, I was the loneliest I've
ever been. It made me realize—I've never been lonely before. I
never even knew what lonely was until now. I looked out of my
dorm window at McMurdo into the pile of metal slapped together
that constituted the buildings and the storage yards of innumerable
gas cylinders and crates and abandoned fifty-five-gallon drums. It
was unfriendly and unhuman outside. And it was the same inside,
too. My dry, dry room. (The air is dry there; it is uncomfortable). It
had two beds and two closets crammed into it, so it hardly had room
for two people to stand in at the same time. But I didn't have a
roommate this time. I didn't have a friend and I was assaulted with
loneliness.

I'd sort of adapted to the fact that this was the way it was going to
be. I was kind of going along with the flow of things and doing my
work and feeling that this is the life I live here in a little tent with
not much of anything. Then my husband sent me a fax because he
had a job offer, and it might mean that we'd have to move somewhere. So he wanted me to respond to his fax within a couple of
days. The fax went through this incredible chain of command
before it got to me. And by the time I did get it, it was past the job
deadline. When I looked at the letter it snapped me back into life,
and it was really hard to take. All of a sudden, I realized that things
were going on back home while I was living this other life in the
Antarctic. I was very unhappy and depressed because of my surroundings. I began to count the days to when I could leave.

I feel like my battery is completely down. No more recharges left.

Both years I was in the Antarctic, I wrote in a journal almost every night. I would write it in the form of a letter. Every week I'd put it all in an envelope and send it home. And the second year, I also had a tape recorder and I taped myself as I walked or sat in my tent. I wanted to try to capture a lot of the feelings so I could remember them and bring them back—just things like the noises and the things people would say. I realized that I wasn't capable of remembering what it was like, and I wasn't capable of communicating it to anyone. The pictures looked so different to me. In reality, Antarctica was much more beautiful and much more enormous and much more awesome than I had even remembered. When I look back at things that I wrote or I listen to the tapes, it seems I couldn't capture what I was trying to capture.

In our group, I had one supportive friend—David. I didn't know him before I went there, and we got to be good friends. We leaned on each other when we were so tired that we couldn't deal with doing the work anymore. He was funny; it made the hard times bearable.

David and I were walking around the lake. I stopped to listen to ice melting in the moat. Like a million tiny ice chimes, tinkling in the moat water. Quiet, calm morning skies at 0400. Blue. And chiming ice. A gentle, mysterious sound. This place is sacred and mysterious. It holds many secrets that I will never understand.

There wasn't a lot of group activity. My boss would try to pull things together. She would put together a special meal or a special event. People would resist her efforts to do that and say, "You're being ridiculous." But I really appreciated it, even if it was hokey or stupid. I don't know if that's sort of a male versus female thing or not.

The first year, the only women were my boss and myself. There were five males. I think I just tuned the male versus female thing out of my mind, although I definitely felt I got more attention for being female. It was annoying at McMurdo—someone in the dinner line would ask if I wanted to take a sauna or if I wanted to sleep

with them. It upset me, and I didn't know how to deal with it—so I ignored it. I wouldn't like the language that men would use to sit around and yuk it up about things or make sexist jokes. I just sort of stayed away from it. I always felt that men would rush in and do things and fix the crates and wouldn't really give me a chance.

There were a couple of people with whom I felt I could connect occasionally. One person had a different schedule than I did; he had to work out on the ice during the night, so I didn't see him very often. When I started seeing him later on, it did really help because I could connect and commiserate with him. I still felt *extremely* isolated because Ted had such control over people. He'd tell them when to wake up, when to sleep, what they could eat, what they could do. He took away from people their own feelings of having any kind of freedom at all.

People went along with what Ted nonverbally implied was acceptable—the sort of thing that I saw as being very twisted. About the only thing that was accepted was reading the *National Enquirer*, a tabloid newspaper. I didn't want to have anything to do with it, and I socially isolated myself. After a week or two I realized that I couldn't survive like this. As much as I disliked these people, I needed social interaction. That was intensely interesting to me, to observe that happening—that I needed these people, no matter how horrible they were. It was almost scary, too, because I just thought, Wow, what am I compromising in order to have a sick social connection? I felt that I had reached this point where I compromised, and I started to have more fun because I just needed some social interaction; I needed to have something, and I had to go along with the accepted way of behaving, according to this psychopath who controlled the whole situation. It was very strange.

Now it makes me especially angry that I couldn't just stand up to Ted and say, "What you are doing isn't right." He did terrible things that endangered people's health. I'd say what I thought but felt powerless to really oppose him. I regret being so helpless. It almost seemed cultlike because Ted would make people think they were important and they were a part of a team, and what they were doing was so great and they were going to be important scientists, and just string them along. I could never figure why no one saw through it and why they would do anything for this guy. They

weren't getting any sleep at all; they didn't have a day off the whole time they were there. They were sleep-deprived, and they were so tired when they left the camp that they fell asleep on the helicopter. I just thought it was dreadful.

> When the wind stops it is the valley of silence. . . . It is so quiet. I don't get to hear enough of it. We work constantly with the scenery only as a backdrop. I want the surroundings to be the main stage. The generator is loud and obnoxious and we are always running around doing science . . . I feel like an intruder here and this is a sacred place. And here we are, intense scientists raping the lake, working all the time to get what we want and leave.

> Oh Steve, I have been here way too long. The situation here at Camp Fryxell is like a concentration camp. I have been here almost 2 months and the only days off were my sneaking off from McMurdo. My body aches like it never has before, even though I try to stretch while having breakfast or meetings or talking to people. My hips have been seriously hurting for about the last week. I think it is from hauling heavy loads on the sleds and standing for long periods of time. My motivation, my sense of humor is fading fast. We have been beaten like dogs here by the schedule and a lot of the stuff has been stupid, I'm sorry to say. I had all the zip and energy of anybody here, then I broke. Now they say, "Sarah is broke."

Both years I was physically exhausted and emotionally drained by the end, like the faucet had been on for too long and there was nothing left at all. And the second year, especially, I was so drained. I had been planning to spend time in New Zealand, and I couldn't do it. I was so tired. Even in the pictures that I have of myself there, I can just tell there was nothing left of me. But still, coming back is like a whole new look on life, to be back where there are smells, and daylight and moonlight, and just life. It's overwhelming to come back to New Zealand after being in the Antarctic. It's the daylight day and night; it's being back in a place where there's a schedule; it's being back where there are people and things are happening. You don't have so much of a sense of time in the Antarctic. Work progresses as it gets completed, rather than by a schedule. In New

Zealand, I would stare at the terrain—stare at trees and think of how funny it looked—that they were coming up out of the ground and they went up into the air. Wasn't that odd? I noticed the life. I'm a biologist, so maybe I'm kind of keyed into that, but it was just so striking to see life and to see color. I anticipated darkness because I hadn't seen it for so long.

For about three weeks after I came back, I could only sleep for about four or five hours at a time, and then I'd get up and I'd want to do things in the middle of the night. I'd wander around in the house. I was disappointed that it was dark outside and I couldn't do anything. The first thing I did was to buy a sun dress and walk around barefoot and feel the pavement under my feet. I ate fresh food. All the things that I anticipated as being exciting, or what other people had told me they got excited about when they came back, didn't turn out to be the same for me.

They talked about the light and probably the food. I don't think anyone had told me about being able to smell. I noticed I hadn't smelled anything the whole time I was there because it was so dry. Nobody told me that I would feel my skin again, and what it was like to go without layers and layers of clothes on. I was in New Zealand a couple of days before I saw stars. I was lying on a beach, sleeping out, and I was staring up at the stars. They were magical, and it was a great tingly feeling to see them.

It upset me that the experience was going to go away—that I would think it was an ordinary experience, that I would habituate to this thing which had been so unusual or nonexistent before. I was sensitive to things for a month and a half. But I know that even when I get together with people who were from the first year from around here, when we have dinners or someone shows slides, or even people who went there years that I wasn't there, all the people who have been in the Antarctic have this sort of Antarctic connection—they know what it's like. They lapse into this other world. And I notice the spouses are left out of what these people are talking about.

I'm in graduate school right now, and my first trip extended the time of my master's degree by about a year. I figured that was worth it. I did give up time away from my husband. It was hard to be away

from climbing. When I'm in Antarctica I get really out of shape for climbing, and that's distressing to me.

My boss has another proposal in to go back, and I've thought about going, if I want to be involved in it, and how to get the social thing straightened out. I really can't imagine anything would be as awful as this last experience. I'd definitely check out the people. I think if I went again there probably would be more trade-offs, mostly being away from family.

It was an incredible adventure, and I learned a lot about myself and the way I interact with people, and what it is that I need from people, which I didn't realize that I needed. My tolerance and acceptance of people has been much improved—just my feelings of being less judgmental of people. Then, the other thing is the part that's horrifying to me, to see what people can be like and what I can be like. I wasn't able to stand up to people who did things that I thought were straight-out wrong or harmful to other people. I thought that I was easy-going. Now I know what my limits are.

It's Just Not a Routine Stop in Life

S. McDonald

Biologist on oil spill

S. McDonald **worked with a team of scientists responsible for studying the results of the shipwreck of the Argentine ship, "Bahia Paraiso," and the subsequent oil spill. During the four-year project, she was down in the Antarctic for the last two years. She stayed at Palmer Station, a U.S. camp on the peninsula of the Antarctic Continent. Her work involved going out on small zodiac boats to sample for traces of the oil spill. She was invited to participate in this project based upon her experience with studying fish physiology for subtle indicators of contaminant exposure.**

Our group basically got started working in the Antarctic as a result of the shipwreck and subsequent oil spill of the Argentine ship, "Bahia Paraiso." Our group does a lot of work with organic contaminations, so we were called in after that spill. We had a relatively short turnaround time to get down there and respond and start monitoring the extent of the oil spill. This last year was our fourth year of monitoring, and we expanded into some other areas, instead of doing straight organic-contaminant monitoring. I did not go to the Antarctic the first two years of this project, only the last two. I was the biologist, and I'd been doing some physiology work with the fish around the area, looking for more subtle indicators of contaminant exposure.

We typically take five or six people down. We take some divers to collect samples, as well as scientists. We do some work off a large ship, the Polar Duke. However, most of our sampling is done in the zodiacs they have at Palmer Station to get to various islands. The divers generally will dive off the zodiacs; they do not dive off the big ship. Then we conduct experiments actually at Palmer Station.

Some of the work I do in nonpolar climates is a sensitive way of detecting exposure to oil. The person that was primarily involved

with that project brought me on it to sort of expand what he was doing. So he had an ongoing project, and when he wrote the grant for renewal, he put me on as a co = PI (co-principal investigator), and that's where I started doing my work.

In science, with the funding often being limited, you take your opportunities where you can. I wasn't quite sure what I was going to think about the Antarctic because I'm not a cold weather person; I'm more a caribbean island person. Really, the only trepidation I had was how I would deal with the weather down there. But other than that, I looked at it as being an interesting experience and the chance to do some research—some funded research.

The only actual risky thing that I think we do is when we are in the small zodiacs around the Palmer Station area. You go from one island to the other, sampling. The water is extremely cold, and if someone were to fall in, you don't have very much time in that cold water before hypothermia will set in. So that's the only aspect that I was concerned about. I'm very careful always when we're on the water. I didn't actually realize the danger until I got to Palmer Station. Also, my first time traveling through Chile, I didn't quite know what to expect.

Everyone was very supportive of my going to the Antarctic. Our co-workers here are a pretty dynamic group, and we're used to going off to all sorts of strange places in the world, so it wasn't that big of a deal. My husband and family were extremely supportive of my going. They thought it was a great opportunity. My husband is a scientist also, so I knew there wouldn't be any problem with him. My parents have always been very supportive of whatever weird things I've decided to do.

If I have the opportunity for an adventure, I'll give it a shot. I've done a fair amount of work in the Gulf of Mexico and other oceans. Since I'm a biological oceanographer, I've spent some time out at sea. Some of the places I've gone, some of the things I've seen, and some of the experiences I've had could be described as adventuresome. Going 8,000 feet below the surface of the ocean in a submersible, I consider pretty adventuresome. I've flown helicopters out to platforms in the Gulf of Mexico in heavy winds. That was kind of exciting. I don't really need that kind of excitement. I've

also done a fair amount of traveling through the United States, as well as Europe.

The first year I was there it was absolutely fabulous; I just had the time of my life. I told my husband that it was the best vacation I had had in years. I didn't have that much required work, and I went out in the field and helped my team collect samples, so I got to see a lot of the surrounding area and had lots of time to play and explore. There were also some people down there that I was very compatible with, and we'd go off and find all sorts of things to explore and to get into. It was a very relaxing experience.

The camaraderie down there is also interesting. If you get a good mix of people, it's really a lot of fun. One of the impressions left on me, when I got to Palmer Station the first year, was the station personnel. I got to the station and watched some of the people who'd been there for a while make an evening out of sitting around together and matching slides. I felt sorry for these poor pitiful people. This is the highlight of their day! But after you're down there for a few weeks, you really do slow down. You stop and you actually have conversations with people; you're not just hurrying to and from, or rushing to get your work done. You actually stop and sit down, and you have a cup of tea or a cup of coffee, and you have philosophical conversations. I generally don't do that too much when I'm trying to take care of a baby, a house, and a job. I really enjoyed being able to slow down, and just getting back to enjoying the company of people.

There were a couple of people that were down there from another group. Our personalities meshed and we really hit it off. I think there were three of us—myself and two men—and we were always going off and getting into things. I got along well with my own group, as well, but one of these two other men was my age and we had basically the same outlook on life. So we'd wind up hanging out a lot, walking up and down the glacier, and going to the islands or something like that. The first year I was at Palmer there were about thirty to forty people, which included both scientists and station personnel. The second year there were twenty to twenty-five people. There were three people in my group, and we were the only scientists.

The second year when I went down, I had a greater responsibility for getting work done. A large part of the work consisted of my experiments, and I had just had a baby, so I left a six-week-old baby

to go down there and do my work. As such, I was only interested in getting out as quickly as I could. I had an opportunity to get out after three weeks so I basically worked the entire time because my priorities had changed, and I wanted to get back to my baby. It wasn't a negative experience because I got a lot of work done and I got a lot of good data, but it wasn't the relaxing experience it was the year before.

I used to get up pretty early, usually between 6:00 and 6:30 a.m. I got up because the sun rose earlier. That was basically the only time on the station that you could actually get any sort of quiet time to yourself because it was a small station, and it was tough to get away from people. In fact, it's very important that your team's personalities all mesh. That's always a consideration when we pick a team—we make sure everybody can get along. So if I get up at that hour, there would only be myself, the cook, and the station manager. I could have my cup of coffee, eat my breakfast, then I would get into the lab and get my work done and be finished, basically, by 10:00 or 11:00 in the morning. By that time, my field team was ready to go out, and I usually went out with them. It was a chance for me to see all the different islands and locations. We'd usually come back for lunch, and then we would go out in the afternoon, typically sampling again. I'd go out with the divers, sampling, and come back for dinner. Then after dinner, I would either read for a while or sit there and listen to my walkman, or I'd go over to the pub and socialize, then go to bed. Or, if I had a free afternoon or morning, some of the other people and I would go off exploring. So this was not a rough life at all, during my first year there.

There's the glacier behind the station that you can hike up and down, and that's what I was doing for exercise. It's about a forty-minute round trip to go up there, and it's a nice site around there. You could go to some of the islands and look around and take pictures of the various animals. So we'd get in the boats and load up our photography equipment. Old Palmer Station was just a hop, skip, and jump away, and there's an ice cave over there that we went crawling through, as far as we could. We'd take the snowmobiles up and down the glacier and have fun with those. Some people would ski down the glacier. I'm not into skiing, so I avoided that. At night

we'd go out and identify constellations. It sounds kind of boring, but it was fun.

I spent Easter there, and we had some birthdays too; they were always a lot of fun. One thing about the people down there and being away from so many things—people have a tendency to get very creative. Birthdays and holidays were always a lot of fun. You never quite knew what to expect. This past year there was a communications officer who's been down there for a long time. He's sort of a hippie—he has long hair and he likes to wear short tunics with goofy-looking rag wool socks and sneakers, and he has a scraggly beard. So on his birthday, they got some wool for a beard, and they all dressed to look like this particular communications officer. The cook had made a wonderful Japanese dinner with sushi and all this great food. We went and got him out for dinner, and he walked into as room of clones; it was extremely funny.

There was a wide variety of communications with home. What I personally used was e-mail since my husband works at the same place where I do, and we would communicate through e-mail. I could have killed my husband a time or two because he marches on a different time scale than I do, apparently, on answering e-mail. I'd expect responses immediately, and he didn't always respond. Especially this past year, when I was concerned about my baby, I was about ready to strangle him. He did not understand my concern about the baby. He could have been a little bit more committed to responding to me.

Other than that, communications were fine. With regard to my work in the United States, when I'm away from it, there's not much I can do, so why tell me about it? I can't make the decisions from the Antarctic! So I usually don't communicate too much with work because there's not much I can do from where I am.

Mainly, the thing that I wanted most was personal information. The weather's great; the garden's doing well; the baby's fine, cats are fine—that kind of stuff. That was more important to me than anything else—getting some sort of personal contact with my loved ones.

In the first group I went down with, I wasn't aware that anybody really needed much personal support. Everybody was basically pretty self-sufficient and didn't need a lot of support from other

people. This past year when I went down, one of my assistants apparently needed a little bit more support because she missed her boyfriend. Unfortunately, I guess I'm not the most patient person in dealing with this type of issue. You're there to do your job, so do it. But I think she got support from other people who were there.

I went to Antarctica with a very defined purpose. I knew what the circumstances were; I knew I was going to leave a young baby. I had resolved myself to that. My mother was going to care for her. So because of those circumstances, I pretty much just focused on my work. I really didn't have much time for anything else since I was totally focused on getting my work done.

There was more cooperation than you would probably find in most circumstances because of the remote location. It's a small unit of people, and that small unit of people is basically making the whole thing run. It's a basic necessity that the station runs well, that you're able to do your work. Because if the heat goes out or something, that's critical. Or if the aquarium room floods, that usually winds up messing up somebody else's experiments. So everybody pitches in to see if they can get the problem solved before it causes any major damage. Because of the remoteness, too, and the difficulty of doing things, you do get the sense that everybody is going to help whenever there's anything that needs to be taken care of.

In terms of gender, the first year there were two women and four men in our group. The chief scientist on the station was a woman. During the second trip, we were the only science group down there at the time, and there were three women in my group. For the station personnel, the ratios were probably one-third women to two-thirds men. I didn't really notice that much of a problem with the male to female ratio because even though it wasn't equal, there were enough women on the station where it was just no big deal. There were enough of us running around there that nobody ever paid any attention to that fact. However, Palmer Station is one of the more unique places I have been, where there is not a real distinction made between whether you're a man or a woman. The first year we were down there we were visited by Greenpeace. I remember a couple of the people came onstation, and they were asking the station manager just that question, "Well, how many women do you have onstation?" And he looked at her and said, "Gee, I don't

know. I'll have to look at the list." She was all upset because he didn't know how many women were there. I just wanted to strangle her! This was the best possible scenario—that nobody had paid any attention to the number of males and females. That's the way it should be. Everybody's doing their job and the specific numbers are not a big deal. It was the same this past year, as well. Among the station personnel, they had women carpenters; they had a woman who runs the boats and maintains the engines. I've never noticed any problem with having women scientists onstation. It's just no big deal. And that's great. It's not something you're going to find in a whole lot of places.

It was different in our research group though. One of the divers was a woman, and she wasn't quite as strong as some of the male divers. She couldn't pull herself into the boat with her weights on. Well, I couldn't either, and there were some comments made about that. You know, we're a bunch of Texans here, so it's very traditional.

The co = PI that I work with doesn't make too big of an issue out of whether you're male or female. As long as you do your job he's happy. Among the field personnel, I think gender came into play a little bit more. And then, another thing that I have to confess is that a female diver we had came down one day and said, "Well, I can't dive today because I have cramps." That was especially hard for me to relate to because our field team depended on all of our divers. I guess I've never experienced cramps bad enough to keep me from doing my work, and that was very frustrating for me because I just wanted to shake her and say, "You can't expect to be treated equally if you do this. This is going to happen all the time. You've got to learn to deal with it." So there were some subtle things like that in our field team; there were some gender differences.

I've heard McMurdo is a lot more stressful place to be, worse than at Palmer. Also, we weren't there during the peak season. I'm sure that people who were there during the peak season probably have a different story. But when we came in, the major season was over, so it wasn't as stressful for the station personnel. You didn't have sixty-some people that were onstation taking up every available space. There really was not a lot of that going on. You could walk in a room sort of at the end of conversations, and you never

really heard them stop, as if they were just talking about you. I was surprised at the professionalism of the staff there.

The first time it was very hard to come home because I came back from a relatively stress-free environment. I was totally relaxed, and then I went into work and the crap had just kind of hit the fan. Letters and problems while I was gone. Our laboratory director called me into his office and dumped a personal problem on me. I found it extremely stressful when I got back to suddenly have to deal with all the petty things again. The second year, I was basically stressed out the whole time I was down there, just trying to get my work done, so I didn't really notice that difference coming home. But the first year it was tough, and it took a few weeks to get back into the swing of things. I remember having a very difficult time, and I know one of the people that I knew down there was having the same problems. When he came back to his job he said, "These people worry about such minor details," and he basically quit who he was working for and went to work for somebody else. After he'd been gone, he did not like what he was coming back to. In that sense it can be a problem. It's a shock, and it's just a very difficult thing to describe. I remember it being very traumatic for me to suddenly have to deal with all this crap. I was angry that people were sitting there trying to ruin my feeling of euphoria—"Why are you doing this to me? Just let me have it a little longer."

Plus, within just a few days of coming back after that first year, I got pregnant. So my whole life was turned upside down. That was fine though—I'd been trying to get pregnant for years! I thought, wow, I need to go down to the Antarctic more often.

My husband was extremely supportive, but he complained a little bit, saying, "Oh, I've been here working my butt off, and you've just been down there having a good time." I heard a couple things like that, but the main problem was coming back to work and having to deal with all those trivial things and then having to realize that, gosh, I've got to go to the grocery store again.

I was down there long enough to have slowed down and wound down, but I had to kick back up again. I've had that comment made to me before. This individual who actually ended up quitting his job said that, the previous year, he'd experienced the same thing. He said that you come back and you promise yourself that you're not

going to get caught up in the rat race, you're going to remember what it feels like to be able to relax and get stress-free. But, as he said, it sucks you back in every time. I guess he'd had it with his job after the second year and quit. I felt as if, after I came back the first year, I wanted to quit too. It was just that frustrating. It probably took about six weeks before I straightened out.

The first year I didn't feel like I gave up anything. The only thing I may have lost, because I was gone longer the first year, was that it took a while to reassert my power base at work. I was gone long enough that people were kind of creeping into it. So that was probably part of the readjustment; I had to reassert my power base. The second year, it was a very difficult decision because I had a six-week-old baby whom I had to leave. I didn't want to do it, but I had a sense of obligation to the grant. I could not live with myself unless there was a good reason—either medical reason with the baby or myself—that I was not going to go. I'd made a commitment, and I thought that I should honor it. But it wasn't that I was particularly wanting to go. I would have just as soon stayed here with my baby. That decision was difficult to make. I lost five weeks, basically, in her life, but between six weeks to three months they don't do too much, other than grow a little bit. My mother did come here to take care of her. Still, I did miss part of my baby's life, which was hard, particularly since I had waited so long to have her. It's the classical thing that a woman goes through—career versus family.

There's no easy answer. No matter what you do, somebody's going to criticize you. And I did hear some criticisms. My boss told my colleagues, "Don't plan on her going. She's not going to leave that baby." I had other people saying, "How can you leave your baby?" I received a lot of mixed signals on that. It worked out though. The baby survived, my mother survived, and life went on. Still, people couldn't understand how I could desert my baby. I think I made the right decision because actually she came out fine. I was the one that was more unhappy about it. I just felt that I had made this commitment to this job and that I had to see it through.

I gained a lot, including some valuable experience for my work. The chance to do some work that, since I'm just starting out in this field, I may not have the chance to do in the United States because there are people who are more established than I am, and it's always

challenging to inch your way up to the top. This was one way to get some work done, even though I was a relatively new person in the field. I also gained a lifetime of memories. I can see myself when I'm older and gray and sitting in a rocking chair, being able to visualize the things that I found and was able to do in Antarctica. I feel, overall, that it has just been a very positive experience.

It's difficult to explain how you feel when you go to Antarctica and see these vivid sunrises and sunsets; you see the mountains, and the snow and the glaciers, and all the animals. The first time I went down there and saw some of the station personnel, I thought, "Boy, these people are definitely a little off the beaten path." There was the one who went around wearing the tunic and another one who liked to bark like a dog, and you're thinking, "Oh God, am I going to survive this?" But by the end of the time I was down there, they started looking more normal.

I recently got a telephone call asking us to go back down for another field season. We had stopped everything, so now we have to try to pick up the threads again, line up divers, and get equipment shipped down there. So it's just been a madhouse. Initially I had been disappointed that we weren't going to get our project renewed. And then I thought, "Well, okay. I had two good years down there. That's the way it goes."

PACKING INSTRUCTIONS

PACK THE FOLLOWING ITEMS IN THE BAG LABELLED HANDCARRY.

1 ea. Parka.
2 sets Thermal underwear.
1 ea Wool Shirt.
1 pr Field Trousers w/ Liner.
1 pr Boots either Rubber Thermal or Mukluks.

1 pr Mittens or Gloves.
1 pr Furback Gauntlets.
2 pr Tube Socks.
1 ea. Balaclava or Pile cap.
1 set Trouser Suspenders.
1 pr Sunglasses.

PHOTO 1. Packing instructions for the flight from New Zealand to the Antarctic (photo by Berneice Albright).

PHOTO 2. McMurdo Station, the largest Antarctic station and the "hub" of all U.S. Antarctic activity (photo by Sandra Kenady).

PHOTO 3. Jamesway dorms, now used only in field camps (photo by Berneice Albright).

PHOTO 4. A penguin between two fuel tanks at McMurdo Station (photo by Sandra Kenady).

PHOTO 5. The MARS (Military Amateur Radio Service) shack, winter 1988/1989. This was one way that the women communicated with family members back home. This has since been remodeled (photo by Berneice Albright).

PHOTO 6. One of the many celebrations on the ice: "Icestock" 1991 (photo by Sandra Kenady).

WOMEN NAVY PERSONNEL

In the early 1990s, the Navy was in charge of transporting people and supplies to the Antarctic and was also in charge of transportation within the Antarctic. People were flown to Antarctic stations and field camps by Navy planes and helicopters. Until 1994, women who entered the Navy were excluded from combat-related deployment. Going to the Antarctic was one of the few ways in which women Navy personnel could be deployed and thus achieve advancement in their careers. The U.S. Naval Support Force Antarctica is based in Port Hueneme, California, and Navy personnel are deployed to the Antarctic for two-year terms. In recent years, about 200 women from this Navy base and twenty-five female personnel of the VXE6 air squadron have gone to the Antarctic each year. Navy personnel lead different lives in the Antarctic than do scientific research teams. They spend two full years on an Antarctic station, including Antarctic summers and winters. They rarely get to travel around the Antarctic, unless they are members of flight crews, but instead stay at one Antarctic station and its immediate surroundings. They are part of the military hierarchy and affected by its policies (for example, the officer's club is open to military officers and all civilians, but not to military enlisted personnel). This section includes three accounts by women Navy personnel.

This Is Kind of Like Being on the Moon

Jane M. Alstott

Avionics technician and loadmaster

Jane Alstott **spent five years from 1989 to 1994 as a loadmaster and avionics technician in the Navy's Antarctic Development Squadron (VXE6). She spent five seasonal deployments (October to March) on the ice. A loadmaster is an enlisted aircrew member who is responsible for loading the aircraft and determining the weight and balance configuration of the aircraft. The loadmaster is also responsible for passengers and knowledge of aircraft emergency systems. Jane has 1,700 flight hours as a loadmaster in VXE6, and most of those hours were over Antarctica. As an avionics technician, she repaired radio and radar equipment in the aircraft. In 1992, Jane was part of the first all-female crew to fly to the South Pole.**

I'm in the VXE6 squadron, and I have two jobs. One is an avionics tech—which means that I work on the electronics in the airplane. And the other one is as an aircrewman—I'm a loadmaster, which means that I load the planes, off-load the planes, deal with passengers, and I deal with paperwork, as far as weight and balance goes, as far as what you're putting on the plane and how it affects the balance of the plane. Sometimes I'm flying, and some days I'm in the shop.

I went to the Antarctic because I joined the Navy, and those were the orders that I got. Ultimately it wasn't my decision, but when they told me that I could get this assignment, I was glad. I was willing to go. I didn't have any real specific concerns because I had no idea, really, what I was going to. I didn't know what kind of conditions we'd be living in or anything like that or just how cold it would be.

I told my family and they just thought, especially my father—oh, what a marvelous opportunity; what a great thing; what an unusual thing that you get to do this. I've moved around a lot, so really the only people I knew when I joined the Navy were my family. I'm not really sentimental about spending the holidays with family or anybody, so it doesn't affect me a whole lot. I've been a lot of places, but this is the only place I would really call an adventure.

Being in the Antarctic was like being on the moon because you look around, and you just have all the mountains, and everything is ice and rock, except for the animals; there are a few animals around. There were even some seals on the ice runway—there was a mother that had her baby out on the road that leads from McMurdo out to the ice runway. Then we saw a lot of them off the road. Since I'm flying, sometimes we fly over the ice edge, and of course, we're a couple of hundred feet up, but we could still see the whales—killer whales. We took some New Zealand scientists on a penguin census. We had the doors open all the time, and we flew a few hundred feet or so above the penguin rookeries. You couldn't actually see the birds; you could only see little dots.

When we're at the South Pole—unless we break down or something—when we do a flight somewhere, we never shut down engines once we're there because it is so cold. If you shut them down, you'd have some problems with operation if you try to restart. When we're on the ground, when we're off-loading and reloading and doing whatever we have to do that we have to be on the ground for, the engines turn all the time. So we just go and do what we have to do mission-wise and then go home. So I never actually spend very much time at the South Pole at all.

The first year that I went there, I did experience a little bit of—I would call it like consumer withdrawal—because in the rest of the world we're so used to running out and buying this and buying that, and it's a way of living and maybe, to some extent, it's entertainment. Then when you're down there, you just can't do that, and you can't really go anywhere. I guess the first year that made me kind of blue. But every year I get a little bit better at how to live down there and what to send and what to take and stuff like that. Sometimes I got a little bit down because I was new in the Navy; I was new in the squadron; I didn't know anything about anything; I didn't under-

stand a lot. I had to learn how to work with people, and I was the person who didn't know anything, and everybody thought I was stupid, and I was female, and all this kind of stuff. I'm very sensitive to that kind of thing, to feeling bad about not knowing the ropes and all of that. On the other hand, when I get further into the planes and the systems and learn even more, the flip side of those challenges is that it's very rewarding once something is learned.

Sometimes flying depresses me because, although I like flying, if I'm on duty for three or four weeks in a row and I fly every day, I go on a mission every day, and then I just come home and sleep and then go again. The first year, the way that they did the flight schedule was very erratic. You might have to get up at 2:00 a.m. one time, and you might have a twelve-hour or an eighteen-hour crew day. Then you'd come back and maybe you'd have eighteen hours off, and your next flight would be at 2:00 p.m. or something. That was a little bit hard to deal with. They've changed that a little. They try to schedule everybody at the same time every day. Also, I get a little bit stressed out because flying in these planes is kind of physically exhausting, even though I'm not the pilot; I'm just in the back of the airplane. But you're in there and you have this headset on your head all day, and sometimes it's either too cold or too hot, and nobody can do anything about it. The planes vibrate a lot, and it's not something you notice as much; it's just something that kind of creeps up on you. That's definitely a physical stress, even though maybe you don't recognize it. When I'm flying, I don't get as much studying done. It's not like when I'm on the ground, and I can go out with the shops and learn more about the systems on the planes, which means a lot to me. Whereas when I'm flying, I don't have time for a lot of that stuff and that stresses me out. I feel like I'm just drudging along and not getting on with my life.

I was older than most Navy people in Antarctica because I didn't join the Navy until I was twenty-one. So certainly for my level of experience, I was rather old.

A few years ago, our squadron had almost zero females, but they have increased it a lot. Right now I would guess that we're about 25 percent. That doesn't mean that all squadrons are 25 percent, but ours was at least 25 percent. It's partly because this is one of those little enclaves. There are a lot of squadrons in the Navy where there

are no women at all. Then they have places—"Oh, well, we can send women here. This isn't combat," or whatever. And so they'll become almost all women, and they can say, "Oh yes, we have so many women in the Navy," even though you only have maybe two or three places where those women are allowed to be, and the Antarctic is one of those places. Actually there's no job in this squadron that a female is not allowed to do. We probably have more females that are in administrative, paperwork kinds of jobs than some of the other jobs. We do have female pilots and female navigators, but there are probably only two females out of every forty pilots. For some jobs one is allowed to do, for various reasons, there aren't as many women.

Among the females, we provide a lot of support to each other. It's still—even though there are more and more females—basically a man's ball game. We definitely provide a lot of support to each other, I would say. There aren't usually any bad feelings between the males and the females. But there are differences. Because you're a female in one job and there's another female in the same job, definitely there's a little more of a special relationship there that's different from the relationship you have to the men who do the same job.

As far as personal things, I'm friendly with everybody, but I'm not very socially oriented outside of work. Because I'm usually in my room with my face in a book, and that's just the way that I live, I don't have very much of a purely social association with a lot of people. It's all pretty much professionally based.

What I gained is all tied in with me being in Antarctica and being in the Navy, since this is the only place I've ever been in the Navy. I've gained so many things because, well, I had to learn so many things, coming into the squadron and going to Antarctica. You learn things about yourself. I guess one thing is that I learned how spoiled I was—well, I learned that when I went to boot camp. When you go to Antarctica, you go through withdrawal from the regular consumer society. You learn a little bit about yourself that way. I've had to learn things about the planes and about being a loadmaster. Definitely one of the greatest things that I've learned is how to work with people—because I'd never really worked with people a whole lot before I came in the Navy, and I haven't always been the most

cheerful person or whatever. But I've worked through a lot of that and I've learned—I guess I would say one thing I've learned is humility.

Also I've learned objective things on my job, because working with aircraft and the kind of thing that we do was a totally new area to me. I was just in college. I was someone who'd never really done anything but read books my whole life, and I'd never taken any physical science. I didn't know anything. I didn't even know how a car ran. When I came to the squadron, I didn't know how an airplane flew. But through learning and through some of my own delving into some of the books, I began putting two and two together here and there. It's an entirely new area of the world. It's a different type of thing from studying something in college.

Some of the conditions when you're down there contribute to growing, certainly. There are a lot of good things to do in the Navy, but this is one of the best ones.

I'm Glad I Did It, But I Can Never Turn the Clock Back to Spend Those Six Months with My Son

Eva Flores

Aircraft firefighter

When *Eva Flores* went to the Antarctic the first time as part of her duties in the Navy, she left her son, who was only a year and a half, with her husband. She was the only woman on the ice, at the time, who had left both a child and a husband. She worked in the Antarctic as a firefighter, a physically demanding and stressful job. Despite the fact that there is so much water in Antarctica, the extreme cold makes it very dry. Threat of fire, especially with the aircraft and its fuel, is quite a serious matter.

Antarctica is majestic. I felt like the serenity and the beauty of the continent was always catching me off-guard. Seeing the mountains and the volcanos was exhilarating. It was a beautiful place—tranquil. I felt that I was away from everything and everyone, even though there were few people around. I felt as if I were out in the middle of nowhere.

I was an aircraft firefighter. There were about eighteen of us stationed in Antarctica. I had orders to go to Alaska, and I didn't want to go there because of my being separated from my family for the whole time. With the Antarctic deployment, you spend half your time in California and the other half in the Antarctic. We decided to do the Antarctic deployment. We could all go to California, and I could leave my family in California for the five months I had to go to the Antarctic. That way I wouldn't have to put them through the weather change and everything that they'd go through if we moved to Alaska. I left them in California and went out to Antarctica.

Going to Antarctica is an experience a lot of people don't get a chance to do.

I didn't think Antarctica was risky in comparison to being stationed in Cuba. The only thing I was concerned about was not being able to communicate with my family. If there were an emergency back home, what would I do, and how would I manage out there?

My family was excited for me. My husband was in the military, so he knows what it's like when they say you have to go. He had deployed in the past, earlier in our marriage, so he said "Okay, now it's your turn to be away." My mom said, "Oh, I wish you wouldn't leave," and she was more concerned about my son's well-being. I was always communicating with them the best way I could, by writing letters. They were doing the same for me—writing me constantly, keeping me updated, and sending me videos. I can't thank them enough for doing that for me. My mom was never crazy about me being in the Navy. She thinks half the stuff that I do is too risky, especially being a firefighter. My husband's reaction surprised me just a little because he was so calm about it. He said, "Go have a good time."

It was an adventure. I'm glad I did it. The only thing is, I can never turn the clock back to spend those six months with my son. As far as his growing up, when I came back, he was a totally changed little person.

In the beginning of the season, our day consisted of waking up about 7:00 a.m. and getting ourselves ready and getting our crews ready to go. We worked twenty-four hours on and twenty-four hours off. We had to man the ice runway. Once we got ourselves and our trucks ready, we went out to relieve the crew that was already down at the ice runway. We would make sure that our trucks were running and functional, and we also did training. When an aircraft came in, we'd just stand by in the trucks from its landing till its departure. That could be up to five or six hours in our trucks, waiting. After all the flights left for the day, we'd still stay out there on the ice runway. We'd stay in our shack until we were relieved the next morning. When we got back to town on our twenty-four hours off, and we weren't out, we would have to respond when the fire alarm went off. We were also the structural support for our small town.

The trucks we drove were special; they're special Antarctic fire trucks because they're track vehicles. They also have heaters to keep the chemicals warm so that they can function. They were different fire fighting apparatus than what I was used to. There was a crew of about four per truck. If it was a larger aircraft, we had to man more trucks. I worked with the same people every day. Toward the middle of the season, there were some changes, and I became assistant crash captain.

This was my first season, and I didn't know anything about fire fighting in such harsh weather. I had to get all my training done in order to let them know that I'd be capable of handling an emergency. I was in charge of all the people in my crew. I had to let them know if the procedures they were doing were okay and make sure that everybody was doing what they should be doing as part of the team during an emergency. I was also in charge of driving the truck. Some of the trucks didn't have steering wheels; they had two sticks, one for turning left and one for turning right. Pull them both back and that's your brakes.

The twenty-four hours off were for unwinding. I'd do a lot of letter writing or I'd go into town. That would give me my chance to get packages mailed or be with friends. At night we used to frequent the clubs. I'm not into the crowds, so I liked going to the bigger club because there was more space. I went almost every time I had a night off. I ended up drinking a lot more than at home.

We had a weight room. For firefighters it's almost mandatory that we have some type of exercise regimen. We'd have a scheduled time for everyone in my group to exercise. I was working out every other day, and it was normally on my off days that I'd spend at least an hour in the gym weight lifting.

Spending the holidays on the ice was okay. At first we weren't guaranteed to have that day off. Especially with us, we have to keep our shift the way it is. We closed down the airport during the holidays for two weeks, but we were still responsible for structural support in town. I ended up working both Christmas and New Year's. The key thing was just trying to make it feel like the holidays. We got together and decorated a Christmas tree, trying to make it feel like Christmas. I love Christmas and decorating, so I made it my business to make sure that everything was nicely decorated.

The weather was unpredictable. One time, my friend and I went hiking, and not too many people knew we were out. Toward the last leg of the hike, it got very foggy. We were scared that a storm was going to come, and we weren't clothed properly. That put a little fear in my heart that we should have prepared better. From then on, we were better prepared for any hikes we did.

A couple of friends and I went out in our truck to see an aircraft that crashed a long time ago. Our truck ended up getting stuck in a big hole. That was very risky because if the truck fell in, we could have just as easily fallen in with it.

Most of our calls were false alarms. People would smoke too much in one area, and the smoke alarm would go off. Or just a bunch of drills that we would have to go through to make sure that we were on our toes at 3:00 or 4:00 in the morning, when you're trying to get some sleep. There was a fire, though I didn't participate in it. The other crew was on duty. It always reminded us that these trucks had to work. These were the only things we had to fight the fire. It was a big challenge. As much maintenance as we did, as much checking as we did of the equipment, there was still a chance that something could go wrong—for example, chemicals freezing up while coming out of the nozzle.

The friends I made on the ice turned out to be good friends. When we got back to the States, we continued to socialize—mostly at work. When we got back, we had our families or people were trying to take vacations, so we didn't really see each other as much. We supported each other on most personal levels. About 80 percent of the people I worked with were single so it was a little bit harder for me being female, having a son, being married, and leaving my family—nobody could fully understand. There were a few guys who had left their wives and their kids, but they're used to that because of going on a ship and having to deploy. So it was more typical for them.

When I was feeling down, I would watch a video of my son or go into my room to do some letter writing or listen to music. I would go to the weight room and work a lot of it out on the weights, making myself feel better. There was one guy that helped me out a lot; this was his second season. I could say whatever I wanted to, and he

wasn't judgmental but just gave me that ear that I needed, which helped out a lot.

Some of the guys that I worked with would come to me to talk, like the newlyweds or the single guys. They would say, "My girlfriend's doing this." Or, "This is what's happening in my marriage." I would try to give them the best advice I could. I am a mother so all the guys looked to me as a mother figure. I guess they respected whatever I had to say to them. And if they didn't, they didn't have to listen to it. I wasn't too judgmental; I gave them the best advice I could. Maybe I've been through what they're going through, or being a woman, I could tell them, "Well, I would have felt this way if you had done that." They could respect that.

Most of my career I've been the only woman working among many men. Here I was lucky because there were three other women besides myself, which was rare for me. I didn't know that many other women existed in this job. It was nice because we helped each other keep our sanity. We would say, "Okay, this person is pulling this macho stuff, and how are we going to handle that?" All the women that were there were in charge, so we got a lot of respect. They had to listen to us. My friend stayed down for the winter season. She's the only female firefighter in her crew. I write to her to let her know even though I'm not there to talk to her, she can write to me and let me know if she's having a hard time with the guys and not to let her guard down. She's worked very hard to get where she's at. I was the only Hispanic, our boss was the only African American, and the rest were Caucasians.

For me, coming home from the Antarctic was traumatic. My son was away. My husband couldn't take care of him so he sent my son to my mother and my mother-in-law. They live about a half hour away from each other, so they took turns taking care of our son for us. When I left, my oldest brother was staying with my husband to help him take care of my son. That arrangement didn't work out. My husband's a firefighter and he works twenty-four hours on and twenty-four hours off. So it's hard to say, "Here, babysitter, take care of my son for twenty-four hours." When I came back, I found some stuff out that I wasn't too happy with, and my life was confused. Getting my son back and trying to get him into a regular routine was difficult.

I came back and discovered my husband had had an affair. That caught me off-guard, because he was Mr. "I'm being ever so faithful to you while you're down there." That totally blew things up for me. It took me a few months to try to figure out why things happened the way they did. The one thing that always came up is, "What could I have done to make things different?" I told him if I was deployed again, I'd do things differently.

I gave up the chance to see my son say his first words and be the person he is today. I gave up that and being there for him. When I got back, he would always say, "Mommy, I don't want you to work, let Dad go to work." He was so afraid of losing me again. I don't know if I changed a lot as a person. I do know I'm a little bit more mature. It was always party, party, before.

I'm More Adventuresome Than the Guys Who Went to Work on Wall Street

Karen

Attorney in the Navy

Karen **was in the Judge Advocate General (or JAG) Corps in the Navy. In order to advance in her career, she needed to get an "operational billet" yet was excluded from most because, as a woman, she could not be on a combat-related mission. Going to Antarctica provided a way to get around the restrictions; while it is not combat duty per se, it is still considered a deployment and thus, a career advance. Karen was the only lawyer the Navy had in Antarctica. She answered to the two most senior officers and was among the highest-ranked women there. She was mostly responsible for dealing with environmental issues, such as hazardous waste disposal and recycling, yet she was also called upon for all disciplinary investigations, as well as any other legal problems that Navy personnel had while in the Antarctic.**

I'm an attorney in the Navy—what the Navy refers to as a JAG officer, a Judge Advocate General. While in the Antarctic, I did primarily legal work. I did a lot of work concerning the environment. I was involved in developing policies for recycling, hazardous waste use and disposal, and other things that involved the Antarctic environment. In addition, since the Navy was involved in the disposal of waste back in the States, through Navy facilities, I was also involved in the legal end of those sorts of things. I also did general legal things, such as advise service members concerning legal issues that might be affecting them back home. I took care of all the disciplinary investigations concerning offenses that were committed by military members. I was also the overall legal advisor to the commanding officer down on the ice.

I worked with a lot of different people. My office was in the administrative section of the building, so I had very close contact with the administration, very close contact with the executive officer and the commanding officer, as well as any other department that might need some kind of legal help or had personnel who were in trouble. I also had a lot of contact with civilians, in particular, dealing with environmental issues.

My first tour in the Navy was as a prosecutor in Norfolk, Virginia. I decided to remain in the Navy for another tour. Part of the Navy career path that is most enhancing to us in the JAG Corps is to obtain an operational billet, meaning working with the line command, working with an aircraft carrier, or any other type of job that did not involve working purely with other attorneys. But my ability to be with an operational command was restricted by the fact that I was not allowed on any combatant. I could never be on an aircraft carrier; I could not be with any kind of command that had a combat mission. I then came across this command in the Antarctic, and it sounded very interesting. The reason I had remained in the Navy was to do things that were a little on the unusual side to what I would be doing if I were a civilian attorney. I thought, "There's no way that any civilian attorney I know of would be venturing to Antarctica." So that's how I chose the command.

I had anxieties about going to the Antarctic. I thought of it as a much more primitive station than it actually ended up being when I got there. I didn't necessarily think I was going to be in tents, but I thought I'd be in open-bay barracks, with bunk beds that you see in boot camps, and very primitive without any extracurricular activities.

I wouldn't say I felt that anything was risky in the sense of my well-being. I wouldn't say that I was fearful for my physical self; I think it was more just the anxiety of the unknown that made me fearful. Other than that, I didn't like the fact that I would be away for Christmas.

My parents were fascinated. Certain friends of my parents were very fascinated with the fact that I was going down there. In fact, one of my parents' close friends would have loved to have been in my position to go down. They were definitely supportive. It was the same way that they've always reacted to anything I've decided.

I have done other adventurous things, maybe not as exotic as this, but I tend to think my entering the Navy was adventurous. I was the only person in my law school class that did that, so I tended to think I was a little bit more on the adventuresome side than the guys who went to work on Wall Street. Entering the Navy wasn't an exotic adventure, whereas I tend to view Antarctica as being a little bit more on the exotic end.

I remember wearing all the cold weather gear that they gave me in Christchurch. They told us to wear it on the plane, and I had everything on. I stepped off the plane and it was just an amazing sight. It was all this white vastness that was just spectacular. You could spot me as a new person because I had all this stuff on, and it was not cold enough to have it all on. The woman who was meeting me at the runway had on leggings, like stirrup pants, and her coat was wide open. So I will always remember that part of first landing in Antarctica; here I am just top to toe in cold weather gear, and it wasn't that cold.

I didn't know a soul when I got to the Antarctic. One thing about the Navy is that you tend to have a very familylike atmosphere. So people were very warm and friendly. I change jobs every three years and have to get to know people all over again. So there was camaraderie that existed, and it was fairly easy to get to know people, and a little bit easier down there because they didn't have their homes to go back to at the end of the day. I'm not a shy individual, so it wasn't like I kept to myself either.

I was in the Antarctic for three of the summer seasons. The beginning of the season, in October, was definitely cold. Toward December and January, it almost was warmer than I've sometimes felt here in Newport, Rhode Island. I was raised on the East Coast and that December and January felt very much like a winter on the East Coast.

To people who ask me what it was like, I say that McMurdo itself was very much like a coal mining town. Very dull in appearance—nothing majestic about it. But once you got out of McMurdo, away from where it was volcanic rock to where there was just white snow, it was sometimes majestic. It amazed me how clear the atmosphere was; you could just see for miles—things that you saw were miles and miles away. Whereas, back in the States, there's always some kind of haze, and you don't have that kind of visibility. It was, at

times, just awesome in its bigness and brightness and what you could see.

My job wasn't routine every day. At any given time, there would be different things that I would be doing, based on what came through my door. My job wasn't as hectic as some other people's jobs were; it went in peaks and valleys. If someone had gotten into a bar fight or there was some drunken incident, then I would have to deal with the investigations and handle the disciplinary actions that would be taken for something of that sort. I might have to deal with that right off in the morning. Or, it could be that I had appointments with people who had problems at home. For instance, we got a lot of young sailors whose wives were having financial problems back home, or they needed a power of attorney or something of that sort. I had meetings that I had to attend—those that were totally internal military meetings, as well as community meetings. I was a member of the Safety Environmental Health Council Committee, and we met on a weekly basis to handle everything from how we were going to advertise our recycling program and safety for the vehicles, to our hazardous waste situation.

I was not the judge and jury. That was left up to the commanding officer, who was the individual who looked over the investigation that I initiated. I made recommendations, and then based on those, he made a determination of how things would be handled. So I was more his legal advisor, giving him what I thought was the best legal way of handling something. Then he took that advice and made the final decision. That was only for military personnel. We didn't have any control over civilians. The way the civilians handled any disciplinary action was that they fired offenders and sent them off the ice right away.

Alcohol was somewhat of a problem because, number one, a lot of people think, "Well, I don't have anything else to do but drink." Alcohol was definitely available, and you got a lot of alcohol-related incidences. Fights, disorderly conduct, where people would be loud, pulling fire alarms—things of that sort. Then you had incidents that were very much military-type stuff—someone mouthing off to a supervisor, for example, or problems with fraternization. That is basically becoming too familiar with someone that you shouldn't be becoming too familiar with, such as sleeping with

your boss, which is taboo in the Navy. Things of that sort. Fraternizing deals with senior/subordinate relationships, either between officers and enlisted people, or between a senior and a subordinate in the work environment. We did not prohibit sexual conduct; we just, number one, required that it not violate any of the Navy's rules and regulations, and, number two, we hoped that they would use birth control because otherwise, if someone got pregnant, we had to send her off the ice for medical purposes.

We had a lot of problems stemming from the winter-over group. We'd come back onto the ice in October, and there'd be many incidences that occurred involving the winter-over group or the group that came down during winfly, which was in August. We had one individual who went off a flagged path with a bulldozer, and it went through the ice. He was lucky enough to get out and climb through the hole that was made in the ice, but we had to pull the dozer out later in the season when we had the icebreaker. We had a fire truck overturned. They were driving too fast, and it was an unlicensed driver, and he overturned the fire truck. We had a fuel spill that required investigating.

We had two very minor types of sexual harassment. My command was in the forefront of this issue because we definitely did the training on sexual harassment. As a matter of fact, I had done a TV spot on the TV station in Antarctica about sexual harassment. We had a program on dealing with it, and I think we had a leadership that was a little bit more enlightened than what we are seeing from some of the leadership from commands back here in the States. It was well known that sexual harassment was not tolerated in Antarctica.

As far as homosexuality, there was a claim that there was homosexual activity between two women, but both parties denied the complaint. The complaint came from a woman who was herself in trouble, and these two women had brought the evidence to light. So it could have been sour grapes on the other woman's part. There was no actual evidence of any homosexual activity. Our problems were more heterosexual. If I had to name the biggest problem, it was alcohol, and that involved both civilians and military.

Socially, it was similar to being back in college, where you had a group of people who had nothing else to do, so you had a ready

social circle. I did more dancing than I do when I'm back home. The people had the time and didn't have other commitments. Essentially everybody was single, so it wasn't like, "Oh, I have to get a babysitter," or "My husband or wife has got this going." I probably consumed more alcohol than I would normally; I'm not a big drinker, typically.

I pretty much stayed in the McMurdo area. You could walk, and they had areas that were flagged for walking. If you were into cross-country skiing, you could do that. As far as getting beyond what would be a walking distance, we did have space available on flights to the South Pole and on the helicopters. You had your name in a pool, and when there was space available on any of these, if your name came up to the top, then you might get a flight to one of those locations. That was very special. I went on one helicopter flight during the three times I was down there, and I did get to go to the South Pole twice. But that was the extent of getting out of McMurdo. If they tell me it's dangerous to go somewhere, I'm not one to then question whether they know what they're talking about. I'm not one who takes risks to endanger my life, as some people did. So I never felt that I was in danger at any time while I was down there.

My roommate and I were very close. It's funny because we lived together, we worked together, and we just got along fantastically. No one got their own room except for the executive officer and the CO (commanding officer). The CO had his own hut. I developed a very close relationship with my roommate. She was definitely my best friend. I also met my husband-to-be down there, so he was the closest person to me then. I had dated him during our time in California so I didn't really start the relationship in Antarctica, but, of course, since we were from the same command, we were down there together for part of the season. So I definitely developed relationships that are of lasting value, which probably are closer than relationships that I have developed since I left college, in the sense that you are living together, working, eating, and sharing a great deal together.

I did a lot of letter writing. My parents were very good about sending me care packages almost every week. I didn't get them every week, but they sent them to me every week. Now I feel, "Gee, I wish I got care packages." My male friends have never

been great letter writers. My female friends are much better at it. So I did hear from friends on a fairly regular basis. And I'd say every two to three weeks I was able to make a phone call home. So I had contact with my parents and friends back in the States. I was fairly lucky in that people wrote to me.

Right now my fiancé is down there, and they're not having as easy a time getting phone calls out. When I was there, the phone wasn't readily available to just pick up and make a call. You had to make arrangements. You could only do it once a week, and it could be only for ten minutes. I was still able to do that every couple of weeks.

As the legal officer, I kind of took on the role of sitting and listening. Also, in the social sense, with just my fellow officers and my roommate, my room became kind of a social center. People tended to gather to watch TV because we had lots of food and things of that sort. So we seemed to gather in my room with other officers. Though they might not have come with specific problems, it was a place where people felt comfortable gathering. My roommate and I generated a lot of social activity.

There are not a lot of women at my rank, but surprisingly, I'm at a command now in the States that has fewer females than in Antarctica. Naval Support Force Antarctica was about half women and half men in the Antarctic. I felt less of a minority there than I do in other areas of the Navy that I've been in. I think that's because the Antarctic was an operational command that gave women sea time. It was the opportunity for women to help their careers. The majority was definitely male, but there was certainly a contingent of females, both civilian as well as military. I never had a female boss, which was very typical.

Racially, the wardroom—meaning the officers—included, I think, three or four black officers. Ethnically, we had, at one time, one Spanish and one Chinese officer. I don't think we had any Jewish officers. It was somewhat of a mix, but it was predominantly white.

We definitely had a "them and us" feeling with the scientists down there, and also between us (the Navy) and the National Science Foundation (NSF). The NSF, I think, was always frustrated with the way the military worked, and we were sometimes very frustrated with the lack of organization that they had, since we were so used to having such a structured organization. I had a fair amount

of contact with the NSF. The senior officers especially had contact with them. Depending on what kind of job you had, some officers, and certainly the enlisted, didn't have very much contact. I hardly had any contact with scientists, based on my job, so I did not really get to know any of the scientists very well. And a lot of them were in and out of McMurdo very fast because they were sent out to outlying camps. So sometimes I thought the military viewed the scientists as—they want so much; they demand so much. And we weren't necessarily totally clear as to all the things they were doing. I think a lack of communication between the groups existed. They're thrilled because this lichen has grown a mere millionth of a centimeter in the last ten years, but they look at me as a lawyer and think I'm merely a shark out there feeding on others. So it was definitely a sense of different communities who were insulated against each other. Unless you really made an effort to get to know another community, you didn't.

To some extent that was true also between the Naval Support Antarctica and the VXE6 air squadron. It's just the nature of the makeup. Whenever you have someone who's telling the other person what to do, there's always going to be a kind of "them and us" situation. The first season I was down there, the groups had separate living situations. We did have living spaces together my last two seasons, and I thought that might help with our getting to know one another and maybe being less "them and us." But it didn't really end up doing too much about that.

I didn't feel so much out of the loop with people from the Antarctic, but I did with the way that the world went while I was there. I went down in October of 1990, when we were not yet at war. We went to war while I was there, and by the time I came back, we were done with the war. So I felt very much out of touch in the sense that, wow, things were just flying by back in the States and back in other parts of the world. We were really out of it in Antarctica.

In all, the Antarctic was a great experience. I do think I changed as a result of being in the Antarctic. I think I've grown. I'm not as timid with the idea of going someplace totally new. Part of that's the Navy, in general, and part is going so far away from home. I was always afraid of getting lost; that was one of my fears growing up. Even going into a new city or driving not that far from home, I'd

want to have it mapped out and someone to go with me the first time. I'm not that way anymore, so I definitely see this experience as making me less timid. I had to drive from California to Pennsylvania by myself in December of last year when I left the command. I was so proud of myself that I did that, and I didn't even give it a second thought. A few years back, it would have petrified me to do that. Going to the Antarctic toughened my skin up a bit.

I don't have any great desire to go back to the Antarctic. It was interesting and I'm glad I went, but I don't understand the civilians who go back year after year, for ten to fifteen years. You're depriving yourself of many, many things by doing that. I think by seeing it once, even twice, you've gotten that experience under your belt.

WOMEN CIVILIAN CONTRACTORS

Antarctic Support Associates (ASA) is the current contractor hired by the U.S. Antarctic Program to build and maintain stations. ASA hires civilian support staff such as construction workers, field engineers, facilities maintenance personnel, power plant personnel, garage personnel, computer personnel, and clerical workers. ASA personnel typically answer advertisements in local newspapers and are hired for one- or two-year terms. It is ASA members that spend the winter in the Antarctic, keeping the station operating while the scientists are gone. In 1990 to 1991, ninety-five women went to the Antarctic through ASA, and thirty-seven of these women spent the winter there. ASA employees are most likely to go to the Antarctic out of a spirit of adventure and to quit their current jobs to have the opportunity to see the Antarctic.

A Little Slice of Heaven

Berneice F. Albright

Computer terminal operator

Berneice F. Albright was ready to do something extraordinary. She saw an ad in the newspaper for people who were interested in working in the Antarctic, and remembering the wonderful stories she had heard in her childhood from her stepfather who had worked in Greenland, she decided to send off a résumé. After weeks of no response, she was finally offered a twelve-month contract (including a summer and a winter in the Antarctic). At that, she felt as if she had won the lottery. She credits her twenty months of experience at McMurdo Station for her deep, personal growth.

I am a mother of six children, and a good part of that motherhood had been spent as a single parent. In 1987, for the first time in approximately thirty years, I had no children to be responsible for in the home, and I had more freedom than I knew what to do with. I also had a very strong desire to do something extraordinary, to do something to climb out of my responsibility curve, so to speak, and to have a good time, go see some of the world, explore.

One day I was reading the Sunday newspaper. There was an ad about work available in Antarctica. It had a long list of jobs; clerical, janitor, boiler fitter—all sorts of different things. Down at the bottom it said, "And if you're willing to do them in Antarctica, send your résumé to this address." When I was a youngster, my stepfather spent several months working on a contract basis in Greenland. He came home with such a glowing story of so many adventures and slides and photographs and souvenirs of Greenland, that it had always left a vivid image in my mind. A few minutes after reading the ad in the *Seattle Times,* my résumé was in a stamped envelope and in the mail.

One evening, ITT Antarctic Services left a message on my answering machine. I went to my employer the next morning and I

talked with my supervisor. He stared at me after listening to my story and he said, "Anything you need, you let me know." I said, "All I have is a telephone interview. I don't even know that I'm hired, but I sure would like to pursue the opportunity, which might mean that in a few weeks I would pack up and leave." He told me, "When I was in the Navy, I passed up an opportunity to go to McMurdo Station, and I have kicked myself ever since."

One of the funniest parts of the story, I thought, was the interview over the telephone. They started out talking about offering me a summer contract. We got to talking about the fact that I had lived in northern Wisconsin for eight years. The minute I said that they switched and started talking about the winter-over contract. I guess they decided that if I'd lived in northern Wisconsin, I knew what cold was like. From then on it was a one-year contract, and they never reversed themselves. So I went and stayed a full twelve months.

When I told my family about my plans to go, three of my children said, "Gee, that sounds great. Go for it, Mom!" And the other three of my children said, "You're going *where?* Why?" When I later made arrangements to go a second time, of my six children, the three who said, "Go for it, Mom," said, "Why would you want to go again?" And the three who said, "You're going where for what?" said, "Well, you must have enjoyed it the first time."

As it was coming right down to the wire, just before the final decision, there was controversy in terms of my physical exam. At one point, I had three doctors with different opinions, and I didn't know who was going to win. I was practically in tears. One of my co-workers was very comforting and tried to help me step back and just remember that I'd gotten this far and to keep my fingers crossed. In fact, the group of people that I worked with gave me a going away party and a big helium balloon with penguins on it before I left. I worked for that company and that group of people until the night before I got on the airplane. You should have seen me; I carried my helium balloon all the way to New Zealand.

I certainly considered this as an adventure. It was like a twelve-month vacation. You have to remember that I was coming from thirty years of being a mother of six, and a large percentage of that thirty years was as a single mother of six. That means that I spent much of

30 years, from before dawn until well after the children's bedtimes, up to my ears in responsibilities and tasks to do. When I got off duty from my job in Antarctica, I had an amazing world—no children, none anywhere, and a minimum of responsibilities. My responsibilities, as far as after work, consisted of keeping my bed made and my half of the dorm room clean. That was it.

Try to imagine yourself in perhaps the most unusual, abnormal situation in the entire world. Picture a community where the population fluctuates and is constantly in a state of turnover. There is no such thing as a stable population in McMurdo. Picture a population that meets much of the criteria of Shangri-La or utopia. The analogy fits because you have 100 percent employment; you have 100 percent of people in good to excellent health; you have no fragile elderly, no nursing homes, no infants, no children, no police, and no homeless people. You have no neon signs, no freeways, no pavement, and no tax collector. And you're on a continent that is dedicated to international collaboration. Imagine having Russians fly into your community hoping for a tour and asking if they can stay and have supper and party with you because they got lonely over at their own station. Imagine being invited to a New Zealand banquet. Imagine being a volunteer telephone operator and having two Italian scientists come to request help for a telephone call to their home country. Or maybe an internationally known photographer comes and chats with you while he's waiting for his turn to make a telephone call.

I was in Antarctica twice. I worked the first time from October 1988 to October 1989. During that contract, I worked as a computer terminal operator at the heavy shop. That's short for heavy vehicle maintenance facility (HVMF). During the second contract, I asked for a different assignment because I thought I'd like to try something else. And so when I hired on I was expecting to be a materials expeditor. Within forty-five days, they came to me and asked if I would go back to the heavy shop because I had some experience up there, and the people who were there were struggling with very little knowledge of the computer. So I went to the heavy shop again and finished out the rest of the contract there.

When I first arrived, which was during the summer, I was assigned to a Jamesway. That's where my bunk was and my personal belongings and such. A typical day in a Jamesway is a very interesting

experience. The Jamesways were in a cluster, and there were four Jamesways side by side, separated by maybe a few feet. At the rear of this cluster of Jamesways was a hallway that led to a group bathroom and shower room. Each one of the Jamesways could house nine of us. We worked different shifts, and so you set your alarm clock to get up when you had to get up. In the Jamesway, it would be relatively dark because the Jamesway had only one window up by the front door. The relative darkness was good because people who worked shift work needed the darkness for their sleeping pattern. You would get up, and you would turn on only just a very small light for your little bunk area and get dressed. Probably you would get up and find your robe and head for the bathroom and the showers. Once dressed, you'd go to chow hall.

I signed up for a calendar year, and until it actually was approaching December, it did not occur to me that I had signed up to spend my first Christmas without my family. It was the first time in my life that I spent my birthday, Thanksgiving, Christmas, and New Year's with my family far, far, far away from me. But, overall, I had a great time. We had a great Thanksgiving banquet. The Navy galley crew made a cornucopia out of bread dough and filled it with fruit. Maybe there'd be an ice sculpture. They'd have a table set up with fresh fruits and cheeses—that sort of thing. The Navy went out of their way to make holidays special occasions. I generally had a companion or more than one companion to go to supper with. The rules were loosened on holidays: people could bring a bottle of wine to their meal with them if they wanted, and little champagne glasses were available. At ordinary meals they didn't use tablecloths at all; you'd come in on the holiday and maybe there'd be tablecloths and candles on all the tables and centerpieces or something. There was a good deal of sharing and talking in terms of different Christmas traditions. It was different, but I was not upset by having Christmas without my family.

Winter is a long time. The last plane flew out in late February. Here is a community that was 1,200 to 1,500 strong, a logistics center with people moving in and out constantly, airplane flights overhead, airplane flights on the runway, vehicles running to and fro from the airport section to town, and in February, the whole thing winds down; the community shrinks to 120.

In March and April the amount of light begins to decrease. It's not

dark yet all day; it's not totally dark, but it's now twilight a good part of the day. We had brilliant, beautiful clear sunshine during much of the summer, but now we were in March and April, and there was no more brilliant sunshine anywhere, not any time of the day. The darkness just gradually grew until we came to the really dark time, when it was dark twenty-four hours a day. I think some of us Americans experienced real honest-to-God darkness for the first time in our lives. Many people don't realize that when it's dark outside and you're standing on a city street, you still don't know what dark looks like. A typical winter day in deep winter in McMurdo, when it was really dark, it was black outside all day long.

In the winter, we still had the rhythm of getting up and getting dressed, going to work and dinner, etc. However, things did change. I was no longer in the Jamesway; I was in a brand-new dormitory, living on the third floor. I had an entire dorm room to myself. What I mean by entire is that I wasn't sharing it with anyone. Usually there are two people in a dorm room, but in the wintertime in 1988, we had a private dorm room until winter was done. Also in the winter, we no longer had water rations because we had actually more water than we could take care of, so we could take long showers if we wanted. We no longer had anyone come and take the agitator out of the washing machine. That was one way they got us to conserve water in summer—you don't put your clothes in the washing machine if the agitator is not in there. So the routine changed.

Now in the winter, it's dark—whenever you go outside it's dark. Doesn't matter—you can go out at noon or at night, it's all the same. Actually it's really kind of fun to lie on your back on the snow at high noon and stare at the stars. That was a whole new experience. You might get up and head for the chow hall and wander in for breakfast, and maybe one of the Navy chiefs will be playing with his yo-yo, or maybe two of the civilians will be playing pretend catch across the expanse of the dining room. Now, here are 120 of us, total, working on shift work and in the galley at different times, and we're in a facility that used to serve 750. It's a whole different experience. The pace is slower; the atmosphere is different—a great deal of tolerance. If you feel like acting a little silly or a little bizarre, nobody gets excited. But the majority of people are still doing their routine thing.

The heavy shop, where I worked, was responsible for the 4th of

July party, which is midwinter in McMurdo. I felt like I knew almost everybody in the room. Everyone had that same feeling, but the feeling can be wrong. It was so funny, the first year we had one employee who worked at the power plant, and the power plant works on a twenty-four-hour schedule, of course. This employee had been a very nonsocial person. He had routinely got up, went to work, gone home, and gone to sleep. Because of the power plant being a twenty-four-hour operation, they had their own kitchen. This young fellow did not show up in the galley all summer, so people in the galley did not know who he was. One day in the middle of winter he showed up for lunch. People were sitting at their tables, and all the heads turned and said, "Who in the hell is that?" There was no way that this new face could have come in on a plane. All of us were sitting wondering, "Where did he come from?" So you can see what I mean, in terms of everybody thinking they know everybody. It was quite an interesting phenomenon. To me, there was an extraordinary closeness the first winter—a very, very special experience—not only between Americans, but between the Americans and the New Zealanders as well. We had just marvelous relationships, as far as I'm concerned.

I made an ongoing appointment for one telephone call per week to talk to my children, plus my mother and father. I rotated my phone calls so that I called my oldest child this week and then the next oldest the week after, and etc., down the line. I gave instructions. Since I had limited phone calls, I set the schedule up before the last plane flew out, so that they knew what day I was going to call and to whom I would talk. They knew that Steve was going to get the phone call on this particular Tuesday night. If they had a question, they could call Steve and say, "Hey Steve, ask Mom about this, or ask Mom about that." It worked out great. I had good communication with home, and that telephone call was always very important to me.

It isn't a matter of what happens or exactly what a letter or call contains; it's just a matter of knowing how they are, what's happening with them, and being able to let them know how I am and what's happening for me. It was the opportunity for the contact, more than what you talked about. I have eight grandchildren. We didn't have that many phone minutes—maybe the whole conversation would be about Jessica. My poor Jessica. She was in first grade. They were studying the family; the teacher gave an assignment that each child was to go

home and ask their parent where their grandparents lived. The next day they went back to class and when it came Jessica's turn she stood up and said, "My grandmother lives in Antarctica." The teacher said, "No, no, Jessica. Nobody lives in Antarctica." Jessica stomped her little foot and said, "My grandmother does!" The teacher just wouldn't believe her, so the teacher called Jessica's father who said, "Well, that's where her grandmother is right now." So the teacher had to more or less apologize to Jessica. When I got back from Antarctica, I did a show for Jessica's second grade class.

There were always more men than women. There were some very strange official attitudes. For example, even in 1991 on my second trip, the U.S. government still hadn't figured out that there's a difference between boys and girls. They issued only male long underwear, and I hated to wear the male long underwear. It's very thick cotton underwear, and it's intended to be used for warmth. But because it is so thick, the male fly shows under women's garments. I think that the U.S. government should grow up a little bit. I bought my own and wore the kind that I bought. The point is women's longies are readily available and equally warm, and both kinds are put on the same way.

I encountered an interesting situation in 1988 in my Jamesway (which is a quonset hut) when I was trying to get settled in. I was putting some of my belongings in my closet and I heard somebody about two bunks down just crying and crying, and sniffling and crying. Here was this little lady, older than myself; she and her husband had signed up for one year at McMurdo. Her husband had been assigned to a brand-new dormitory room, and she had been assigned to a lowly, scroungy Jamesway. Now, all around us there were men and women who were becoming roommates because they wanted to, not because they were married, but just because they wanted to. She hadn't noticed that. She was sitting on her bunk crying because they had assigned him to a dormitory room and her to a Jamesway. She had been married for over thirty years and, in that time, had never slept anywhere without him.

I said to her, "You know, all around I see these people are making private deals, switching rooms so that they can be roommates with whom they want. Lots of them are men and women who are doing this." I said, "If they can live together unmarried in the same dorm room, surely you can make some kind of deal so that you can live

together with your own husband in a dorm room. And if the management wants to make a big issue out of it, we'll talk about these issues." She stared at me a little while and finally I said, "Make a deal with your husband's roommate. Buy him off. Give him fifty bucks. Encourage him to find some other room to switch to." Within forty-eight hours she was gone. She made some kind of a deal with her husband's roommate, and she was gone. I never will forget the company trying to put married people in two different dorm rooms! I was pleased that during my second contract, ASA handled room arrangements more realistically.

Ice romances are strange things. Sometimes they cause a great deal of friction; they cut across marriage lines and all sorts of things, and yet they seem to be very necessary for the people involved. My relationship with a New Zealander turned into a very ugly rumor that he and I were having sex and that we were an ice romance, when in fact we weren't. Not that I wouldn't have if he wanted to. He was a very attractive man—very attractive and very marvelous socially and very nice to get to know. Romance wasn't the case, but it didn't matter whether it was the case or not. When there's only 120 of you, or 132, counting the New Zealanders, the rumors do run.

During my winters there, one of the things that happened was a very heightened awareness of the roles of people. Numerous times I've used the classic example that when I went into my dorm room and flipped the switch to turn the light on, I knew who was making the electricity. I became very much aware of how we all depended on each other. The power plant came up to the heavy shop because they needed to repair a generator, and they thought that perhaps our inventory might have a part that they needed. Now, basically we didn't stock parts ordinarily for power plant generators. But we did have numerous parts for Caterpillar tractors, and Caterpillar generators were related. So we helped each other out. ASA has set into motion a unified inventory system that should increase this interaction between facilities. Take a shower in McMurdo—I knew the person who was running the water plant. That's something I can't say here in Seattle. I knew who was baking the bread and who cooked the omelets. It was a thing where, if you wanted something, you could, by thinking about it for a while, probably figure out how to get it—how to accomplish it— whom to contact and whatnot.

I am just now trying to return to a normal life, and I have to tell you, I'm having trouble. I'm having troubles I've never experienced before, and I'm going to counseling at the moment. I'm battling with depression, the doctor says, in spite of the fact that I'm trying my usual techniques of having something to look forward to. I keep wanting to go someplace else, either to go back to Antarctica or there's an opportunity that I've learned about where I might be able to go to Japan and teach English as a second language. That sounds like a wonderful experience. I've been teaching English as a second language to Vietnamese people here in Seattle. I find that I am enjoying that experience. It's as if half of me wants to go off and adventure some more, and the other half of me is trying to talk me into settling down. I don't know what I want to do the most. I had no trouble making a decision to go to Antarctica, and I enjoyed the adventure. I have many, many memories that are absolutely indelible. But now, trying to fit back into the real world is like a shock. It's very hard to describe.

I gained a tremendous amount. During my time down there I gained insights into my own personal needs and I gained some insights and perspectives of my own strengths that are even more valuable to me. By and large, I coped with the winter much, much differently than some of the people around me. I had certain kinds of strengths and coping strategies already in place, in terms of dealing with limited circumstances. I hadn't really been so much aware of that. I think I changed as a person. I think that it has had a big impact on my life. And I don't think the impact is done yet because I don't know yet what I want to do with the rest of my life. I have options and I have dreams, but I really can't choose a direction at this moment.

I think that there was another major factor for me, in terms of McMurdo, and I've only just identified this recently with the counseling that I've gone to. McMurdo for me was like a cocoon. For some people, the limited personnel and the limited physical area were big problems; they felt that their freedom was diminished. It's been one of the only times in my life where a really strong sense of security and strong relationships emerged. I come from a background of extensive change; I come from a background of always having had to scramble to deal with my next meal. In McMurdo my situation was like guaranteed security. So long as I functioned on my job, I had three meals a day, a roof over my head, free transportation to and from work, and

people to talk to, and things to do and supplies for those activities. For me, I guess it was similar to some other people's childhoods, where you always have somebody who provides for you. I have not always had somebody who provides for me. I have had years and years where I was the only person doing the providing for a family of five and six, and I had to do plenty of self-sacrificing in order to make things work. In McMurdo it was the complete opposite. I did what I wanted to do. It was a little slice of heaven. So it wasn't reality, but it sure was fun for my personal situation. I think that a tour of Antarctica functions that way for some people, over and above myself.

The Silence Was Incredible

Kathy Bojack

General laborer, administrative assistant, and lab worker

Kathy Bojack **has been to the Antarctic six times including an entire twelve-month stint. She and her then-husband heard about the possibility of working in the Antarctic when, while on a bike trip in New Zealand, they met an American woman just returning from Antarctica. Her husband pushed her to apply with him. They then went down together as general laborers. At first it was wonderfully exciting, although due to the rules, they could not live together. However, they grew apart over the years. After their divorce, Kathy continued to return to the Antarctic, mostly because of the salary. She also met her next husband there.**

I went down with my first husband; we had been married about a year at the time. We originally heard about the program while bicycle touring in New Zealand in 1983; we met some people coming off the ice who told us about the opportunity. I hadn't met them before. When we were cycling along the South Island, we stayed at a campground and I ran into an American woman while we were both hanging out clothes. She was wearing an Antarctica sweatshirt. I hadn't met another American in the entire three or four months, and curious about the origin of her shirt, I asked, "How do you explain your sweatshirt?" She said, "I just came back from working in the Antarctic," and I said, "No kidding. I didn't realize there were people working down there." She said, "Oh yeah, there are quite a few of us." So we chatted a little bit, and I got a bad feeling. It was really funny. After speaking to her a little bit I said, "I'm not going to tell my husband about this, because knowing him, he's going to want to try to pursue this. I'm not sure it's the right thing for us."

Anyway, I tried to keep it from him, but something made me tell him. That night I said, "I can't stand it anymore. I have to tell you

about this woman I met. Something is just pushing me to tell you," and immediately he was excited and had to meet the woman and her husband. He then really pushed to go down there. I did not want to go, to be honest. I was ready to quit the nomadic life we'd been living. At the time I was living at a guest ranch in the summer, and I was ready to cut out this "doing your work where you live." I knew if we got into this it would become a habit. I don't know what made me know that.

But, it was true. I applied, got my first job in the Antarctic as a general laborer, and I started moving up. I hit it off well with the men I worked with. There were very few women that year, about thirty total, and there were about 900 men. It was kind of a crazy ratio. I had a wonderful time in my department, wound up liking it, and was eager to come back. My husband and I did not live together down there; we weren't allowed to, especially since we had no seniority. That, and the fact that we were just laborers, put us at the bottom of the totem pole. We were both young—twenty-five when we went down. We went back together for two more years.

But we started growing apart, and finally split up after our third year. I'll return to that later. After that, I kept returning because I needed the money. By my fourth season, living conditions were much better and my new boyfriend and I were able to live together. That's my basic history—what made me go down there. So I kept going back after my divorce because, number one, I needed the money to help me through my divorce, and number two, I'd met someone new and I didn't want to blow this relationship. I decided, "If he's going to keep going back, I might as well too." I was offered a job in the Chalet, which is the administration building, an excellent job where I learned stress management, as mine was a stressful job. My job title was administrative assistant, but the job was coordinating and scheduling helicopter operations. It was also a good way to meet other people. By this time, 1988, it was time to do something new, so the Chalet job offered the perfect opportunity.

In the Chalet, I worked with women for the first time. It was nerve-wracking at first, trying to get to know other women. I hadn't known many women in my life, yet today, I don't know how I survived all those years without female fellowship. Originally, I felt at home with the men but not at all with the women. In 1984, there

were so few and they were very cliquey. It reminded me of high school. At the same time, one couldn't help but meet new people, and pretty soon the ice became like a second home. It was also a sure job. Every year after the ranch closed I had a job that paid fairly good money. I didn't take the decision to work in Antarctica lightly; it took some serious thought on my part, and I worried how my mother and father were going to feel at the time.

My dad was all for it—a bit nervous, because he's rather conservative and would worry, but he encouraged me nonetheless. My mother, on the other hand, was always very negative toward things like that. She would say, "When are you going to become a lady?" When I was running marathons, for example, she would say, "How can you sweat? It's so unladylike." Until I came home with trophies, and then all of a sudden it was, "My daughter, the runner." It was the same thing with the Antarctic. Of course, after she started telling her friends, "My daughter is in the Antarctic," it became a status thing. That's how she dealt with it. Overall, however, it was considered kind of an adventure, especially for protective parents from New Jersey who'd grown up in that suburban atmosphere and raised me in the same way. This was totally different, totally off the wall. It was a Big Adventure.

What's it like being in the Antarctic? The winter-over was the best part about it. The winter-over was where I found my privacy. I loved it. That in itself was an experience so worth doing that if I were ten years younger I'd do it again in a heartbeat. I loved the winter-over and the darkness. I felt like I was in a cave and it was great. I never had problems sleeping at night. When night was night, that was it. Some people said they had trouble sleeping. I never understood that. The twenty-four hours a day of darkness was the only time I could find privacy. I really felt invaded when people came back in August, but that's a very common feeling among those who winter-over.

In 1984, my first job was shoveling snow—lots and lots of snow. It was wonderful. We were a small group who made up the general labor pool. Eventually they farmed us all out to different departments, and I went to the sheet metal department. I started by fabricating sheet metal radar reflectors for landing strips. Then I was installing flashing, pieces that protect the sides of the building, then ductwork and roofing. All fun stuff like that. We had a fun-loving crew, lots of joking, lots of singing and laughing—really and truly a

good, fun group of people. They were heavy drinkers, though. I thought I was going to become an alcoholic. In fact, I wouldn't doubt it if I've got it in me because I could keep right up with them. There was a lot of drinking down there. It's scary when I think about how much drinking occurs down there; it frightens me.

Take the Christmas of 1988, for example. The night before, there was a Christmas party, and by this time I hated the large parties, but I went to it because a friend was playing in the band. As my boyfriend and I walked in, a bunch of drunken military guys were in a fight over a woman and they started hitting me. I had just walked into it and I got rather banged up, and my boyfriend practically killed the guy. It took several guys to drag him off this guy, quite seriously, because the guy had hurt me and he was drunk, and my boyfriend was pretty much just holding him to the ground saying, "Are you going to stop it? Are you going to stop it?" And all of this fellow's cronies were kicking around at my boyfriend; it was just such a bad scene, and I thought to myself, "This is awful! What on earth is going on?" I was so stunned. So that ruined our Christmas that year, and of course, the rest of the year was unpleasant.

Nothing happened to the guys. The guys got slapped on the wrist, and the excuse was, "Oh, well, they were drunk." It's okay to be drunk. It's an accepted thing down there. "Oh, it's okay. He was just drunk. He wouldn't have done it had he not been drunk."

My belief is that you are responsible for your own actions. If I drink, I am responsible for my actions. And if I do not drink, I am responsible for my actions. During the winter-over of 1991, something else happened. We spent most of the winter-over with three or four friends—a small crowd, a very quiet crowd. Lots of excellent Sunday brunches, nice times. Well, one night, it was 11:00, I guess, we decided to go over to the club. It was pretty empty, and we went up to the bar. My husband was standing there—by this time we were married—and he had his arm around me. A man who was old enough to be my father came over and pinched me low on the butt. He came back and he did it again. I told my husband what happened, and well, my husband was very protective and I thought he was going to kill this guy. I asked him to not do anything. He said, "Don't worry, I won't." He went over to the guy and he said, "If you ever so much as look at my wife, so much as *look* at her, I'm going to kill you. I'm going to

turn you upside down and use your bald little head as a mop." (The guy, by the way, was sober.) We left the club.

Back in 1986, after my second year, I had called home while traveling in New Zealand and was told that my mom had cancer. It just sunk me—I was so shocked. We passed the rest of our vacation in New Zealand quickly, and I went home to see my mom. At first, I thought she was going to get better.

By now, my first husband and I were arguing—especially over going back to the ice. He'd say, "Well, I like it." I'd say, "Well, I don't." So we'd argue back and forth about that, and yet, we went back down. My dad got a call through to me in November 1986, saying, "Mom is going in for another operation. She's sick. Come home for Thanksgiving." So they flew me home. I couldn't believe it. I thought, "This is really happening. It's happening to my family, and I'm in Antarctica. What is wrong with me? Why am I not with my family?" My then-husband kept saying, "You gotta come back to the ice; we need the money." I returned to the ice the day after Thanksgiving, and the last memory I have of my mother is when I was standing at the door and she was crying. I said, "Bye. Love you, Mom. Bye." I got into the taxi and went away, and I never saw her again. I thought to myself, "What is wrong with you? Why aren't you staying home? You're not getting along with your husband anyway." Things were really feeling weird, and I was thinking this was not good; this was not healthy. I went back anyway.

That January, in 1987, I got word that my mom had died. I was at work and a station official called me there and said, "I suppose you realize your mother's dead." Isn't that nice? I said, "Oh, well, thank you for telling me." He said, with the same degree of tact, "I suppose you want to make a phone call." I told my boss that my mother died. He said, "Go on, make a phone call and go home." I couldn't even cry. I didn't cry for four months. On my way down to the Chalet to make my call, I stopped to see my husband. He said, "What's up?" and I said, "My mom just died." And he said, "Do you need me?" I said, "Nah." I went down to the Chalet and someone was there getting ready to put the phone call through for me. I had to call collect. At that point they wouldn't let you make a call; you had to pay for it. It was a terrible connection, but I heard my dad say, "Don't bother coming

home; it's not worth it. You came home already. Stay there and I'll see you when you get back." So I stayed.

Once I got back to the States, I separated from my first husband and went back to my dad's place. I went to visit the Antarctic office, which was near my dad's, because I needed a job and I needed help, and I didn't know what to do. So I went to see the deputy director. He said, "I heard about your situation and I'm really sorry." He added, "Well, you're going to need to get on your feet." I said, "Yeah, you're not kidding." He said, "Well, I need help for the summer. Would you be willing to work as my clerk?" I jumped at it: "You bet." He took me over to personnel, and then Dennis, this guy I knew from the ice came over. He said, "So what are you doing for lunch?" I just said, "Word travels fast in this office." He said, "Yeah, you're separated," and I said, "Yup. Well, let's go to lunch." That started another episode of the Big Adventure.

I made some interesting observations about the female relationships down there at first. During my first year, it seemed as if the women who had been there before were threatened by new women, and I don't really know why. Then that group of women seemed to kind of disappear after that year, and new women came in; suddenly there were more and more women. There was a whole new feeling. Even I started to befriend some women. I'm still close to several women that I have worked with down there, particularly from my fourth year. I began to develop and maintain female relationships that have proven to be very important to me. I'm really thankful for them, and to think I never knew I needed female companionship! I'm very fortunate right now. In fact, I live in an area where I've got some very close female friends; we're all on the same wavelength and the same plane. To me it's genuinely necessary for mutual support, which I didn't have my first three years on the ice. I can't help but wonder what it would have been like if I had cultivated friendships among females then.

There are so many different types of personalities in the Antarctic program. The powers-that-be administer psychological tests to screen people who are potential winter-overs, but it's such a bunch of baloney. Anybody with half a brain can get through that test if he or she really needs to get down there. One classic rumor was that there were people hiding from the law. I think even I believed it could be so. One of my volunteer efforts for the winter was typing up Mars-

grams for people to send home—messages that are sent over the radio. So one day I went down to the Navy's quarterdeck to get the book and the key to the Marsgram box, and a Navy watchman was looking at the TV set—he seemed entranced by it. I said, "What are you watching?" And he said, "It's a television show called *America's Most Wanted*." (Everything's on tape down there.) He said, "I want to see how many ASA-ers I can recognize." I said, "You're not!" He said, "You never know the types of people you're going to get down there. What a perfect place to hide out." So I don't know how carefully they check records. I really don't.

Going to the Antarctic is great; it's just not something I wanted to do for too long, because it's easy to get a warped sense of what's reality and what's not. For example, when I came off the ice in October of 1991, I needed sunshine in a bad way, not just any sunshine; I needed *warm* sunshine. So when I got off the plane in Hawaii and through customs, I made a rash decision. I took my bags and walked out of the airport and went to a hotel, and I spent three days in Hawaii on the beach, just enjoying the sun. But I started to see new people, and I had to react to them. All the people I had interacted with throughout the winter were the same people over and over again, for an entire year. All of a sudden I was seeing all these strangers, and I found myself really becoming impatient.

The first time you come home from the Antarctic it's exciting because you want to tell everybody about your Big Adventure. The last time I came back, nobody wanted to hear it anymore. It was old news. But what was unusual about the last time I came back was that I felt a sense of finality. Now, at this very moment, I'm picturing what the weather's like down there, and I'm thinking, oh boy, in a few months I'll be in New Zealand. It's as if you always look forward to leaving. Crazy, isn't it? But in September 1992, I had a hard time because usually in September I was always leaving to go to the ice. When my husband left without me in 1992, I actually had a sense of panic. I had committed myself to a job and I was here. Here I am every day, five days a week, for the next who-knows-how-long, I'm in this job. And before, there was always a sense of ending one adventure and renewing another. Oh, goody, goody—two months off, hiking in New Zealand and playing Peter Pan and Tinkerbell again, and it was terrific. Now, all of a sudden it's, uh-oh, responsibilities. I've always been

fairly responsible, so I shouldn't say I'm not, even though you'd never know it by the things I've been describing!

There has been a trade-off. I gave up any chance of trying to start a family. I still don't have children. Other trade-offs? I never had a chance to have any sense of normalcy in my life, really. What's normal? Who knows. I've got a normal life now, you might say, but I'm not so sure. I haven't been to graduate school. I'd often thought about going to law school and there's no way. I would never have that kind of money now.

In 1984, I went to the Beardmore Glacier camp with a group of total strangers. I was the junior member of the entire team, and there were a couple of other females there. The cook was the wife of the Beardmore camp manager. Another female was a carpenter who kind of kept to herself. But I had a neat experience that I don't think can be duplicated or even explained well. I experienced, for the first time in my life, utter and total silence. There was a place, over a plateau, where I went for a walk with my friend, Kevin Roy, from the station. Once we got a couple miles away from the camp, you could no longer see it or hear it, and there was no wind; there was nothing around us at all except frozen ice. We stood there for a second. This was on Christmas Day, in fact, and Kevin stood still and said, "Hey, Kath, stop." I stopped and he said, "Don't move," so we didn't move. He said, "Hold your breath." So I held my breath. He whispered, "And listen." The silence was incredible. The silence scared me. I'd never in my life experienced the feeling of deafness. That's what it felt like. I mean there was *nothing*. Nothing. No sound at all. You could almost hear the blood going through your veins, that's how silent it was. Our eyes were getting wider and wider, and we just burst out into laughter, and he said, "Have you ever felt that?" And I said, "Oh my God, it's haunting." To this day it haunts me. I wonder if Kevin remembers that!

I think experiencing that silence changed my life. It really did. I will never, ever forget that. It's absolutely impossible to explain, and it was the weirdest experience. It doesn't really mean anything, but it's just something that has always stood out in my mind. Then the slightest breeze picked up, so slight, and it started to brush a couple of ice crystals across the frozen terrain, and you could hear them. It was an intense magical experience.

I Went to Antarctica When My Children Were All Married

Sandra Kenady

Computer operator and office manager

Sandra Kenady decided that she was interested in having an adventure once her youngest child got married. The kind of person who always fulfilled her responsibilities, she wanted a change and an opportunity to travel. While in the Antarctic, she met a man whom she eventually married. Her time while in the Antarctic was shortened, however; she was injured and had to be sent home.

The first year that I went to the Antarctic, I took any job I could get, so I went as a clerk/typist terminal operator. I was a secretary for the head of logistics. It didn't start out that way. I was to be a secretary in one of the warehouses, and that warehouse was not turned over from military to the civilian personnel in the timely manner that they had anticipated. So in the meantime, they brought me in to work in the office where the manager of logistics was. Well, when she found out the skills I had, she kept me.

A man I'd met socially in Denver told me about the program and helped me get an employment application. He walked it through for me, got it into the right places, and was very helpful. That's how I got to the Antarctic the first time. While I was there they learned about me—that I had managerial skills, etc.—and that my background was in real estate (I'm a broker) and property management. So the second year, I went down as the housing coordinator and handled all that for them. Then I was injured and sent home.

The injury took place one morning when I had a big meeting with the head of NSF and my boss about housing and how we were going to handle things. I'd been up all night making charts. I got out of my truck, started into the chalet, and the wind was unbelievable. It picked up all my paperwork right out of my arms and blew it all

over. I got everything except the big spreadsheet that I'd been up all night doing. So I went into the office and I told my boss and he said, "Well, girl, you'd better go get it." They were sitting there waiting for me, so I sat down on my nylon parka and slid down a hill of ice. I laid back and zipped under a pipe, then went on down. It was great going down, no problem, and I did find the paper. It was blowing around in a corner, thank God. It had headed for the bay. I got the paper and I stuck it inside my coat, zipped it up, and started back up the hill. There was not even a chance for a toe hold; it was solid ice. I just started climbing. I had on regular shoes and regular gloves and this slick nylon parka, and I certainly was not prepared for climbing, but it was the only way back. I got up about fifteen feet, probably, and I fell. I landed on my knee. Because the ice was just like granite, it didn't absorb the blow, and the force from the blow went up into my back, broke a bone, and shattered three vertebrae. I had to have spinal surgery. I had three vertebrae fused and rods inserted. Now it's very doubtful that I'll be able to go back because I probably wouldn't be able to pass the physical with all that steel in my back.

My husband is there now, and I would like to be there, too. I met him in the Antarctic. He was one of those people I worked for the first year.

I'm forty-five now, but the first time I went down I think I was forty-two. I had raised my children alone, since they were ages two, five, and eight. I went to Antarctica right after my youngest child got married. I was tired of going from home to the office, to parent-teacher conferences, to the grocery store. That's all I'd ever done. I'd never been out of the country; I haven't traveled extensively in the United States, even, and I had fulfilled all my responsibilities, so I wanted to do something for me. When I heard about Antarctica, I knew that's what I wanted to do, and that I wanted to see the continent. Very few people have ever been. I wanted to know for myself what it was like, and I wanted to travel. You get to go through New Zealand; I'd never even been to Hawaii. So it was wonderful. It was something for me.

Quite frankly, I was worried about flying over so much water, between here and there. My children thought I was crazy. They were happy for me, very cautious and worried about it, too, but

supportive. I don't think I worried about some of the things I should have worried about. You don't realize until you're there what the isolation is, and that you very well could be hurt badly there, and that you very well could be isolated there for long periods of time, which we were. Everything depends on the weather and machinery. If the weather is bad, they can't bring those planes in; and if the planes aren't working, they can't come in, whether the weather is good or not. So the isolation factor is something that really plays on people. If you're not a strong individual and at ease with yourself, then you have problems. People who have those problems begin to drink there and drink very heavily.

It starts out as sort of a lark, and then when you get there, the lark comes to a screeching halt. You suddenly realize that you're in a work camp, and you're not there for your own little bit of adventure—that is extremely limited because of danger. There are crevasses; there's just danger that you don't know about that's in the ice. You can walk out over ice or you can walk out over snow, and it may be a crust only and you'll fall in. If you're in that water twenty seconds, you're dead. If you fall in a crevasse, the chances of anyone finding you, although they have a system set up for that, are almost none. I didn't anticipate all of that. You're very controlled there. The scientists get to do a lot of things, but the average person doesn't get to go do anything but work. So you're pretty well taken to the bottom of the world and then locked up in a several-mile-square area. There's all this beauty and all of these fantastic mountains and interesting people that you meet coming through town, and scientists and grantees and foreigners who are stopping there to get supplies to go on to their bases, etc. They're the ones that are actually seeing Antarctica: the dry valleys, the digs for the dinosaurs, the research camps.

I've always wanted to travel. I've always had a desire, for example, to live on a lake in Canada somewhere, where a plane drops my supplies twice a year. Of course, I'd have to have a generator so I can have my refrigerator and dishwasher and everything!

When I first landed and got off the plane, there were all these foreign vehicles that have been developed specifically for use there, such as half-tracks or track vehicles similar to snowcats. As you step out of a military plane (the first military plane you've ever been in),

and here are all these foreign-looking vehicles, people dressed like Eskimos, and mountains coming 15,000 feet up out of the bay. You're landing on sea ice, and you know that there are whales and whatever under that ice. I expected to see James Bond with some busty blonde, whizzing past on a snowmobile! It was so unrealistic.

I actually was on an island in Antarctica. I was on Ross Island, and we faced the mainland, but it's connected with solid ice. The ice in the bay where we had landed when we first arrived melts. Eventually it's too thin, and they have to land on permanent ice, the Ross Ice Shelf, which connects the Ross Island with the mainland. We had a live volcano on the island with us that steamed every day.

My second time in the Antarctic, I went during winfly. It's called winter inward flight, and that's the worst weather time, during August and September. It's really bad. Here in Colorado, the end of the winter is extremely blustery, and spring is blustery, and it's all combined. Well, multiply that by a thousand, and that's Antarctica during August and September. The weather is very bad, but the light is starting to come in, and you have a four-hour window of flight that you can fly into. Because of the priority of my job the second year, I had to be on the first flight. No one has landed on this ice for a whole season. You don't know what it's like; you're landing on skis; they have to use the wing flaps on the plane as brakes; your heart's in your throat. It was really exciting.

Not too many people go back to New Zealand on the first return flight. They're sending out scientific experiments, specimens, etc. But if someone's been fired or injured or whatever, they're taken out on the first flights.

The temperature was nearly 100 degrees below zero and ninety-knot winds in August, when we went in. It was bad. It was the coldest I have ever been in my life. When you go in during October, it's chilly—well, it's damn cold sometimes, but you have to realize it's zero humidity. That's a high, dry area. It never rains. It's an arid area, a desert. The cold doesn't affect you the way it does in other countries with humidity. It's the wind that makes it cruel, so it's not that bad. The worst time of all is winfly.

The wind would sometimes pick my feet up from underneath me, when it was behind me. When you're walking into it, it'll take your breath away. Of course, all that's exposed are your eyes, and they're

covered with sunglasses. You have all the ECW gear, too—extreme cold weather gear—so you're dressed for it. It's not as if you're in shorts and a tank top, trying to survive.

Being in the Antarctic was the most awesome thing that's ever happened in my life. I can remember walking down from the building I worked in; we were the second highest building in town. We would walk back down to the galley and to the dorm and whatever, and there would sometimes be mirages. These mirages occurred because of the way the sun hits the ice, and of course you have ice everywhere. Over on the mainland, a beautiful range of mountains called the Royal Societies rises straight out of the bay. You can see strata; they're gorgeous. They're the most beautiful things I've ever seen in my life, and I'm a mountain person, having been born in the Cascades and now living in Colorado.

Once my fiancé—my husband now—and I were walking home from work one night, down that hill, and there was a mirage halfway up the mountains. They seemed to be raised up off of the ice. What it did to the mountains that afternoon was to show you the bottom half of the range; then the fuzzy mirage went halfway through; and then the whole mountain range was refracted above it. It looked like it was half again as high as it really was, and yet there was this misty quality through the middle of it.

I've sat on the top of a hill in the middle of the night and watched minke whales go into a feeding frenzy. There must have been a school of fish or something out there, perhaps cod. When they settled down after they'd eaten, they played and they talked to each other. I feel so fortunate to have been able to see mountains like that and to have listened to whales.

I once had a single penguin come up to me. They never travel alone unless they're hurt or sick or something, and you could tell he wasn't just right. He rubbed all over my leg. I just wanted to reach down and hold him and support him, but I couldn't touch him. He rubbed and rubbed on me, making this funny little noise. His feathers were all different directions. I don't know if he'd been bitten by a whale or a seal or what had happened, but that was sad, and I couldn't do anything. We are not allowed to touch them.

That's part of an international treaty. We can be there, but we are not to interfere at all with the natural fauna; there's no flora. We can't

introduce anything foreign. Plants cannot be brought in; nothing can be done to disturb the ecosystem. My children and I have saved all our bread crusts for years in the freezer, and when we get a bunch, we go feed the ducks at the park. Well, you're not allowed to do even that sort of thing there because that would mess up their ecosystem.

Every day brought something different. There were a lot of personality clashes to deal with because it's the military; it's the civilian workforce; it's the National Science Foundation. The National Science Foundation was your boss, and a lot of those scientists were egomaniacs. They're brilliant people, but they don't seem to have a personality, so sometimes that's hard to get by. They're not all that way. Some are warm and wonderful. So you're working with all these different personalities; they're coming from nowhere; you don't have the equipment that you need to do your work; you're expected to be absolutely perfect all the time because it's a crunch situation. You have X number of jobs to get done in X number of days.

You're not supposed to send plants down there, but my mother, this sweet little old lady in Oregon, sent me a Christmas tree, the kind you buy at the store, a little ten-inch tree in a pot. She mailed one down there, and she wrote on the customs form what it was and everything, and they sent it in. Also, in the mountains near where she lives there's a holly farm. She sent me holly in a box that advertised the holly farm, too. So I told everybody that I had it, and I took it to the incinerator after the holidays to be burned correctly because you have to be so careful.

I'll never forget this one kid named Jim who was such a precious person anyway; he was close to my oldest daughter's age, and I just loved him. He called me Mom and we had a good time together. There were two boys, Jim and Doug, to whom I really was attached. They helped me fill my nesting needs. I missed my own kids. When I got the Christmas tree, I told the boys about it and they came to my room. I had it sitting on a little nightstand, and Jim got down beside that nightstand on his knees and smelled it and felt it, and the tears just rolled down his cheeks.

The male to female ratio was challenging. You have to prove yourself. Of course, not in the secretarial position I had the first year because I was expected to be a secretary. But when I was in management, I went head to head with some of those guys, and I didn't

back down. My experience in managing properties here in Colorado was extremely valuable. I often was in charge of homeowners' associations, condominiums, or townhouses where there was still construction going on in new buildings, etc. I bucked those construction guys all the time, so the men in Antarctica didn't affect me at all. I did very well with them. I was able to elicit unbelievable support from those guys when I was there because I knew how to deal with them, and they did everything they could for me.

For trips, you can go out to a place called Castle Rock. You can walk, or you can go on your cross-country skis and climb up the rock. It's only a mile and a half or two miles out there, and that's nice. There's a lot of foot traffic back and forth because that's about the only place you can go. You're also allowed to go to Scott Base, which is the New Zealand base two miles away, also within walking distance. They're in a very nice place, a little cove, but you are not allowed to go in there without an invitation. They have a bar and they're nice about issuing invitations. For example, they'll send an invitation to the construction department to come on Thursday night, or logistics to come on Monday night or whatever, and they have interaction all the time. They have parties back and forth. Otherwise, you can just walk around town. Town encompasses a lot, though—extensive shoreline, including one of Scott's huts. The hut is very well preserved, and the Navy opens it up on Sundays for tours.

It was amazingly difficult returning home. When I got off the plane in New Zealand in February, it was fall there (our spring here at home). They still had grass, and the leaves were turning on the trees, and it was gorgeous. I hadn't seen a piece of grass for a long time, and I took off my shoes and my socks and I ran my toes through the grass on a little island dividing the parking lot. And I was feeling the leaves on the trees. I remember we were driving in a cab to go to our hotel, and I heard a dog bark, and I had to see where that bark came from; I had to see that little dog. He was trotting along, and my heart just swelled; it was so great. And small children, I'd see them and I just had to touch them.

Then there was this long airline trip back. It was wonderful to be with my family again; it was terrific. My daughter had just had a baby a few days before my return. She loves Mexican food and she was craving this, so I said, "I'll go get us some for lunch." I was

there to help with the baby. Taco Bell is close to a high school and it was noon. It was crowded and noisy when I walked in and, if Lisa hadn't wanted that Mexican food so much, I would have left. I kept balking. There were too many people; it was too tight an area; there was too much noise; and I wanted to be away from there. A few days later, on Saturday, I went to a large food chain here. It took me an hour and a half to get through there. Sometimes I just had to hang onto my cart because there were people coming from everywhere. It was tough.

And driving—my God, it was such an experience because I had been living at such a slow pace. Then to come back to a town the size of Denver, and everybody's moving so rapidly. I would look down at the speedometer and see I was only going 35 mph on the turnpike, feeling frightened when the cars were whizzing around me. It was amazing.

Some people stay in the Antarctic for up to fourteen months. They call them "toast." When they leave down there, they say they're "toasted," and they are.

I loved the spirit of the people there; it was something that amazed me. The people have so little privacy anyway, and they have so little time away from work, but they were willing to give all of that time to make it pleasurable for the mass, for the group. They had a thing called Icestock, mimicking Woodstock, where seven bands got together. Somebody pulled down an old wagon and made a platform out of it, and the guys from the heavy shop, where they repair the equipment, brought down a trailer off a truck. They took their personal time to pull it down; the sheet metal guys took their personal time to make a structure so that it could be covered and protect these kids from wind; and the electricians wired it. It was a joint effort, and those kids played from 10:00 in the morning till 10:00 at night, over and over. We danced in the rocks all day. The bars were open, and you could bring your drinks out. The Coast Guard ice cutter was in then. Those kids very seldom get off that ship. To watch them with all this energy coming out was amazing. They needed to release it. They got crazy and stupid, but it was a necessity, and it was okay.

The whole Antarctic experience was wonderful and truly the most awesome thing to take place in my adult life.

I Don't Mean to Exaggerate When I Say It Was the Best Decision I Ever Made

Janet Gluck

Communications operator

A temporary employee at *Janet Gluck's* company had worked in the Antarctic and told her about it. Janet was not pleased with her present job and decided to apply to go to Antarctica. She had also just ended an eight-year relationship and was wanting to do something "uncharacteristic." She talked her new boyfriend at the time into going with her. In retrospect, this was not a good idea. They had not been together long; being in the Antarctic really changed him, and their relationship became very difficult. Janet's job was doing secretarial work. Janet initially went to the McMurdo Station and later worked at Palmer Station as well.

I was working in Boulder when a woman came to work at the company as a temp. I knew they were going to offer her a full-time job in the Boulder company. I said, "Are you going to take it?" She said, "No, no. My husband and I do this thing every year, and we're waiting to get rehired." Then she told me about the program. I dismissed it because I'm not an outdoor enthusiast; I don't like cold weather, although I am from Colorado. I said, "Oh, that's interesting, but I could never do that, with the darkness and all." I got to know her a little bit better and discovered she worked for personnel. So one day just on a whim, because I was frustrated at work, I sent off my résumé, and didn't hear anything for about two months. They called me for an interview. I got the job, gave notice the next day, and started packing, and it was like that—fast. It was the best decision I've probably ever made in my life. It was a very good step for me to take.

I'm not an outdoor enthusiast. I'm a homebody; I've lived in Colorado my whole life. I'm very domestic. So for me it was a

major decision to quit a permanent, salaried job, take a pay cut, take a contract position that would expire after six months, and then be unemployed. These are all security, stability-type issues that I had to be comfortable with.

I'd never really heard of Antarctica. I knew where it was, of course, but what is it? In deciding to go to this continent, the type of living conditions and the extreme cold were all considerations I had to take into account, as well as many of the unknowns. It was really a major upheaval of my life, and I was about twenty-six at the time. I'd never adventured out before then.

I went for a number of reasons. I was overqualified for my current position, and I didn't like the man I was working for. I had confidence that I could come back and get a job. I just knew it. You get to that point where you get secure enough that you can say those types of things. I'd just gone through a major relationship breakup about nine months prior. I'd ended an eight-year relationship, and so I thought, "Why not go?" It was so uncharacteristic of me—to be in an environment as harsh as Antarctica—I bitch and moan if I have to shovel snow off my car. I like creature comforts. I don't particularly like roughing it. I like bone china. I like silks, and I like dry cleaning. All those kinds of things you can't have down there.

I talked to my current boyfriend about going with me to McMurdo. He had a job at a lumber yard, but my comment to him was, "You can always come back and get a job. I can come back and get a job. Why not? We don't have mortgages; we don't have kids." The fact that he was going with me also made it an adventure. He came down to McMurdo about the same time as I did. We didn't travel together, but it was within a week. So that helped. But I'm a very verbal person and I'm sociable, and so it's very easy to meet people while traveling. I had accepted the position before I talked to him about it. And, in hindsight, it would have been better if I'd done it alone. But hindsight, of course, is twenty-twenty, especially when it concerns men.

So I went to McMurdo—Mactown—despite all the reasons of how uncharacteristic it was for me. I did it, and I was very success-ful at it. I became one with the computer. At the time I thought, "Oh I took a pay cut, and this is a geek job, and no one's really notic-ing." When I got done, I was amazed at how many people noticed.

And when the contract changed hands, I was amazed at how many people wanted to hire me because they had observed my positive performance.

I've gotten more confidence in myself, and I really do attribute a lot of it to being on the ice because it was so different. There were some adverse things about it; there were some hard things about it physically, interpersonally, and emotionally. But I guess, considering some other things I'd been through in my life prior to that, it wasn't hard by comparison.

Once I got down there, I started sending letters. I never, ever knew my father had a sense of humor. He wrote really great letters with a dry sense of humor. I'm grateful that I got to see that. When you're both living in the same area, you never write letters. Personality really comes out in written communications.

The reason my lifestyle was this way was because the boyfriend that I took down—a wonderfully social, gregarious, outspoken person in the United States—changed. We got down there and were there a few weeks, and everything was great and really fun, and then they put him on nights. There was not enough work for him to do because construction was so overstaffed. I mean, literally, they would say move these boxes here, and that's all you have to do for eight hours. To have to stay awake for such limited tasks was difficult.

So it really twisted my boyfriend's personality, and he became incredibly possessive and jealous and insecure, and he couldn't sleep during the day. It really messed up his biological rhythms. He'd have to wake up and look at the greasy, gross dinner food; everyone was getting ready for the evening and having fun, and he had to go to work. He just warped. He drank; he started drinking abusively. There were times that I would encourage him, I'd say, "Go talk to personnel. Tell them this is really horrible. This is not what you expected. I understand that someone has to work nights, but they didn't warn you." So anyway, my way of assisting him was to stop my social interaction. One time I said, "Oh wow, after work I was invited to the construction people's party, and I went and I had a good time." And he said, "Oh, well, I never get to go." So my reaction to help him was I just stopped having fun, to try to be supportive of him because he was so jealous—possessive and jealous and insecure of my going to social events without him.

If you're a woman at McMurdo, you can walk around looking absolutely disgusting, and men still follow you around. You're a woman; and that's all they see. So it's not like you're consciously going out and flirting, or trying to look good, or wearing bright lipstick or anything that you think would attract attention; just by being female you attract attention. So that twisted him up even more because obviously I'm female. We'd be standing in line at the galley, and some guy would come by and talk to me. That would set him off. That was really bad because that was not his character at all in the States. Actually, our relationship ended on the ice because he drank too much and became potentially physically abusive with me. He didn't hit me, but I was sure he was going to. He wouldn't leave my room; he wouldn't be reasonable if he'd been drinking. That's just unacceptable.

I would love—at some point, if I ever got tired of what I'm doing now—to go to McMurdo as a single person, just as a single woman with a job that I liked, and to experience it that way. Because my whole trip there was rather twisted. Maybe I'm too old mentally now. I'm in a relationship now, and I'm comfortable with it. I didn't date until I was twenty-six. I was with one man for eight years, and then I met a new boyfriend and I went to the ice with him. I just think it would be so much fun to go to McMurdo as a free spirit.

I would do it very differently, just for the personal aspect. Other women were going out skiing and dancing and to parties, and out on snowmobiles, and all the other forbidden stuff you get to do because you're female. At McMurdo, I remember going into the bar and having eight men surround me at once. Talk about an ego rush.

Actually, I prefer being away from home for the holidays because I was raised Jewish so I celebrated Hanukkah. In the eight-year relationship I was in, we celebrated Christmas sometimes. My birthday is in December also; it's the 22nd. I prefer being out of the country in December. Holidays are not significant to me. I know everybody has different reactions to Christmas, but last year was difficult because in America you're just bombarded by this Christmas crap, and if you're a single person, you're nothing. If you're not celebrating Christmas, you're an alien. So for me, I'd much prefer being out of the country.

I don't mean to exaggerate when I say it was the best decision I ever made; it gave me confidence in my ability to put myself into unknown situations and cope with them. That simple statement is applicable in just about every area of your life, and most people don't ever challenge it, or they don't ever contemplate it. I'd never done that myself before this. I'd always taken the safe, traditional—"This is how your life has got to be because this is how it is"—approach. I feel I've gained a lot of self-esteem, which has been continuing. I've gained a whole new profession, which I love. I've doubled my salary from what I used to make as an administrative assistant, and the money is nice. But even when I proposed a promotion for myself, a restructuring to turn my current position into a department, hiring someone else and making me the supervisor, and that was all approved, the money was not the motivator; it was more that I want more control over what goes on in my area. I've become much more aggressive about controlling things in my life.

If I knew it was going to be the same, would I go back? Oh yes—yes, definitely. It would have been nice if things were different, but again, I wouldn't have changed anything. Because of karma or fate or whatever, it needed to happen, for whatever reason. And also, the self-imposed isolation that I put on myself at the time was strengthening, in a way. Because I do take care of myself, I don't really take strength from other people. If I have a bad time, then I talk to people, but ultimately I rely upon myself. So it was good to do that. Yeah, I would allow it to happen that way again.

DISCUSSANTS

There are a number of common themes that run through these women's Antarctic accounts. In this section, Marie Thomas and Patricia Thomas describe issues facing the Navy women in particular. Joni Seager, a feminist geographer, discusses the women's experiences from the point of view of the Antarctic as a "gendered" place. Jacqueline Weinstock, a developmental psychologist, focuses on life in the Antarctic as it affects women's interpersonal relationships.

Although almost all of the examples our discussants draw upon are present in the versions of the women's interviews printed in this book, a few come from interviews or portions of interviews not included here for space or confidentiality purposes.

Navy Women in the Antarctic

Marie D. Thomas

Psychology Department California State University
San Marcos

Patricia J. Thomas

Navy Personnel Research and Development Center
San Diego, California

Marie D. Thomas, **PhD, is an assistant professor of psychology at California State University, San Marcos. Previously, she was a research psychologist at the Navy Personnel Research and Development Center, San Diego, California, where she conducted research on issues related to women in the Navy.**

Patricia J. Thomas, **MS, is a research psychologist at the Navy Personnel Research and Development Center, San Diego, California. Since 1975, the primary focus of her research has been women and minorities in the Navy. She is currently working in Washington, DC, as a scientific and customer liaison for the research center. She has been serving as research advisor to the Secretary of the Navy's Standing Committee on Military and Civilian Women since 1992.**

There are a lot of good things to do in the Navy, but, well, for a woman this is maybe one of the best ones, I think. (Jane M. Alstott)

As research psychologists, currently and formerly employed by the Navy, we have been in a unique position to observe the changes that have occurred with regard to women's participation in the military.

Note: The opinions expressed in this chapter are those of the authors, are not official, and do not necessarily reflect the views of the Navy Department.

Navy women have been the focus of our research efforts for many years (Edwards et al., 1994; Rosenfeld et al., 1991). Although we are civilians, our research, friendships with military women, and relationships with project sponsors have given us an appreciation of the benefits and difficulties associated with being a woman in the Navy.

WOMEN IN THE NAVY

A Brief History

A phenomenal change has occurred in the number and representation of women in the Navy, paralleling the trend occurring in the other military services. In 1970, 8,800 women were in the Navy, representing 1.6 percent of the force. A decade later, their numbers had risen to 34,700 (6.5 percent of the force), and by 1990, there were 60,500 women (10.1 percent of the force) in Navy uniforms. Several events were responsible for this unprecedented growth. The most influential were the advent of the all-volunteer force, the decline in the birthrate (hence, the pool of available men), and the feminist movement.

Prior to the 1978 modification of the federal law that prevented Navy women from serving aboard ships, the maximum number of enlisted women who could be accommodated was 30,000. This limit was a pragmatic one, arising from the alternating sea/shore assignments basic to a Navy career. Until 1993, when Congress repealed the relevant law, the representation of enlisted women never exceeded 10 percent of the force. Even then, the Navy did not modify its policy limiting the number of women recruited until shortages of male applicants in mid-1994 forced a change. Today, accessions into the Navy are gender neutral.

Generally speaking, women's roles in the military have evolved from being female-traditional, to restricted access, to nontraditional jobs. Often, federal laws applying solely to female military members determined that most nontraditional jobs would be closed to women. Curiously, however, the first American women to be accorded full military rank and status were not constrained by law. Because of what was later viewed as an oversight, legislation authorizing the raising of a Navy referred solely to the enlistment of citizens. This oversight

was corrected by the Naval Reserve Act of 1925, which limited service to male citizens of the United States, thus effectively delaying the entry of women into the Navy at the start of WW II. A forward-looking Secretary of the Navy, Josephus Daniels, made use of this loophole in 1917, and created the Yeoman (female) to help meet the wartime need for clerical personnel. (Josephus Daniels also displayed considerable ingenuity regarding the section of the law that required all Navy personnel be assigned to a ship. He assigned the women to a tugboat that was firmly stuck in the mud of the Potomac.) Almost 17,000 "Yeomanettes," or "Marinettes," as they were popularly called, served as telephone operators, camouflage designers, typists, fingerprint experts, and translators before the program was discontinued two years later (Thomas, 1986).

It took the exigencies of WW II to make women a valued military resource again. In July 1942, the WAVES (Women Accepted for Voluntary Enlisted Service) were formed with the proviso that Navy women would not be allowed to serve overseas. They were permitted to work in almost every type of stateside shore billet, however, even in such nontraditional jobs as machinist's mate, instrument flying and gunnery instructor, metalsmith, and air controlman. When peace came, the WAVES numbered 8,000 officers, 78,000 enlisted personnel, and 8,000 women in training (Hancock, 1972).

The legislation giving women permanent status in the Navy is the Women's Armed Services Integration Act of 1948 (Public Law 625), which applies to all of the services. This act established differential treatment of women and men. Some of the more restrictive clauses, all of which have been repealed, provided that:

1. Women (but not men) had to be twenty-one years old in order to enlist without written parental consent and could not enlist before their 18th birthday. This was repealed in May 1974.
2. The number of enlisted women could not exceed 2 percent of the male enlisted strength, and women officers could not exceed 10 percent of the enlisted female strength. This rule was repealed in 1967 when the military's personnel needs skyrocketed because of the Vietnam War.
3. Women officers could not have a permanent commissioned grade above commander. This was repealed in 1967.

4. Children of military women would not be considered dependents unless their father was dead or their mother was their chief support; male spouses were not eligible for the benefits given female spouses of military personnel. A 1973 Supreme Court decision on a lawsuit filed by a woman officer resulted in women being entitled to the same benefits for their family members as are military men.

The most far-reaching law affecting the careers of Navy women, however, was Title 10, United States Code, which is a statute that carried forward provisions in the Women's Armed Services Integration Act. Section 6015, which applied to the Navy, originally stated that, "Women may not be assigned to duty in aircraft that are engaged in combat missions nor may they be assigned to duty on vessels of the Navy other than hospital ships and transports."

In 1976, a suit was filed by six Navy women, charging that the statute was discriminatory. The Congress, following a decision by a Federal District Court judge who supported the accusation, subsequently amended the statute to permit the assignment of women to vessels similar to hospital ships and transports that are not expected to have a combat mission (destroyer tenders, submarine tenders, repair ships, oceanographic research ships, and tugboats). In 1987, the wording of section 6015 was again amended, opening up combat support ships to women. Finally, women became eligible for assignment to all types of aircraft in 1993 and to all classes of ships in early 1994 when section 6015 was repealed.* Navy regulations still do not permit women to serve in submarines or mine hunters, or with SEAL commando units. Thus, Navy women have yet to be allowed to participate in all aspects of the Navy mission, although they are no longer restricted by law.

In addition to assignment restrictions, codified in law, biological differences and societal norms have resulted in gender-specific rules. Prior to 1971, women could not marry and remain in the Navy, though, of course, men could. Navy regulations prevented mothers from enlisting or being commissioned and required that women

---

*Of the 50,696 Navy women on active duty on March 31, 1997, 3,487 were assigned to combatant ships and 4,108 were in noncombatant ships.

who became pregnant or who acquired a child through marriage or adoption be discharged. In 1972, this regulation was modified to allow a waiver to be granted in special cases. In 1975, at the direction of the Department of Defense, the involuntary discharge policy for pregnancy was abandoned.

Effect of Restrictions

Gender-specific laws and regulations have affected Navy women in three major ways: (1) By not allowing women to be assigned to combatant aircraft and ships (over 80 percent of all platforms), the range of jobs open to women was limited and a ceiling was placed on the number who could serve; (2) because women could not serve in jobs critical to the Navy's mission, their careers were constrained and they could not aspire to the highest, most meaningful positions in the Navy; and (3) due to regulations regarding pregnancy and motherhood, many women had to curtail their military careers or forego having children. Another result of the restrictions is that men are more valuable to the military than women. This fact subtly influences management decisions and perceptions concerning the two genders.

The unique laws and regulations applying only to women also have had an effect on group dynamics. Women have been resented because they seemed to reap the rewards of military service without incurring the responsibilities and discomfort. In the past, women were accused of extending the amount of time men had to spend at sea. This perception was based on the land-locked careers of women, which meant that fewer shore positions were available to men than if the Navy had been all male. Today, when women can serve in Navy ships, they are accused of becoming pregnant in order to avoid sea duty.

Women at the military academies have had to endure the verbal harassment of men telling them that the academics have lowered standards and women don't belong in an institution devoted to training wartime leaders (Government Accounting Office, 1994). Because of the small quotas on women in nontraditional jobs, those who became trained found themselves greatly outnumbered in the work groups to which they were assigned. Like blue-collar women in industry, they have been blamed for the attention given to the prevention of sexual harassment, accused of being lesbians or whores, and generally made to feel unwanted. This situation can be particularly stressful when the

position they occupy is highly valued by men. At least part of the impetus for the severe harassment of women at the 1991 Tailhook convention resulted from male pilots' recognition that women soon would gain access to fighter squadrons—the most elite positions in naval aviation.

New Career Opportunities for Women

The abolishment of the statutory restrictions on the assignments of women is very recent, and Navy policy to implement the changes is still being promulgated. Thus, the effect on women's careers has yet to be felt.

Now that enlisted women may enter any rating, without ceilings placed on their representation, a gradual increase in the number of women in senior positions is anticipated. This restructuring will occur because advancement opportunities are greater in the sea-intensive jobs that have been barred to, or that severely limited the number of, women.

The recent disestablishment of the General Unrestricted Line (GenURL), the designator (job specialty) in which over 90 percent of women line officers serve, will have a major effect on the occupational distribution of women officers. Currently designated GenURLs who are fairly junior are being encouraged to transfer into warfare special-ties. New women officers will enter designators traditionally chosen by men. As women's careers become parallel to men's, more will assume command positions, in ships, aviation squadrons, and major shore establishments than is possible today. They also will become competi-tive with men for the most senior positions in the Navy.

Equality of opportunity and responsibility of the sexes should have a positive effect on group dynamics. When two groups are not treated the same, a heightening of the differences occurs and cohe-sion is difficult to achieve. Thus, the removal of ceilings on the number of women, gender-specific regulations, and gender-based assignments should encourage the acceptance of women as fully contributing members of the Navy.

THE THREE ACCOUNTS—THEMES AND ISSUES

Before considering the common themes of the three Navy women in this book, a distinction should be made between the account offered by Karen, the one officer (the attorney), and the accounts of the two enlisted women, Eva (the aircraft firefighter) and Jane (the avionics tech and aircrewman). Within the Navy, all officers are college graduates, trained to lead those they supervise in pursuit of a common goal (the military mission). Enlisted personnel are skilled workers with a defined set of duties. Although senior enlisted women and men can rise to positions of responsibility, their role is to oversee a group of personnel in their skill area only. Officers are generalists who move back and forth between management positions to assignments in their specialty area. The officer versus enlisted distinction is very apparent in the three accounts in terms of the jobs the women performed, their experiences with male co-workers, and their language. Karen, as an officer and an attorney, had a professional administrative day job with a long lunch period and, during busy times, a little overtime. The enlisted women, on the other hand, worked long hours and/or difficult shifts in often physically demanding jobs. Karen discussed sexual harassment at McMurdo as a problem that she had to deal with as a manager, not as something she experienced directly as a woman. This is in contrast to the incidents of direct harassment described by the enlisted women. Finally, an interesting distinction in language is seen. Karen refers to women as "women;" the preferred term for an officer who is female is "woman officer." In the enlisted accounts, Eva and Jane refer to themselves and other women as "females." Reference to enlisted "females" is common practice in the Navy, just as men are referred to as enlisted males. The use of the biological terms "male" and "female" seems to accentuate the differences between enlisted men and women. When we were studying pregnancy among enlisted women, it was quite disconcerting for our participants to be referred to (and to refer to themselves) as "pregnant females"!

Karen's personal account would be somewhat different from the experiences of the other two women, simply because of her higher status and the fact that her male peers are college graduates. Despite such differences, however, common themes do run through the accounts.

Benefits of a Tour in the Antarctic

A tour in Antarctica is an unusual assignment for Navy personnel. In each account, the women touched upon the sense that they had done something unique. As Eva said, "It was an adventure. I'm glad I did it." Interestingly, before the women arrived in the Antarctic, it was primarily family and friends who conveyed the sense of adventure through their own excitement, surprise, and envy. Karen described her parents and parents' friends as "fascinated" while Jane said, "I told my family and they just thought, especially my father—oh, what a marvelous opportunity; what a great thing; what an unusual thing that you get to do this."

Eva went to the Antarctic because the timing was convenient and because of family considerations, and Jane was sent to Antarctica as her first assignment. Only Karen specifically chose an Antarctic tour as a positive career move. As an officer, an operational billet (a position that is somehow connected directly to the Navy's mission, i.e., warfare) would clearly enhance her career, yet restrictions on women's assignments limited her opportunities. ". . . [M]y ability to be with an operational command was restricted by the fact that I was not allowed on any combatant. I could never be on an aircraft carrier; I could not be with any kind of command that had a combat mission. I then came across this command in the Antarctic, and it sounded very interesting."

Yet, the benefits of this tour clearly went beyond career considerations; each of the women described a process of growth and change that occurred during her time in the Antarctic. Eva reported that she had matured. She also realized that her little son was her top priority and her major regret about the time she served in the Antarctic: "The only thing is, I can never turn the clock back to spend those six months with my son." Jane's tour in the Antarctic was her introduction to the Navy. Finally, Karen's tour changed her view of herself as someone "afraid to venture off the straight and narrow." She continues: "I think I've grown. I'm not as timid with the idea of going someplace totally new . . . Going to the Antarctic toughened my skin up a bit."

The reasons that brought these women to the Antarctic differed, but they shared the sense that their experiences were unique and important. Each woman learned new skills, matured emotionally,

and returned feeling more competent and capable of handling new challenges.

Working in a Predominantly Male Environment

The Navy is an environment overwhelmingly populated by men. Most Navy women are concentrated in "traditional" job classifications, such as hospital corpsman or personnelman. Fewer women choose blue-collar or "nontraditional" types of jobs such as weather observer or avionics technician; it is not unusual for women in these ratings to find themselves the sole female in a work center filled with men. The jobs and training of the three Navy women in this book often placed them in work situations where women were a small minority. But because the Antarctic is a "good" place for women career-wise (as Jane says, ". . . this is one of those little enclaves"— an operational command that was open to women), the gender ratio was sometimes more balanced than they expected.

Beyond numbers, however, the Navy is a bastion of male culture. Through blatant experiences of sexual harassment or the insidious nature of a hostile environment, many women have received the message that they do not belong in the Navy (Culbertson, Rosenfeld, and Newell, 1993; Thomas, 1995). Such experiences are familiar to women who enter blue-collar or other nontraditional jobs in the civilian world.

Karen, the attorney, did not see sexual harassment as a problem at McMurdo. She reported that her command was in the forefront on this issue; prevention of sexual harassment training was held, the leadership was enlightened, and it was made known that sexual harassment would not be tolerated. During her tour she dealt with two minor incidents of sexual harassment.

It seems unusual, however, that sexual harassment would be so rare in an environment dominated by men. Perhaps as an officer, Karen was less likely to be a target of sexual harassment. Or perhaps, the types of harassment experienced by women were not viewed as "severe" enough to be labeled sexual harassment. Research conducted by one of us (Thomas, 1995) on how Navy enlisted personnel conceptualize sexual harassment suggests that both women and men view behaviors such as sexually oriented jokes, remarks, and whistles (the most common forms of sexual harassment) as part of the enlisted

milieu and are reluctant to label such behaviors as harassment. However, there is a consciousness, particularly on the part of senior enlisted women (and also in some men), that such behaviors create a hostile environment for women.

Although Eva and Jane briefly allude to the fact that women were sometimes looked down upon by men in their work groups, another Navy woman (not included in this book) described blatant harassment of women by men. For some women she worked with, the harassment was "a nightmare." Not only did men harass their female peers, but they tormented a woman who was senior to them in the chain of command: "My senior female has been brought to tears from these guys . . . these guys would just outright call her incompetent, ugly, old, lazy." She reported that as soon as women arrived, they were classified by men. Because she chose not to associate with many of the men, she was labeled a dyke. She said, "It was questionable for the other women for a while, until they made it known that they were seeing men on the ice, and they were obvious and blatant about it. Then they were just called sluts. So either way, you lost."

Remarks of senior Navy enlisted women in focus groups conducted as part of a Navy sexual harassment study (Thomas, 1995) echo this woman's words. These women, most of whom were in nontraditional job classifications, also complained about the labeling and harassment male co-workers had subjected them to during their years in the Navy. Some women described how prevalent mild, ambiguous forms of harassment, such as sexually oriented jokes, whistles, gestures, and remarks, were in their various environments, and they understood that these behaviors were related to Navy men's attitudes toward female sailors. It is interesting to contrast the information provided by the senior women with focus group data collected from junior enlisted women in the same study. The younger women were relatively new to the Navy and were trying to fit into the culture. They were reluctant or unwilling to consider that they were being sexually harassed or subject to a hostile environment, especially if the behaviors they experienced were relatively mild or ambiguous. Jane demonstrates a similar attitude in her account. It is necessary to read between the lines, but it seems likely that she, too, was exposed to negative attitudes about women in the Navy. She describes how she was depressed at first because she was new to the Navy and to the squadron. She says, "I had to learn

how to work with people, and I was the person who didn't know anything, and everybody thought I was stupid, and I was female, and all this kind of stuff." For at least some of her co-workers, being a woman and being stupid were related. We can't help but wonder what opinions were expressed in her presence.

In the sexual harassment study discussed above (Thomas, 1995), the senior enlisted women made an interesting point about the labeling of women. They said that often the only women who escaped being labeled by men were those who were married, especially those married women who had children. Motherhood seemed to confer a certain amount of protection from harassment. Despite the fact that men in the Navy often left their families at home while they were deployed to different parts of the world, Eva mentions in her account that her colleagues in the Antarctic had a difficult time relating to her because she was a *woman* who left her husband and child behind; she was the only one in that category. She took on the role of dispenser of advice to young newlywed and single men: "I am a mother so all the guys looked to me as a mother figure" (for a full discussion of issues related to motherhood and the military, see P. J. Thomas and M. D. Thomas, 1993).

Slut, dyke, or mother—it is difficult for Navy women to escape categorization. It is likely that for some women in the Antarctic, the work center could be a very hostile place.

Women As Support Group

In their accounts, the three Navy women mentioned the importance of working and living with other women. Karen and her roommate became best friends; they were able to share the joys and frustrations of their Antarctic tours. For Eva, the presence of three other women in her work center was a welcome change: "I didn't know that many other women existed in this job. It was nice because we helped each other keep our sanity. We would say, 'Okay, this person is pulling this macho stuff, and how are we going to handle that?'" Jane, who felt that there weren't usually bad feelings between the men and women in her work group (although she says that "it's still . . . basically a man's ball game") admitted that the women provided support to each other: "Because you're a female in one job and there's another female in the same job, definitely there's a little more of a special

relationship there that's different from the relationship you have to the men who do the same job." The remarks of these women underscore the importance of ensuring that women in nontraditional jobs are assigned to work centers where they have contact with other women.

CONCLUSIONS

Three major topics were discussed in this chapter on the account of Navy women in the Antarctic: the benefits of the tour, working in a predominantly male environment, and the importance of other women for support. The issues we have considered here are relevant not only to women who work in the Antarctic, but to all Navy women, especially those who are in nontraditional job specialties.

What changes might be expected in the lives of Navy women now that combat-related environments have been opened to them? The Antarctic will still be an interesting and unusual tour of duty, but it will no longer be one of a few career-enhancing assignments for women. With new billets open, the Navy is attempting to attract more women to nontraditional job specialties. While the Navy will probably always have more male than female sailors, it is conceivable that in the future, women in these nontraditional jobs will regularly have female co-workers. We hope that a changed gender mix in these jobs will eliminate the negative attitudes toward women that still exist. It is also our hope that women will continue to provide each other with support and understanding.

REFERENCES

Culbertson, A.L., Rosenfeld, P., and Newell, C.E. (1993). *Sexual harassment in the active-duty Navy: Findings from the 1991 Navy-Wide Survey* (NPRDC-TR-2). San Diego: Navy Personnel Research and Development Center.

Edwards, J.E., Rosenfeld, P., Thomas, M.D., and Thomas, P.J. (1994). Navy research into diversity: An update. *International Journal of Intercultural Relations, 18,* 521-538.

Government Accounting Office (1994). *DoD service academies: More actions needed to eliminate sexual harassment* (GAO/NSIAD-94-6). Washington, DC: Author.

Hancock, J.B. (1972). *Lady in the Navy, A Personal Reminiscence.* Annapolis, MD: Naval Institute Press.

Rosenfeld, P., Thomas, M.D., Edwards, J.E., Thomas, P.J., and Thomas, E. (1991). Navy research into race, ethnicity, and gender: An historical analysis. *International Journal of Intercultural Relations, 15,* 407-426.

Thomas, M.D. (1995). *Gender differences in conceptualizing sexual harassment* (NPRDC TR-95-5). San Diego: Navy Personnel Research and Development Center.

Thomas, P.J. (1986). From Yeomanettes to U.S. WAVES to women in the Navy. In D.R. Segal and H.W. Sinaiko (Eds.), *Life in the Rank and File.* Washington, DC: Pergamon-Brassey's, pp. 98-115.

Thomas, P.J. and Thomas, M.D. (1993). Mothers in uniform. In F. Kaslow (Ed.), *The Military Family in Peace and War.* New York: Springer, pp. 25-47.

Women Out of Place:
The Gendered Geography of Antarctica

Joni Seager

Department of Geography
University of Vermont

Joni Seager **is a feminist geographer teaching in the Geography
and Women's Studies departments at the University of Vermont.
Her research interests include the "gendering" of landscapes, the
environment, and urban structures. Her most recent books include**
***Earth Follies: Coming to Feminist Terms with the Global Environ-
mental Crisis*** **and** ***The State of Women in the World Atlas.***

Antarctica is a "no-man's" land. There are no indigenous peoples
with ancestral ties to the land; by international agreement, this is the
only place on earth that is not claimed as the sole property of any
nation. For more than a century, Antarctica has been visited by a
steady stream of whalers, explorers, scientists, tourists, and military
personnel, but people only "dwell" in Antarctica for short periods of
time; no one "lives" there. Antarctica is the only uninhabited continent on the planet. Human presence on the ice continent can only be
sustained with the assistance of elaborate artificial support systems.
The material culture and the cultural norms that prevail in temperate
or tropical lands have little relevance on this continent. Although the
imperatives of nationalism and the possibility of commercial gain
have drawn adventurers to Antarctica, these have proved ephemeral,
and the enduring magnetism of Antarctica is its iconographic role as
a massive *terra incognita.* Although the blank spots on the Antarctic
map are now few and far between, the continent still symbolizes a
"last frontier" of sorts. Unlike other places that were explored and
"discovered" by Euro-Americans, Antarctica had no prior cultural
fabric; figuratively, it might be thought of as a social *tabula rasa.*

211

Despite its possibilities, then, both geographic and cultural, as a place of unfettered imagination and new beginnings, the experiences of women in the Antarctic paint a portrait of a place where old patterns of gender-typing and sex-specific constraints have been imported as a set-piece, although tailored and fine-tuned to the particulars of a new environment. On the one hand, this continuity is discouraging; on the other hand, though, it means that Antarctica is a place where we can see in stark relief, with little "background noise," how social relations and gendered norms are created and maintained.

Within the past decade, geographers have started to examine the role of place, location, and space as sites of social struggle, examining the extent to which assumptions about "appropriate" or "normal" behavior are constructed in relation to the geography (literal and meta-phoric) within which cultures operate.[1] Feminist geographers, archi-tects, and anthropologists have made clear the extent to which these struggles are gendered—that the relationships of people to land, land-scape, and place are always gendered.[2]

It may be considered a "geographic fact" that people are "out of place" in Antarctica; for women, however, this has also been construed as a "cultural fact." The exclusion of women from the Antarctic is rooted in the history of exploration. Euro-American exploration and discovery has always been cast as a prerogative of men; women have been largely excluded from the exploration tradi-tion. In Antarctic exploration, the tradition of male exclusivity is hardened and heightened by the harshness, danger, and remoteness of the place. In a recent study of the history of polar exploration, Lisa Bloom argues that:

Ideologies of gender were central to polar "discovery". . . polar exploration narratives played a prominent part in defining the social construction of masculinity and legitimized the exclusion of women from many public domains of discourse. As all-male activities, the explorations symbolically enacted the men's own battle to become men. The difficulty of life in desolate and freez-ing regions provided the ideal mythic site where men could show themselves as heroes capable of superhuman feats. The polar explorer represented the epitome of manliness.[3]

Until recently, Antarctica was almost entirely the domain of (male) explorers; thus, the imagery of the Antarctic — its "meaning"—has been filtered almost entirely through the lens of its early explorers, and, early on, this continent was claimed as men's space.

By the 1970s, when the first women in this book went to the Antarctic, the "boy's own adventure" form of polar exploration was long a thing of the past. But the definition of the continent as men's space had become frozen in place. Most of the women—certainly in the 1970s, but even in the 1990s—report astounding resistance to the notion that women could or should be in the Antarctic. For women such as Irene Peden and Sister Mary Odile Cahoon, among the first to get to the Antarctic, the gendered assumptions about the Antarctic were explicit; they were told in no uncertain terms that the Antarctic was not considered a place for women. Many functionaries in the bureaucracies (especially the military) that controlled access to the continent only begrudgingly accepted the presence of women.

Although the whole continent had been defined as "off limits" for women, the gendering of Antarctic space was also finely textured. For example, resistance to women "wintering-over" was more fierce than allowing women to visit for the summer, and women's presence on the coast was more acceptable than in the interior, as the narratives of Irene Peden and of the Ann Bancroft expedition make clear. This gendered coastal versus interior distinction is especially intriguing, although apparently not unique to Antarctica. In the history of European exploration of, and "penetration" into, North America, Africa, and Australia, there are suggestions that in those continents too the *interior* of large land masses has long been considered the core of men's preserve. For example, the author of a recent feminist study of Australian landscape argues that:

> the singular vision [of Australian landscape] is the Interior, the outback, the red centre, the dead heat, the desert, a wasteland . . . The central image against which the Australian character measures himself is the bush . . . "no place for a woman." (p. 22)[4]

Thus, the "marginalization" of women is perhaps not only a metaphor but a particular geographic device.

Although the exploration tradition (and certainly its historiography) was predominantly male, there have been female explorers for

as long as there have been male explorers. In the late nineteenth century, so many upper-class European women took up a passion for exploration that they have been dubbed the Victorian "lady travelers."[5] Similar to their male counterparts, some of these women were casual adventurers and others serious scientists, traveling to satisfy intellectual curiosity and for personal challenge. But, unlike their male counterparts, virtually all of the early women travelers were explicit about the extent to which they were motivated to adventure in foreign places as a way of escaping the constrictive gender sphere to which they had been assigned. As Etta Close, a British adventurer who strayed off the beaten track in East Africa in the early 1900s, reported:

> It is hard to be content with a very few luncheons strictly for "ladies only," to find it sufficient just to be useful to relations, to meet dear Tommy at the station and take him safely across London . . . To take care of darling Elsie at the dentists . . . even when women have health and the money to be free, they seem to like the feeling of being anchored . . .[6]

Many of the Victorian women travelers, stepping outside the boundaries (literally) of acceptable behavior for their sex, often spoke of the empowerment they felt when they were exploring and of their despair on losing that power when they returned home.[7] Overcoming the dangers encountered in their travels was a source of challenge and pride for these women, allowing them to prove their abilities in ways that could not be tested at home.

The narratives in this collection of women, who are striving to overcome and challenge the resistance to their presence in the Antarctic, echo contemporary struggles of women all over the world who are challenging "men's clubs" in the myriad guises in which they occur. But they also echo, uncannily, the experiences of the nineteenth and early twentieth-century women explorers. Although the women scientists and base workers who traveled to the Antarctic in the past two decades do not face the same challenges as their explorer foremothers, many of the women in this collection speak with similar enthusiasm about leaving behind the constraints of the "normal" expectations they faced at home. Most of the women in this collection, while not necessarily describing themselves as adventurers, describe their experience

as an adventure, and many of them were consciously testing their independence in making the decision to go to Antarctica. Janet Gluck, for example, recalls that "it was probably the first adventure I've taken in my life . . . and the best decision I've ever made."

Women in the Antarctic have moved outside the bounds of what is usually considered to be women's place—metaphorically, but also literally. In leaving behind their "normal" roles, women in the Antarctic are also leaving behind the demands and expectations that those roles entail—whether it be doing the dishes, making meals, or serving as the primary emotional prop for their families. Berneice Albright, a mother of six children, waxes enthusiastic about the release from her domestic responsibilities: "I certainly considered this as an adventure. . . When I got off duty from my job in Antarctica, I had an amazing world . . . I mean, I went to the galley to get my food; I didn't have to wash the dishes; I didn't prepare the meal; I didn't have to stop by the grocery store and pick up the ingredients . . ." Berneice's sentiments are echoed by S. McDonald, who describes her first year in the Antarctic as "the best vacation I'd had in years."

Virtually all of the women in this collection speak with clarity about the extent to which they were shedding gendered expectations as they assumed new roles in a new—and unfeminized—place. Many of the women use the language of "finding themselves" (emotionally and psychically) through their Antarctica sojourn. This metaphor is not incidental—sense of place is often deeply implicated in sense of self, and changing places with changing images of self. Most of the women in this collection speak eloquently about the process of self-discovery catalyzed by their decision to go to Antarctica and by their time there.

For early "lady travelers," the tensions between being a woman and being an explorer were made manifest in many ways, including difficult choices about how to dress (in mannish clothes, for ease of movement, or in constricting but "proper" women's garb) and even what vocabulary to use to describe their experiences.[8] The contemporary Antarctic is still an environment where women operate on the borderlands of both geographical and social place. This fluidity opens up new opportunities for women, but at the same time, it exerts particular demands and stresses on them. As with the lady travelers before them, women who are "out of place" have to negotiate demanding—often conflicting—gender roles and expectations. The women in the Antarc-

tic in the 1970s were told that they carried the responsibility for their whole sex—that all other women who wished to come to the Antarctic would be judged by their behavior and their work. Irene Peden was told, "If you fail, there won't be another woman on the Antarctic Continent for a generation." Women who came to the Antarctic in the 1980s and 1990s as workers at the bases had to balance demands that, on the one hand, they be "just one of the boys" and yet, on the other hand, that they not be perceived as unsexed, "unfeminine" women. It is clear from many of the narratives that women in the Antarctic are still typically considered to be doing work that women "shouldn't" do, in a place where women "shouldn't" be, and yet, they are expected to retain (and even exaggerate) "feminine" behavior. Most of the women report considerable anxiety about forming appropriate social interactions with the men they worked with—whether or not to date, whether to join the men in the bars—and many felt policed by an aura of potential sexual harassment and the wildfire rumors that swirled around their sexual and personal lives.

The sexual innuendo and pressure, which many report as being virtually ubiquitous, sends a clear message to women that they are entering an environment which they do not control. Many of these women would agree with Jane Alstott's observations of life in an Antarctic base or station as "still . . . basically a man's ball game." The nature of social relations clearly sets this tone, but this social message is also reinforced by the spatial structure—the built environment—of the Antarctic stations and bases. Women do not control the social space of everyday life on Antarctic bases. Many women report that much of the social life of these small communities revolves primarily around the bars, described by several women as dark, noisy, male-dominated places, where fights and fights over women are not unusual. Bar-culture, virtually everywhere in the world, creates spaces that put women at a social and physical disadvantage. Sexual pressure, and the possibility of sexual threat, is heightened by the confined spaces in which the men and women live in the Antarctic. Janet Gluck and Kathy Bojack talk about fears for their personal safety from men whom they literally can't escape or avoid. Other women talk about seemingly more minor problems of living in spaces designed for and populated largely by men, such as Irene Peden's difficulty in climbing the ladders at her station because the rungs were widely spaced,

designed "for young adult males with long legs," or Paige Martin's observation that the lack of toilets and showers in the winter at Cape Byrd was a more significant problem for women than for men. In the constructed settlements of the Antarctic, a myriad of spatial clues send a subliminal message that women are "out of place" there. Even in the 1990s, when the presence of women on the ice appears to be widely accepted—and the facilities to accommodate them are in place—most of the women are aware that they are not moving through a space which is their own.

Similar to the stories of the early women travelers, the narratives of these Antarctic women are diverse. Still, one of the common threads they share is the explicit recognition of the personal goals of their travels. For the early women explorers, the "objective" discovery of new places was not separate from, nor more important than, the discovery of themselves:[9] "The women travelers followed invisible red lines across a map into a distant unknown. But the pot of gold they were chasing was not the mountain, the source of the river, or the oasis in the desert, but the long shadows, cast by the tropical sunlight and mountain glare, of themselves."[10] Similarly, many of the women in the Antarctic express satisfaction in an internal exploration process, in experiencing a world in which they could participate in their own definition. The women of the American Women's Trans-Antarctic Expedition were especially articulate about the dual imperative of their journey: "We didn't just have the objective of getting across the continent through the Pole; we also set objectives that I think male expeditions tend not to articulate. . . . to bond as friends and to have fun."

Human responses to place—especially to new landscapes—is shaped by a myriad of influences, including personality, religion, age, class, politics—and, by gender. In the 1980s, historian Annette Kolodny published an influential study of the American frontier that exposed significant differences between European men's and women's experiences of that new encounter.[11] Feminist geographers have since pursued similar scholarship, expanding the rubric of "landscape study" (a well-defined subfield within the discipline of geography) to include an exploration of the differences between men's and women's experience of place, of nature, and of "wilderness."[12] A close reading of narratives of women in the Antarctic

might provide a rich source for new landscape study. It is clear that many of the women in the Antarctic were moved and awed by their encounter with the land, describing it as "beautiful," "majestic," or "stunning," and exulted in the experience of deep silence. Surprisingly few women were fearful of, or deterred by, the rugged land they were seeing for the first time. However, without having a parallel record of the experiences of their male counterparts, it is not possible to make gendered generalizations about this encounter experience. A comparative study of men's and women's landscape assessment in Antarctica remains to be written.

NOTES

1. Recent works on this topic include: J. Nicholas Entrekin. *The Betweenness of Place.* Baltimore: Johns Hopkins, 1991; Michael Keith and Steve Pile (Eds.), *Place and the Politics of Identity.* London: Routledge, 1993; Derek Gregory. *Geographical Imaginations.* Oxford: Blackwell, 1994; James Duncan and David Ley (Eds.), *Place/Culture/Representation.* London and NY: Routledge, 1993.

2. See, for example: Daphne Spain. *Gendered Spaces.* Chapel Hill, NC: University of North Carolina Press, 1992; Women and Geography Study Group of the Institute of British Geographers. *Geography and Gender: An Introduction to Feminist Geography.* London: Hutchinson, 1984; Vera Norwood and Janice Monk (Eds.), *The Desert Is No Lady: Southwestern Landscapes in Women's Writing and Art.* New Haven, CT: Yale University Press, 1987; Audrey Kobayashi and Suzanne Mackenzie (Eds.), *Remaking Human Geography.* Boston: Unwin Hyman, 1989.

3. Lisa Bloom. *Gender on Ice: American Ideologies of Polar Expeditions.* Minneapolis, MN: University of Minnesota Press, 1993, p. 6.

4. Kay Schaffer. *Women and the Bush: Forces of Desire in the Australian Cultural Tradition.* Cambridge, MA: Cambridge University Press, 1988, pp. 22, 52.

5. For information on women explorers, see: Dea Birkett. *Spinsters Abroad: Victorian Lady Travellers.* Oxford: Basil Blackwell, 1989; Mona Domosh. "Towards a feminist historiography of geography," *Transactions of the Institute of British Geographers, 16,* 1991, pp. 95-104; Elizabeth Fag Olds. *Women of the Four Winds.* Boston: Houghton Mifflin, 1985.

6. Quoted in Dea Birkett. *Spinsters Abroad: Victorian Lady Travellers.* Oxford: Basil Blackwell, 1989, p. 30.

7. Mono Domosh. "Towards a feminist historiography of geography," *Transactions of the Institute of British Geographers, 16,* 1991, pp. 95-104.

8. Mona Domosh. "Towards a feminist historiography of geography," *Transactions of the Institute of British Geographers, 16,* 1991, pp. 95-104.

9. Mona Domosh. "Towards a feminist historiography of geography," *Transactions of the Institute of British Geographers, 16,* 1991, pp. 95-104.

10. Birkett, p. 71.

11. Annette Kolodny. *The Land Before Her: Fantasy and Experience of the American Frontiers 1630-1860.* Chapel Hill, NC: University of North Carolina Press, 1984.

12. See, for example: Vera Norwood and Janice Monk (Eds.), *The Desert Is No Lady: Southwestern Landscapes in Women's Writing and Art.* New Haven, CT: Yale University Press, 1987; Vera Norwood. *Made From This Earth.* Chapel Hill, NC: University of North Carolina Press, 1983.

The Psychology of Social and Personal Life on an Isolated Frontier: U.S. Women in the Antarctic

Jacqueline S. Weinstock

Department of Integrated Professional Studies
University of Vermont

Jacqueline S. Weinstock **is a Developmental Psychologist with research interests in women's development and interpersonal relationships, particularly friendships. In the following chapter, she examines both the similarities and differences the study participants noted between life on and off the ice in an attempt to better understand some of the current constraints on human development and human relating that pervade much of U.S. society. She also examines differences among the women participants themselves, especially with respect to their attitudes toward, and preferences for, various kinds of interpersonal relationships.**

INTRODUCTION

The stories gathered in this book represent a diversity of women's experiences in Antarctica, starting from the early years of women's presence on that continent. These stories are told from several vantage points—the differing experiences of women scientists, Navy personnel, support staff, and expedition members. These women varied in the length of their stay in the Antarctic, their reasons for going, their ages and life-cycle phase at the time of the venture, and in the seasonal and historical moments of their Antarctic experiences. While these differing vantage points and the individual characteristics and life circumstances of the women them-

selves combine to yield quite diverse stories, there are also several common themes that run through them.

Viewed positively by some, and negatively by others, the experiences the women describe are shared experiences of living in an isolated, frontier-like setting with a (relatively) small number of people, in a context previously open only to men and continuing to consist disproportionately of men relative to women. Yet life in the Antarctic, although remote and isolated and away from any of the modernities that pervade late twentieth-century life in the United States, reflects as well the social problems of our times. Some of these problems are highlighted by the women's descriptions of their personal and social lives during their time in the Antarctic *in contrast* with their lives and social relationships in the States. Other problems are highlighted because of their pervasive presence even in such a remote setting as the Antarctic. Despite the distance from the States and from any of the trappings of the twentieth century, the same social and political hierarchies are in place, along with ways of relating that reflect and perpetuate these. We see, for example, class and gender divisions, with some women more aware of, and reactive against, these divisions while others more unaware and/or more accepting of the divisions and their (perceived) benefit from them. There are other differences as well. Although the stories in this book, and in the larger research project, are not representative of all women, nor even of women who go to the Antarctic, they can be usefully examined for insights into women's shared and differing experiences of self and relationship along a variety of dimensions.

LIFE IN THE ANTARCTIC:
TECHNOLOGY RICH AND TECHNOLOGY POOR

The ability to live in the Antarctic today is due to the advances of modern technology; yet, life in the Antarctic itself is experienced in many ways as a return to life before the mass availability of leisure-oriented technology. There is limited access to electronic leisure activities (e.g., stereo systems, television sets, computer games), and the living quarters are sparse. Individual homes with kitchens, washers and dryers, vacuum cleaners, stereo systems, televisions, and other modern-day appliances and games are absent. The women at

the large U.S. bases eat prepared meals in dining halls and have only their small rooms, their laundry, and themselves to take care of when work is over. Overall, there is a relative absence of external, easily accessible and already structured leisure activities, as well as new individuals to meet and communities to join. Conditions are relatively harsh then, not only because of the external environmental conditions but also because of the limited availability of daily amenities. Work is hard (or at least time-consuming) yet plentiful. There is a sense of adventure coupled with danger, and the people interact frequently with each other because they live and work in a small, isolated area.

Such conditions may foster a greater interdependence among the individuals present on the ice. Indeed, a sense of comradery or community was experienced by many of the women, especially when they found for themselves a group of people with whom they felt they belonged. A small-town feeling (and at the field camps or on the expeditions, a small-group feeling) seemed to be created, complete with a sense of everyone knowing everyone's business, and no one being able to get away for any privacy.

In fact, for several of the women, the lack of external demands and the absence of contact with family and friends back home combined to create a sense of physical time and mental space for engaging in social and community life in new ways; several women noted that they began to relate to others (or recognize their desire to relate to others) in a more reflective and intimate manner than was usual for them. Limited standard social options, along with the slower pace of life (aside from the work itself, which seems, at least in the summer season, to be quite time-consuming), also seemed to foster greater than usual attention to philosophical musings and introspection.

Still, while some women experienced and valued the ways they began to live life at a slower pace—engaging in (due to limited access to) few external and nonrelational distractions and more philosophizing about life by oneself and/or with others—other stories in this book indicate that not everyone experienced life in the Antarctic in this way. Some, as with Sarah and Paige, seemed to have wanted more connections with others than did those they were surrounded by. Others, such as Jane, preferred to remain as nonsocially oriented as they tended to be off the ice.

It seems as well that the different settings the women were in while in the Antarctic interacted with their individual personalities. At the larger bases, for example, those who liked to be social and to spend time with others—to develop connections and emotional as well as physical intimacies—appear to emphasize in their stories the comradery of the group and the value of interconnectedness. But those who preferred more independence and separation from others—who liked solitude and privacy—focused on their experience of the Antarctic community at these same bases as too small, and the pressures on their interpersonal selves too great. Additionally, it appears from the stories that there were those who did not find a group within which they fit—perhaps because they differed from most of the Antarctic residents in terms of their sexual behavior (or lack of it), their physical appearance, or their greater need for time to themselves. These individuals are likely to find it difficult living at the large Antarctic bases. In general, while most of the women described creating and desiring some balance between social interactions and privacy, it appears that those whose preferences tilted toward social interactions had an easier and better time at the larger Antarctic bases (at least during the summer seasons) than those who preferred fewer social interactions.

In contrast to the larger camps during the summer season, the reverse appears to be true for the smaller field-research camps and expeditions. There it appears that those who prefer isolation and privacy were more likely satisfied; thus, those who felt a greater need for connection often found themselves struggling to meet their needs in the midst of others who preferred more separation. It seems, perhaps, that there is a greater expectation of isolation in these camp settings and/or lower expectations for social activities and social interactions. The people at the smaller camps and on expeditions may recognize that there are fewer options for social interaction and fewer ways of escaping tensions should they arise among individuals.

An additional consideration is the season of the year when the women were in the Antarctic. The number of people decreases and the darkness lasts twenty-four hours a day during the winter season. The pace slows down, and more space is available for each person to claim, making it easier for people to spend time by themselves. Thus, we can see in the cycle of seasons in the Antarctic shifts in the

balance between time for privacy and time for social life—the same shifts observable in the women themselves within each season, and in the balances preferred by different women at the same points in time.

The women's stories in this book suggest that needs for isolation and for connection change over the course of time in the Antarctic, but also that individual women come to this experience with differing preferences for each. These differing individual characteristics and changes over time do not in themselves appear to be problematic. Rather, it is when individual preferences do not match either the environmental context or the preferences of the others with whom one is working and/or living that problems may arise. For example, Sarah's story of her field-camp experiences and Anne Dal Vera's description of her experiences during the American Women's Trans-Antarctic Expedition suggest that, for both, their needs and desires for affiliation and connection were not in balance with the needs of the others around them. What this highlights is not only the importance of matching individuals and contexts with respect to these kinds of needs, but also how, within a sample of women, there are a variety of balances and preferences for affiliation and isolation. The diverse experiences of the women whose stories appear in this book serve to impress upon us the diversity of needs for connection and independence both within and across this sample of women. This is perhaps best exemplified by an examination of the stories of Sue Giller and Anne Dal Vera, two of the women on the American Women's Trans-Antarctic Expedition. These women clearly express diverse personalities and perspectives. While Sue sought separation and independence at the personal/emotional level (she, as with the other women on this trek, recognized and valued their physical interconnectedness and strived during the expedition to maintain communication and connection with respect to the team's functioning), Anne found herself wanting more of an emotional interconnectedness with her expedition partners.

Overall, like small-town life, there were those who were more satisfied by the possibilities as they experienced them in the Antarctic and those who were less so. Despite differences of these kinds, however, the women were all aware of the different pace of life in the Antarctic compared to their lives in the States. Far from their

lives in the States, they found themselves with few responsibilities besides their work; indeed, they were free from "the second shift" (Hochschild, 1989). All in all, there was something appealing and freeing to most of the women about the limited options for activities, the lack of daily household chores, of access to cars and fast-paced means of getting around town, of not being able to go too far, and of seeing the same people everyday. These elements of Antarctic life, while often complained about during the Antarctic experience, seemed to be reflected upon afterward in ways that suggest it was just these elements which combined to provide for an important, meaningful, and substantively different personal and interpersonal experience for the women while on the ice. People's creative energies are called out in contexts where there are limited external, readily available activities. Many learned, in this environment, how to pay attention to their inner thoughts and feelings, and how to connect with others at this level. When not in a context where family, work, and social obligations extended one beyond one's limits, and where each person went home to her separate abode and responsibilities, the women found themselves with more time to simply be—either with themselves or with each other. The beautiful starkness of the Antarctic environment appears to contribute to these forms of self-reflection and interpersonal connection as well.

The sense of feeling a part of a group also seemed to be important to the women, even if the group consisted of them and one other person. Issues of belonging are important for most people in many contexts, but they seem to come up strongly for the women interviewed for this book. When there are limited means for leaving an environment, and few alternative social groups to join, the need to find a group to fit in with may increase.

The freedom to be whoever you wanted to be was, however, limited, especially for those who were quite different from everyone but who also wanted or needed interpersonal companionship and connections. Diverse perspectives and bizarre behavior may be accepted to a point, but it seems likely as well that certain behaviors or styles may lead one to be excluded from the various groups on the ice. There clearly seem to be norms for acceptable behavior guided by Navy policies but also by the preferences within the various subgroups on the ice. For example, sexual behavior, dis-

cussed further in the next section of this chapter, appears to be highly rule-bound. Those who fall outside the norms—for example, lesbians, bisexuals, or gay men—may find it rather difficult to fit into existing social networks. They may have to suppress parts of themselves in order to form connections with the people available to them. Isolated from one's own family and friends back home, there may be greater pressures for conformity—at least to the norms of a subgroup of people—so as to be able to make connections and experience some sense of belonging during one's time on the ice.

One additional aspect of life in the Antarctic that differentiates it from life in the States involves the notion of "home." No matter how much the women came to like the Antarctic and to find in it a sense of place and community, they could not call it home. The Antarctic is a place where they can work for some months at a time, and maybe through an entire year cycle, but they cannot live there year round, year after year. If they do not have work, they must leave the continent; even if they do have work, they cannot stay continuously through two winter seasons. The Antarctic community is a transitory one; while some do continue to return year after year, most of the women interviewed went for only one or two seasons. The Antarctic is also not accessible to friends and family, nor can one leave the Antarctic for a visit home on the holidays. Although there is now good access to communications between the United States and the Antarctic, it is this separation between friends and family off the ice and those relationships developed on it that highlight for the women that the Antarctic is not home. In addition, the Antarctic appears to be viewed as a place so separate from home, and from life prior to arrival on the ice, that the women can in effect be whoever they want to be. Indeed, for many women, the Antarctic experience provides an opportunity to discover just who they are and how they want to be. They can try out different personalities and behaviors than they may have felt able to in their lives off the ice. They can also, if interested, experiment with relationships with men. Overall, most of the women seemed to have experienced their time in the Antarctic as important in their own development and also as a time-out from the normal course of their lives.

Overall, in contrast with modern life off the ice, the women in the Antarctic describe their daily lives as similar in several ways to

women who lived in what Aries (1965) has described as life in seventeenth-century Europe. At that time, social life was a daily and public activity; social skills were purposively developed and broadly valued. Friendships were interwoven with other social and familial relations. But as more and more two-parent families were formed to live together in isolated, private homes, social life and social loyalty came to be focused on this smaller relational unit. Time spent socializing with friends and neighbors came to be seen as time away from building the family. Over time, Aries (1965) argues, sociability was reduced—and social life was in essence removed from the community to be privatized in the family. But for the women in this book, the Antarctic was a place where social life reemerged from the family and moved back into the community.

The ability of the women to make this shift is greatly facilitated by the structure of Antarctic life. Keeping house in the Antarctic is not necessary, and children are not allowed, so caretaking demands are limited. Living and eating arrangements are institutionalized; no one is responsible for these things after their own work is done. Rather, for some people, this is their work. Furthermore, the work is plentiful; Antarctica has no unemployment (although it does have underemployment). Still, there is a clear gender imbalance on the ice, with men greatly outnumbering women. Some of the gender-related issues that emerge out of this context are explored next.

GENDER ISSUES ON THE ICE

While imbalances in terms of racial and ethnic identities, socio-economic class status, sexualities, ages, and physical abilities remain pervasive at U.S. Antarctic bases and field camps, the focus in this book on women's experiences in the Antarctic highlights only the gender imbalance. The women's experiences and the conditions of social life they describe also highlight issues of sex discrimination and sexual harassment. It is these conditions, then, that I focus on. First, however, it is important to note some of the other forms of discrimination and oppression that are as present in the Antarctic frontier as they are in the United States.

Class differences and discriminatory and oppressive practices on the basis of class are frequently described or alluded to in the

women's stories. One of the ways class differences were played out was in access to the environment. There seemed, in fact, to be delineations by employment, which were associated with class, in the opportunities available to the women during their time in the Antarctic. That is, employment as scientists, Navy personnel, or ASA workers also appeared to both create and reflect class differences on the ice. The women scientists and Navy officers had greater access to resources and to the Antarctic Continent itself, while most of the ASA women had to rely more on themselves and their co-workers to create social activities and new experiences. In addition to differential access to the natural environment based on employment and/or class status, some of the women describe gaining access to the environment because they were women. Those perceived to be pretty, or at least available, were more likely invited to parties on the ships, flights to the Pole, drives in the trucks, and so on. Thus, discriminatory practices based on gender and physical attractiveness were present on the ice, as they also are in the United States.

Most striking, perhaps, are the different perceptions of diversity with respect to the people in the Antarctic. Some women were clearly struck by what they perceived as a great diversity of individuals available to meet and get to know, while others were struck by a lack of diversity. When diversity was emphasized, the focus was on diversity with respect to employment and/or careers (e.g., Navy personnel, scientists, ASA workers of various sorts) and cultures and/or citizenship, as well as diversity at the individual personality level. When the limited diversity of people on the ice was noted, the focus seemed to center on gender in particular as well as age, class, and physical ability. Rarely do the women mention the limited racial and ethnic diversity among the U.S. Antarctic population.

The older women and those who were mothers seemed particularly aware of the absence of elders and children, but so too did some of the younger women notice the limited diversity with respect to age. There was, however, much reflection on the gender imbalances in these stories—much by virtue of the interview schedule itself but also, it appears, because this was a salient aspect of the women's experiences. Turning to the gender imbalances, I begin by examining the experiences of the four women who went on the American

Women's Trans-Antarctic Expedition (AWE). While the AWE women differ from the other women in the Antarctic, with respect to
their experience of an all-women's group in contrast with the dispro-
portionate number of men relative to women at the U.S. bases and
field camps, they still experienced a gender imbalance with respect
to finding funding and support for their expedition. Similarly, across
expeditions, there is a clear imbalance in terms of gender; men far
outweigh women on Antarctic expeditions. That the AWE women
had such difficulties finding funding and support and never did
receive corporate sponsorship also highlights some of the persisting
assumptions about appropriate gender behavior that are seen across
the interviews. As Anne Dal Vera suggests with respect to the AWE,
sponsorship may have been denied them because of a fear of the
women getting hurt during the expedition. Since women are supposed to be protected from danger, the association of a corporation
with women in potentially dangerous situations is too risky. Additionally, taking on the trek itself was probably perceived as unfeminine and outside the norms of appropriate gender behavior; thus, the
women were assumed to all be lesbians, and sponsorship denied due to
an aversion to supporting such women.

   Similar concerns with protecting women and enforcing appropriate sex-role behavior are noted by the first women scientists in the
Antarctic. Perhaps less directly, but no less pervasively, these concerns are seen in the stories of the women who more recently spent
time in the Antarctic. The Navy women, for example, talk about
Antarctica as one of the few places where they were (as of the time
of their interviews) allowed to be deployed. Women employed by
Antarctic Support Associates (ASA) and those scientists funded by
the National Science Foundation (NSF) describe the concerns
raised by these organizations about the imbalance of men to women
on the ice and the likely behavior of the men under these circumstances. In essence, what all the organizations seemed to be afraid
of was their inability to protect the women from the men on the ice.
As with the debate regarding the ban against gays and lesbians in
the military, the problem appears to be the anticipated behavior of
those already there (heterosexuals in the military; men on the ice)
toward the new arrivals. Yet the debate in both cases is often framed
in terms of the newcomers' abilities to perform their jobs, or even to

tolerate the conditions of these jobs, given the likelihood of oppression within these contexts. There is a blame-the-victim mentality at work. While the women describe efforts to ease their problems while on the ice, and while there appears to be a sense of commitment to improving women's circumstances, there is also a sense of adjustment to the conditions as they are articulated in some of the women's stories. These women view it as their responsibility to be able to survive sexist comments and harassing work environments. Some do so by learning to fit in within this context, others by learning to tolerate, and a few by standing up against these situations. But they all have to deal with sexism in the Antarctic; in this way, it is no different from their home environments in the United States.

In fact, the circumstances of isolation, frontierlike bases, previously male-only environments, continuing male-dominated environments, and the military rule that comprise the Antarctic atmosphere, may combine to make matters worse for women in the Antarctic than elsewhere in the United States. As one woman, whose story unfortunately is not included in this collection, put it, "The minute you walked off the plane, you were already classified with some kind of label from men." In this woman's experience, the options for women were to be labeled either a "bitch or a slut or a dyke." She suggests that this labeling process may be harsher in the Navy than elsewhere on the Antarctic, but while the labels themselves differ, the focus on women's sexual availability to men remains. The attention women receive on the ice tends to be greater than off the ice as well, due to the limited availability of women relative to men. Whether they like this situation or not—and there are women with both reactions on (and off) the ice—the women do note that they receive a great deal of attention in the Antarctic because they are, as women, so disproportionately represented.

It is important to note that some of the women describe this kind of attention as pleasurable while others view it anywhere from bothersome to physically threatening. In all, it seems that ASA, NSF, and the Navy, from early on in women's experiences on the ice to the present, were right to be worried about the conditions for women in the Antarctic. But what these stories help to highlight is that it is not the women that they need to worry about but rather the

behavior and attitude of the men and the organizations that structure, create, and perpetuate the objectification of women in the Antarctic environment. Although the roles, expectations, and options for women are expanding in the Antarctic, they are still largely based in a patriarchal framework. Sexual harassment is directly mentioned, alluded to, or implied in many of the women's stories and is evident in the labeling—and treatment—of women in terms of their sexual attractiveness and availability. By focusing on the gender imbalances and tensions in gender-role expectations reflected in the women's stories, we can also see the ways in which cultural and societal expectations and norms are replicated in new and isolated settings, even as some of them—specifically, letting women into the Antarctic interior—are broken.

Before closing this section, it is important to highlight the implications of the lack of racial and ethnic diversity in the Antarctic, as well as the lack of persons of differing physical abilities and, at least publicly, differing sexual orientations or preferences. As the first section of this chapter described, many of the women developed a greater awareness and understanding of themselves and others while on the ice. They also learned to relate to others in more honest, direct, and accepting, nonjudgmental ways. These outcomes, and the Antarctic setting itself, are reminiscent of the findings from various social psychological experiments on in-group/out-group tensions in the 1950s and 1960s (e.g., Aronson et al., 1978; Sherif et al., 1961; see Wilder, 1981, for a review of some of this early work). The study findings suggested that increased contact between members of in-groups and out-groups, when it occurs in settings that demand cooperation and interdependence among equals, encourages the development of the ability to better understand and like those previously unknown and/or disliked. It also may encourage increased commitment to community building (see Daloz et al., 1996). The Antarctic experience, as described by the women in this book suggests its potential as such a setting. While there are clearly status differentials depending on one's work, there are many equalizing factors in the Antarctic when it comes to life outside of work. Everyone truly is dependent on each other for their physical, social, and mental well-being, and building community becomes more of a central focus; it is a shame, then, that we do not take advantage of this setting for

fostering understanding of and respect for diverse racial and ethnic cultures, physical abilities, and sexual orientations or identities. But not only does the absence of diversity at the Antarctic bases reflect a lost opportunity, one must wonder about the implications of this group of people returning to life in the United States. When they describe their Antarctic lives as so ideal in many ways, there is a potential danger in their associating the ideal Antarctic experience with the lack of diversity among people along racial, ethnic, ability, and sexual orientation or identity lines.

CONCLUSION

The women's stories of life in the Antarctic highlight some of the differences among women with respect to their desires for relationships and their sense of self in relationships (see, e.g., Gilligan, 1993; Jordan et al., 1991). The stories also highlight some of the best and the worst about human relating, community, and twentieth-century life. One common—and in my opinion, positive—theme that appears in many of the stories is the development of more self-aware, self-reflective, interconnected, direct and honest ways of being with oneself and with others while on the ice. For some, the setting brought out submerged aspects of themselves—submerged in response to the multiple demands of family and work lives and of the structure of modern twentieth-century life in the United States. For others, the Antarctic setting helped them to develop these new ways of being and new skills for relating. Both circumstances highlight the ease with which we lose track of, and time for, developing connections with others in the fast-paced life of twentieth-century United States (see, e.g., Gouldner and Strong, 1987).

Yet another common theme in many of the stories in this book is the replication of various hierarchies and problems of twentieth-century, big-city life in the small, isolated community of the Antarctic. For example, the prevalence, use, and abuse of alcohol; the long work days; the class-based hierarchies between and within the members of the Navy, NSF, and ASA; and the gender hierarchies, stereotypes, and discrimination toward and the oppression of women are all evident in the stories collected for the larger research project. Although those in the Antarctic were able to create rather

positive ways of relating to each other, they seem to have replicated the worst of twentieth-century life as well. Their ways of relating do not appear sufficient to tackle these problems either. Specifically, the women seem to be describing the development and practice among people on the ice of constructive means for dealing with many forms of interpersonal tensions and problems that arise when small numbers of people interact together in isolation from others for extended periods of time. It is when the problems among individuals surpass the realm of interpersonal tension and are embedded in power hierarchies and misuses and abuses of power that these individual and interpersonal strategies fail. Such problems as these include: abuse toward women from their boyfriends or ex-boyfriends, verbal harassment by male co-workers on the job toward female co-workers, physical harassment in the bars by drunken men, drunken men engaging in physical fights with other men, and supervisors demanding unfair work hours from employees and/or unfairly distributing the available resources of supplies and person-power to benefit their own particular projects and leisure activities.

In trying to redress these problems, it seems important to keep in mind that much of their source derives from imbalances in power as well as misuses and abuses of legitimate power. Thus, the bringing in of civilian police forces and power hierarchies in an effort to deal with severe discipline problems and abuses of power might, in effect, increase the problems already present and/or detract from the residents' abilities to deal with many of the interpersonal and work-related problems themselves. Hopefully, instead, solutions can be developed that build upon the interpersonal connections and ways of relating which the women describe as prevalent in the Antarctic and which address individual differences in needs for privacy and social interaction. The great availability of alcohol should also be examined. It was suggested by several women in the larger research study that the free-flowing alcohol at the bases may be one way to keep people from rising up against the stress of Antarctic life and work within it. It seems, instead, from these stories and the kinds of interpersonal abuses that are described within them that alcohol itself may be the greatest problem. Given the ways of relating and being the women describe as part of their experience on the ice— among themselves, other women, and many men as well—perhaps

the problems might be lessened if, without alcohol so freely available as an escape or social activity, the women and men on the ice had to rely more fully on their creative energies for dealing with personal and social problems.

In closing, let me note that there are implications which can be drawn from the women's experiences on the ice for life off the ice as well. The aspects of that experience, which many of the women appear to value most, are just those elements of life that are easily lost in the hustle and bustle of modern-day twentieth-century city life and the corresponding reduction of social life to the privatized family. Friendships, and social and community relations more generally, had room to develop and grow in the Antarctic context, where they were not perceived either as luxuries nor as interfering with the private world of the family or with occupational success. The women's experiences of self-reflection, friendship, and community serve to remind us of the importance of examining the contexts of individuals' lives and relationships when seeking to understand relationship experiences and the patterns of their days (see Trickett and Buchanan, 1997). While many of the women were glad to return to their families and their jobs in the States, both they, and those who were more ambivalent about their return, describe missing the connections and community they experienced on the ice. Their stories highlight for us the importance of reexamining the structures and demands of our lives and seeing whether and how we might make more room for the kinds of self-reflections and interpersonal relationships with friends that the women found the time and space for in the Antarctic.

REFERENCES

Aries, P. (1965). *Centuries of Childhood.* New York: Random House.

Aronson, E., Stephan, C., Sikes, J., Blaney, N., and Snapp, E. (1978). *The Jigsaw Classroom.* Beverly Hills: Sage.

Daloz, L.A.P., Keen, C.H., Keen, J.P., and Parks, S.D. (1996). *Common Fire: Lives of Commitment in a Complex World.* Boston: Beacon Press.

Gilligan, C. (1993). *In a different voice: Psychological Theory and Women's Development.* Cambridge, MA: Harvard University Press.

Gouldner, M. and Strong, M.S. (1987). *Speaking of Friendship: Middle-class Women and Their Friends.* New York: Greenwood Press.

Hochschild, A. (1983). *The Second Shift.* New York: Avon.

Jordan, J., Kaplan, A., Miller, J.B., Stiver, I., and Surrey, J. (1991). *Women's Growth in Connection: Writings from the Stone Center.* New York: Guilford Press.

Sherif, O., Harvey, O.J., White, B.J., Hood, W., and Sherif, C. (1961). *Intergroup Conflict and Cooperation: The Robbers Cave Experiment.* Norman, OK: University of Oklahoma Press.

Trickett, E.J., and Buchanan, R.M. (1997). The role of personal relationships in transitions: Contributions of an ecological perspective. In S. Duck (Ed.), *Handbook of Personal Relationships: Theory, Research and Interventions.* (Second edition), pp. 575-593. New York: John Wiley and Sons.

Wilder, D.A. (1981). Perceiving persons as a group: Categorization and intergroup relations. In D.L Hamilton (Ed.), *Cognitive Processes in Stereotyping and Intergroup Behavior,* pp. 213-257. Hillsdale, NJ: Lawrence Erlbaum.